# *Benedict Arnold*

## *Misunderstood Hero?*

by

Audrey Wallace

BURD STREET PRESS
SHIPPENSBURG, PENNSYLVANIA

Photographs by author unless otherwise mentioned.

This Burd Street Press publication
was printed by
Beidel Printing House, Inc.
63 West Burd Street
Shippensburg, PA 17257-0708 USA

The acid-free paper used in this book meets the guidelines for permanence and durability of the Committee on Production Guidelines for Book Longevity of the Council on Library Resources.

For a complete list of available publications
please write
Burd Street Press
Division of White Mane Publishing Company, Inc.
P.O. Box 708
Shippensburg, PA 17257-0708 USA

Library of Congress Cataloging-in-Publication Data

Wallace, Audrey, 1924-
    Benedict Arnold : misunderstood hero? / by Audrey Wallace.
        p. cm.
    Includes bibliographical references and index.
    ISBN 1-57249-349-6 (alk. paper)
    1. Arnold, Benedict, 1741-1801. 2. American loyalists--Biography. 3. Generals--United States--Biography. 4. United States--History--Revolution, 1775-1783. 5. United States. Continental Army--Biography. I. Title.

E278.A7W24 2003
973.3'82'092--dc21
[B]

                                                                          2003057729

*To the lady, Sister M. Rosarita Canowsky,
O.P., 1885–1954, who started it all,
and to Vere A. Arnold, 1902–1994,
great-great-grandson of Benedict Arnold
and Peggy Shippen,
who helped me find the answer.*

# Contents

December 15, 1781—Benedict Arnold leaves New York for
the last time, though he does not realize this at the time. He
has plans to submit to the king that he hopes will reverse the
current situation. He sails on the *Robust*, a British war ship.
His family—wife and two children—and one maid sail in the
same convoy aboard a merchantman. Arnold's companions
on the journey are Lord Cornwallis, Lieutenant Colonels
Tarleton, Lake and Dundas. Due to severe storm at sea the
*Robust* is considered unsafe. Cornwallis, Arnold, Tarleton,
Lake, and Dundas are transferred to other vessels. The Arnolds
arrive at Falmouth, England, safely, as does Cornwallis, but
Tarleton, Lake, and Dundas are captured and ransomed.

Birth. Family. Apprenticeship. Young soldier. The move to
New Haven. First business ventures. Hannah's French love.
Travel to the West Indies. The Mason connection. Marriage.
The pot begins to simmer.

To arms. The flame of rebellion is lighted. Fort Ticonderoga
and Ethan Allen. Easton and Brown. Disenchantment and
return home, following death of wife. The plan for Canada.
Up the Kennebec to Quebec. Wounded. Defeat. Easton,
Brown and Hazen make trouble. The Congressional Commissioners. The Cedars. Retreat.

The threat from the Lakes. Building a fleet. Assumes
command. Battle at Valcour Island. The battle lost, but time
gained. A new love, Betsey DeBlois. Passed over for

decision to return to Canada is taken. Peggy and the children remain in London. This marriage is examined. The Aaron Burr incident. A daughter, Sophia, arrives.

# Foreword

Recent years have seen a great increase in the number of books appearing with the subject matter being the life of Benedict Arnold and particularly his participation in the War of Revolution and subsequent change from the American to the British side.

From the time when she was at school and became captivated by Benedict and the enigma of his life, Audrey Wallace has put enormous research into his life and has included visits to most of the areas where he lived and grew up, fought during the war, or spent his later days in England after the war.

It is refreshing to find words uncovering kinder reasons for the steps Benedict took and which led to his change of side. As his correspondence was destroyed by Peggy, his wife, one can only conjecture his motives; perhaps Audrey comes closer than many before her.

Peter Arnold
Descendant of Benedict's Uncle John

## Preface
## Why? The Author's Reasons

"West Point occupied an important position at that time. It overlooked the Hudson Valley at a point that could stop the British if they attempted to approach from New York City in an effort to split the Colonies. It could also stop an attempt to pass it from the north. General Benedict Arnold, of the Continental army, was in command of the fort. He had also been in communication with the British conspiring to hand the fort over to them.

"When Major John André, the British officer who was in this plot with Arnold, was captured, their plans were halted and the fort was saved. Major André was hanged as a spy and Benedict Arnold escaped to join the British. For this infamous act he has gone down in history as a traitor."

---

The strident voice had read the above quotation from the history book, in use in the American school system in the 1930s, to a group of eighth grade students gathered for a special teaching session in the office of the principal, Sister Rosarita.

When she finished reading she closed the book abruptly, slapping her large, strong hand loudly on its cover. Her piercing black eyes snapped as she added in the silence of the small room: "But that's not the whole story! I have read this to you and you will be required to remember it in order to pass your history exam. This will have been the first time you have heard the name *Benedict Arnold* mentioned. I intend that you should know more about him."

Sister Rosarita was an excellent teacher, but one of whom we were very much in awe. She was a tall, heavy-framed woman, not at all attractive, but rather commanding. Her authority was absolute, and we knew it. As a result our attention was riveted on her every word. We didn't dare otherwise.

The room was silent. We waited for her to continue. Finally she spoke again and we listened — not because we had to, but because the words she spoke began to weave a spell around us about a man who began to seem very real to us.

Sister had always had the ability to make her classes interesting. History ceased to be a long boring list of names and dates which had to be committed to memory. People lived — truly lived — as they had all those years ago, and the dates which concerned them, while they had to be learned, seemed relatively unimportant.

So it was that Benedict Arnold came to life in that room as though he had opened the door and come to join us. Sister recreated his image — gave him life. She spoke of how he was a merchant in New Haven when the war with England began and that he had immediately answered the call to arms. We began to become excited by the fever pitch of those days.

Sister's eyes glittered with a bright smile, lighting the strong face, softening the hard lines. She always liked to tease a bit, and we never knew quite how to react.

"Bet you never knew that Benedict Arnold stood beside Ethan Allen at Fort Ticonderoga when he knocked on the door of the officer's quarters and announced that the fort had been captured!"

We hadn't, of course. The history book had never mentioned it. We relaxed. Sister was in a good mood. This was going to be an interesting lesson.

"There's a lot you don't know about this man, a lot you should know, and — what's more — you should remember."

She detailed the famous march to Quebec through the Maine wilderness — the privations of the men — the unbelievable route through which they passed (still impassable in many places to this day), and she told us, too, how Arnold shared all of this with his men, encouraging them to continue when they could not walk another step, prodding them on and on.

We heard of the attack on the citadel of Quebec in a raging blizzard, by the handful of ragged, half-starved men who survived that march, and how it very nearly succeeded. She told how he had fed his men out of his own pocket, using credit established before the war during his trading in Canada. She also told us how he fell before the walls, wounded in the leg.

The room fell silent until she spoke again — this time softly. "It was not the last time he would lose blood for his country. The next time would be at Saratoga, but that comes on a bit later. Before that he did a few other things your book doesn't mention."

Now we were really in the palm of her hand. No one moved. We listened enthralled as she told us about the small fleet he designed and helped to build, working with his men as they cut down trees to provide needed timbers, sweating in the summer heat along with the rest of them.

We laughed along with her as she spoke of how, once the ships were on Lake Champlain, he had to teach the men how to sail the ships they had built, and how to aim the cannons they carried. The man seemed to be a one-man "army" — or, was it "navy"?

The battle that followed and the escape of Arnold's ships in the fog of the night ensued. We were told, too, of how the remnants of this small fleet were burned on the beach of the Vermont shore, the men escaping overland through Indian studded country to Crown Point.

"Sounds like he lost, doesn't it?" The black eyes snapped, waiting for our nods.

"Well, he did. He knew he would. He also knew that what he intended to do he would do, and that was to buy us more time. He bought us one whole year. Winter was not far off and the British returned to Canada. They would try the next year. Hopefully, we would be stronger then."

Then she swept on, telling us of that next year when the British came down again from Canada. This time there was no fleet on the lake to stop them. Ticonderoga and Crown Point fell, and they continued to come. They had also landed another force and approached from the west to meet the northern invasion. Albany was sure to fall, and then the Hudson River would be open to them all the way down to New York. Nothing would stand in their way this time.

"Nothing but Benedict Arnold, of course!" she said, almost with a snicker.

She had us laughing again at his ruse planted amongst the superstitious Indians that had them running back along the Mohawk Valley as though the devil himself were chasing them, instead of Benedict Arnold with a far inferior force compared to their own. By the time he reached Fort Stanwix, which they had under siege, they had dropped everything, including supplies, and had run back to their ships on Lake Ontario.

"Then came the big one — Saratoga. The battle that would be known as 'the turning point of the American Revolution.'" Benedict Arnold was not in command, another man was, a General Horatio Gates. Arnold was to serve under his command."

At this point Arnold had become such a hero to us that we could hardly believe her words. Arnold was not in command! How could that happen?

She spoke of the shuffle amongst the officers which had caused General Philip Schuyler to be replaced by General Horatio Gates. It all seemed very confusing to us, but then she told us of the battles at Saratoga — BOTH of them. Our hero Arnold was on the field once again and this time we could almost picture him dashing through crossfire, exposing himself and his horse to fire from both sides. We heard of his anger at the ridiculous treatment by Gates, which finally erupted in a royal row between the two men, followed by Arnold's resignation.

Silence fell in the room. Sister had led us into a situation where we sensed the danger. With no Arnold on the field, what was to become of our army? We remembered that the history book had told us we had won the battle, but that the man responsible for the victory was General Gates. How could that be?

"Well, Arnold was mad — really mad — but he didn't leave the camp. His men begged him not to. They had no confidence in Gates. When John Burgoyne, the British general, began to move, and really move this time, because he had to — we had cut off his retreat route and supplies — Arnold expected Gates to go out to meet him. He didn't."

She told us how Arnold, without a command of any kind, leaped on the first horse he could get his hands on and galloped out to meet the enemy, calling to his men to join him. They did (and so did we, in our imaginations). The excitement grew to fever pitch and Sister knew it all, as though she'd been there herself.

When Arnold leaped the barricade at Breymann's Redoubt and crashed down, his horse dead, pinning him to the ground, his leg — the same one — wounded, we, too, were crushed. But the victory was ours. The enemy was defeated.

"Arnold didn't receive credit for what he did — Gates saw to that. When he accepted Burgoyne's sword in surrender, the man who should have taken it was suffering agony in an army hospital in Albany."

Sister Rosarita talked then of the treatment Arnold received at the hands of his jealous fellow officers. She told how George Washington, Arnold's friend, attempted to make up for this.

Finally, she shook her head, and the flowing folds of her black habit moved in her annoyance. "Never was a man treated with more ingratitude. Even to this day Americans try to erase his heroic deeds and continue the bitterness of his treason at West Point. You will perhaps feel this bitterness, too, and feel disappointment in the man you had begun to admire. That I cannot do anything about. You yourselves will have to make the choice. All I ask of you is to remember what happened *before* and weigh everything very carefully before you judge this man who was one of our greatest heroes and one to whom we owe more, as Americans, than we can ever hope to repay."

The "end-of-period" bell clanged in the hall and we jumped– liberated from the spell Sister had cast over the class.

"One more minute, if you please!" the sharp voice stopped us as we rose to leave. "Go to the library and read Kenneth Roberts's two books *Arundel* and *Rabble in Arms*," she snapped. "Write down what I tell you!" We did. "Then, if you're still interested, have the librarian get a biography of Arnold for you from the State Library." We made hasty notes.

I was one of those children who did as I was told. Anyone who has read the Roberts books will understand the fascination which begins when Arnold first appears. The thread of fascination continues through the two books; echoing the author's own opinions, it is quite true. All the same, the seed had been planted, and through the years I have studied Arnold, studied the good along with the bad sides of the man. I have read other novels, too, but I didn't need their descriptive flair to further intrigue me. The man had long ago captivated me in that class. I was one of those young children that was reached by Sister Rosarita. I don't know if any of the others were to the same extent. I do know, though, that I owe a debt to Sister Rosarita that I wish I could repay. She is dead now, has been for many years. Somehow I hope she knows what she started. Perhaps she even knows how it will end.

A novelist's talent is not required to capture the imagination when studying this fascinating man. One can never be bored. A gamut of emotions sweeps one along, depending upon what one happens to be reading at the moment. Contemporary treatment can reach near adoration, just as it can reverse to bitterness and hatred. Through all of this run the factual accounts of the heroism of a man who risked everything at times—money, bodily injury, reputation. When the fever was upon him he was glorious. That he could also be impudent, insubordinate, incautious, pugnacious, and even a bit obnoxious, must also be admitted. His impatience and lack of consideration for others at times, makes one cringe. No man is perfect. Arnold, least of all.

And yet, there is this magic, when one comes away from studying the man as a whole, that remains and provides, long after, hours of contemplation. With all his faults and brilliance, he has captivated me for years, and I cannot see an end to my interest—ever.

If we Americans are truly interested in our heritage, we must now review this man, look behind the shadow of his treason and accord him the understanding that is due every man. Through understanding perhaps we can feel forgiveness, which also is the right of every man.

May 21, 1982, was a very special day for me. I was to meet Vere A. Arnold, great-great-grandson of Benedict Arnold. I had found his name in the registry of St. Mary's Church, Battersea, London, where Benedict, his wife, Peggy Shippen, and his daughter, Sophia, are buried. He had been at the church for the dedication of the lovely stained glass window commissioned by the American Vincent Lindner. Mr. Arnold and I had exchanged letters for some time, but on this day I was to meet him.

Despite his still frail health following recent hip surgery, I had been invited to stay at his home "Ardmore," near Chester, England. It was such a privilege meeting this fine gentleman, a Cambridge University graduate, and retired magistrate, who placed various pictures and papers for my perusal, and gave generously of his time. I shall always remember his kindness, and particularly his answer, when I asked him how he felt about Benedict. Having lived in England always he had never had to experience the stigma of the name "Arnold," so often felt by American and Canadian descendants.

"I am very proud of him. I don't know' of anyone who was braver than he was. It is family tradition that his final act was to end the war because he felt it was ruining the country, and he believed Congress was selling you down the road to the French. You must realize that England was then in a very bad situation once France came to your aid. This meant she had to fight the French on two fronts, across the Channel and across the Atlantic. She could not maintain two such fronts much longer, and if she relinquished the American Colony, leaving you extremely vulnerable, France would not scruple to take you over. France, a Roman Catholic monarchy, could mean a return to Roman Catholicism for the Colonies. Benedict, and many New Englanders who had left these shores in order to embrace Protestantism would have been very unhappy. He felt it would be imperative to remain a British Colony."

He smiled gently: "You know he stuck his neck out for you many times. His final decision was just one more time."

Vere passed away in 1994 and I still feel his loss.

*Vere A. Arnold, great-great-grandson of Benedict Arnold and Peggy Shippen, in front of window in St. Mary's Church, London, England.*

*St. Mary's, Battersea, London*

Benedict Arnold is buried in crypt at the church.

*The crypt of Benedict Arnold, Margaret Arnold,*
*and Sophia Matilda Phipps*

# Chapter 1
## The Last of New York

Dawn—December 15, 1781. HMS *Robust*, 74 guns, lay anchored off Sandy Hook. Stationed in the North River, she had taken aboard her passengers, one of whom was the Earl, Charles Cornwallis, enthusiastically cheered aboard by the crew. In haze and snow she had moved to her present anchorage the day before. She would weigh anchor that morning when the convoy had assembled.

It was a large convoy of 120 empty victualers, transports and merchantmen, protected by the *Robust*, commanded by Captain Phillips Cosby, and the *Janus*, 44 guns, under the command of Captain W. H. K. O'Hara.

He'd slept fitfully, listening to the wind and the slap of water against the hull. Now he rose and dressed in the heavy clothing he knew he would need on deck. It was December and once out of the relative protection of the Jersey coast and into the open water, seas would be heavy and the cold penetrate to the bone. He'd been to sea often enough to know that.

He took care not to disturb his cabin companion who slept on unconcerned. It was the restful, trouble free sleep of a man commencing a journey that would end at home.

England was home to Charles Cornwallis, never mind that there would be questions to be answered when he arrived, many unpleasant no doubt—it would be home with family, friends, and remembered pleasures.

At the door, Benedict Arnold stopped and looked back in the dim light at the sleeping man. He envied him, even in his

1

defeat, he envied him. How different were their prospects at this time.

He hunched his broad shoulders and went out on deck.

Light was increasing, though there was no sign of the sun. The sky gleamed like polished pewter — a wintry sky.

"Prepare to weigh!" came the shout to the crew, and the scramble to get away began.

He thought of New York where there would be movement in the streets soon, horses, carts, carriages, and the people. New York was a busy place. Scattered lights would begin to appear one by one in houses ashore, as people awoke to a new day, as he'd awakened, not to just a new day, but a new beginning.

As the light grew he began to see more clearly the other ships that had joined the convoy. They'd been assembling for several days, all eager to join a group that would enjoy the protection of British navy vessels. The French, blockading the port, would hesitate to put to test the might of the *Robust*, *Janus*, and *Addamante*, shepherding the covey of merchant ships. Somewhere out there on one of the smaller vessels, were his wife, Peggy, and their two sons: Edward, a toddler of nineteen months, and the infant, James, four months. They were accompanied by a maid. Their accommodations were decidedly more comfortable than his, though he remembered how Peggy had fretted when she heard they could not travel together.

Sir Henry Clinton advised him to travel with Cornwallis, aboard a navy ship, for his own safety. With the French at sea in the area stopping merchant ships more often than not, he would run the risk of being taken and returned to the rebels (Clinton still would call them that), who would no doubt be delighted. They all knew of the unsuccessful kidnap plots and it was very probable the French were told to watch for him. Intimidating a merchant ship and stopping her for a search was a small matter, not so when the vessel was of the British navy.

So it was settled and here he was, aboard the *Robust*, amidst the bustle of departure, alone by the rail with his thoughts of what might have been, as well as what lay ahead.

Beyond the city he thought of the land upriver — the hills of the Hudson Valley, Albany, and still further north, Saratoga. Impatiently, he shifted his weight from the leg that carried the scars of Saratoga — a leg shortened by two inches, accommodated by a specially constructed boot. He'd said it should have been his heart, as they pulled the dead horse off him at Breymann's Redoubt. He'd meant it then, and even now.

But why this depression? Someday he'd be back, he felt sure of it. The war would be over and he'd come back again. Yorktown was by no means the end of it. There was still a chance that the situation could be reversed. He intended to exert everything in his power to see that it was. He had plans and would present them to the king. Clinton had commissioned him for this purpose.

If only they had trusted him. The petty jealousies amongst the British officers who looked down on any officer who had been a tradesman before the rebellion, and the lack of trust amongst those others who had faced him in battle when he'd fought on the other side, held him back from appointments where he could have exhibited his talents. The story could have been so very different. It still rankled him.

He gripped the rail firmly with his strong hands and vowed he would return. This was his home; no place anywhere else would ever seem so. He knew every cove and headland of this coast. He'd sailed it all many times long before the war was ever a threat. He'd worked hard to build his trade between Canada, New England, and the West Indies. That had meant very often sailing his own ships. Yes, he knew this coast and he would return to it one day.

He became aware of the increasing tempo around him, the shouted commands, the rattle of tackle, the snap of sails unfurled. At last the anchor was apeak, and with topsails aback before a light breeze, the *Robust* slowly moved out of her anchorage and signaled the convoy to close up. The pilot was discharged.

Yes, he would return. He would entertain no other thought! When the war was over, England would continue to rule, but very differently than she had in the past. There would be new respect for the Colonies. They had shown their resolution, if not their qualifications, for home rule. They would be given representation in Parliament. There would be no denying them this privilege. The threat of the rabble-rousers, whom he'd grown to distrust so thoroughly in the last months of his service in the Continental army, would end. Life under the king of England, a king with altered feelings towards his people across the sea, would establish a stable government, not like the one he knew all too well. The selfishness and petty bickering between the States would be over.

He liked to think of what it would be like to return and take up his life once again in such an atmosphere. His eternal confidence rallied once again.

He raised his head and inhaled deeply of the sea air. The blue eyes flashed in the increasing light, the weathered tan face firmed with resolution. He squared his shoulders and turned away from the shore, once again confident, as his mind shifted away from the past.

It was good to feel the deck of a ship beneath his feet again. England lay ahead, a whole new adventure, and that was the breath of life to this man, as it had always been. There were people he intended to see in England. His plans, which he would lay before the king, were strong, sensible plans. If only they would listen to him. All was not lost here.

The moderate to fair winds of the 15th and 16th of December quickly changed to squalls and gales on the 18th. There was heavy rain, hail, and lightning.

On Christmas Day the *Robust* began to leak—leak badly. Her topgallant masts were struck. Seas were huge and the ship labored, taking in water continually. Bearings at noon were: Bermuda SW & S 153 leagues.

The atmosphere in the cabins was tense with concern for the ship. There was also tension of another sort. Lt. Col. Banastre Tarleton, of his Majesty's Dragoons, was also a passenger. His dear friend had been the unfortunate Major John André, hanged as a spy. His silence, tangible as cold steel, was evidence that he held Arnold responsible.

The pumps were going constantly, and on the 26th, the *Greyhound* was signaled to follow the *Robust.* An attempt to repair the leak with thrummed sail was made, but with little success. The pumps continued to be manned.

On the 28th, Lord Cornwallis was transferred to the *Greyhound* and Arnold to the armed brig *Prince Edward.* Lieutenant Colonels Tarleton and Lake and Colonel Dundas were transferred to the merchantman *London.* The *Robust* left the convoy and limped into English Harbor, Antigua, for repairs.

Tarleton, Lake, and Dundas did not fare as well as Arnold and Cornwallis. The French had been waiting for the convoy and had stationed about a dozen privateers off the southern coast of England, near Cape Lizard. The *London* was captured, but they were eventually set ashore at Dungeness, after paying a ransom of 400 Guineas. Surely no such arrangement would have been made for Benedict Arnold had he been aboard the *London.*

When Arnold watched the land of his birth recede from sight that day in 1781, it was not for the last time. He returned to North America, much further north, several years later, in 1785, to try to establish a trading business in what was called at that time St. Johns and is now known as Saint John, New Brunswick, Canada. There were voyages to and from the West Indies when he could bring his brig in close, daringly close, to the shore he knew so well, hoping for a glimpse of home. Nowhere else in the world would ever be home to him. He could never sail into New Haven, Boston, New York, or anywhere else in these newly created United States, because the hatred lived on, and he knew it.

What he could not know was that there were those who would see that not only would the hatred live on, but that all his brave deeds, his sacrifices, his love for his country, were to be struck from the hearts of his countrymen as though they had never existed. His name was to become anathema to Americans. The children of future generations were to be taught only one thing about him — that he was a "traitor." They would be introduced to a new word, one they'd never heard before, but one they would quickly learn to associate with his name until they merged and became synonymous.

For many generations they would not be taught about the man who had led his men into battle like a living flame, brandishing his sword, urging them on to impossible feats; rash, mad feats, until they were as mad and fearless as he, until nothing remained but the tasks they had to accomplish.

They wouldn't hear about his incredible march through the Maine wilderness in an attempt to capture Quebec. A march against unbelievable odds, in tempestuous weather, through country much of which remains inaccessible to this day. A march compared often to that of Hannibal crossing the Alps.

They wouldn't be told that he had stood beside Ethan Allen at Fort Ticonderoga, nor that he had designed and helped to build the ships, as well as instructed the men who would have to sail them in our first naval engagement at Valcour Island.

They wouldn't be told that he had volunteered to relieve Fort Stanwix, nor that he had been on the field for *both* battles of Saratoga (though his presence on the first day of battle is argued to this day), nor that it was his storming the redoubt of the Hessian, Colonel Heinrich Breymann, that broke Burgoyne's back and brought about the turning point of the American Revolution.

All this would be withheld from our youth for generations, while his name would grow in infamy, because of the one deed he did that cannot be understood — will not be understood. Benedict Arnold became our first major traitor, and regardless of whoever followed, he would not be forgiven.

# Chapter II
## The Early Years, 1741–1775

On January 3, 1741, in Norwich, Connecticut, a second son was born to Hannah and Benedict Arnold and was named Benedict, after his father. He was the fifth in line to bear this family name, following his great-grandfather (governor of Rhode Island), his grandfather, father, and an earlier brother, who lived just thirteen months. It is this last Benedict, the child born January 3, 1741, with whom we are concerned.

A daughter, Hannah, followed a year later; another daughter, Mary, in 1745; a son, Absalom King, in 1747; and lastly, a girl, Elisabeth, in 1749. With the exception of the second Benedict and Hannah, the other children lived briefly, dying either in infancy, or during an epidemic of yellow fever in 1753. The daughter, Hannah, survived the fever; Benedict, away at school in Canterbury, was untouched.

Young Benedict, a sturdy, active child, grew and thrived, much to his mother's relief. That she adored him is evident by letters she wrote to him at school, a few of which have survived. However, she was sore put to keep him in school, due to an increasing lack of funds.

Her husband, at first successful in the coastal and West Indies trade, had begun to suffer reversals. Trade fell off, and in his frustration he began to turn to drink. Complete responsibility for the family became that of his wife. A Christian woman, with strong moral convictions, she was well liked and admired for her fortitude. Her husband, despite his deterioration, remained respected in the community, but it was evident that the fortunes of the Arnold family had begun to topple. In 1755, Hannah found it necessary to withdraw Benedict from school.

Norwich, at that time a thriving town at the head of navigation on the Thames River, contained a varied lot of industry. There were cotton, grist and paper mills, a pottery, silk stocking and chocolate factories, along with ship building and busy wharves where ships arrived from England and left for the exotic ports of the Indies. Exciting fare for a young lad recently released from the strict discipline of school, looking for an escape from the depressing circumstances at home. For an active, robust child, there were horses to ride, ice skating on the nearby ponds, swimming, and sailing small boats on the river. He became proficient in all sports and soon was leader of the local lads, creating mischievous pranks which often led to serious trouble with the local constabulary, adding to his mother's worries. She soon came to the conclusion that this young son of hers must be seriously occupied, and if she could not afford to send him away to school, or his father could not provide the guidance he required, perhaps, through her cousins Daniel and Joshua Lathrop, his energies could be channeled into a worthwhile profession.

The Lathrops were successful apothecaries, reputed to have founded the first drug store in Connecticut. Young Benedict became one of their apprentices. Training with them gave him a foundation for the profession he would practice later in New Haven, but his boredom with the monotony of confining work was soon relieved by the commencement of the Seven Years War. The news of fighting ignited the ever-present tendency for excitement, and Benedict reacted by running away from home to join up—at age fourteen. Through the efforts of his mother and the Reverend Dr. Lord of her church, he was returned home very shortly.

The next time he enlisted, at age seventeen, it was with his mother's permission and he joined the militia company of Captain James Holmes in New York. Preparations for Amherst's drive north to Ticonderoga and Montreal were begun and Benedict was to be involved briefly. When news came that his mother was dying, he left, apparently without benefit of permission. His love and respect for his mother were not to be denied. Following her death, he rejoined the army, this time Bloomer's Company, and there does not seem to have been any censure for his leave of absence.

When the war came to an end shortly thereafter, Benedict, now nineteen, returned once again to Norwich, and the shop of the Lathrops. This was a more mature Benedict; the days of the scamp were over. He took an active interest in the drug business, storing up many of the innovative ideas of his uncles, which he would put to use when he opened his own shops in New Haven.

That he had changed is evident by the journey entrusted to him by the Lathrops when he was sent to England to purchase drugs, books, and various other merchandise, arranging for their shipment back to Connecticut.

In 1761, Benedict's father died, setting him and his sister free of the old bonds, but the years of humiliation brought upon them by their father's predilection for the bottle were not easily forgotten, and so came the decision to make a new life for themselves in new surroundings. They prepared to sell the house and move to New Haven.

While Hannah remained behind until the house could be sold, Benedict, in his inimitable fashion, quickly became involved in a business in New Haven, which eventually encompassed three stores. He not only stocked drugs, but books, spices, artist's paints, watches, jewelry, prints, maps, stationery, wall papers, tea, sugar, and rum.

His selection of books ranged from the classics, theology, home treatments, self-taught professions, Latin, Greek, and French text books, to the popular novels of the time.

Before the sale of the house in Norwich could be finalized, Benedict returned there to discover that Hannah was being courted by a young French dancing master. Whether he objected to the young man's profession, his nationality, or his sister seeing a gentleman unattended, is not clear. It is true that he did not favor the French. After all he had fought them as the enemy not long before, and they also represented the Roman Catholic faith, which he abhorred.

He took an instant dislike to Hannah's young man and asked her to stop seeing him. Hannah determined to do no such thing and continued to allow the visits in her brother's absence. Matters came to a head when Benedict arrived unexpectedly from New Haven to discover the young couple meeting again. The hasty departure of the suitor, accelerated by a shot Benedict fired over his head as he exited the house through a convenient window, put an end to the budding romance. Hannah, properly chastised, if proudly rebellious, soon joined her brother in New Haven, following the sale of the house, to keep his books and help in the stores. She never married. Whether or not opportunities presented themselves is not known.

Life in New Haven opened up a whole new life for Benedict. Besides the stores and hustling for business, there was the opportunity to become involved in the shipping trade. Money was to be made in commerce with the West Indies. Benedict acquired interests in ships at first, and then acquired his own, often sailing as super-cargo. Adventure and the experience of new horizons always intrigued him.

In the Bay of Honduras he ran afoul of a Captain Croskie, an Englishman, from whom a social invitation had been extended. Benedict, as always placing business before pleasure, did not attend and neglected to send his regrets. When he attempted to rectify this in person the next day, Captain Croskie became abusive, shouting: "You damned Yankee, have you no manners?"

The result was a duel, from which, after an exchange of shots, Arnold received an apology. There would be other duels. This man never took kindly to abuse, verbal or otherwise. Moreover, his incredible abilities caused jealousy amongst his rivals, a jealousy that would follow him all his life. To be outwitted by an opponent is never a pleasurable experience, but coming from an opponent who is often arrogant, and not very familiar with tact, the encounter can make a lasting imprint upon one's memory which will rankle a long time. If opportunity presents itself to return the injury in kind, human nature usually dictates that one do just that.

Affairs in New Haven were not always of a business nature. Arnold's generous contributions to the Long Wharf, where town-born had special privileges, did not guarantee his acceptance for membership. Still, there were others who found him very acceptable. Colonel Nathaniel Whiting presented Arnold for membership in the Hiram Masonic Lodge.

The facts concerning Benedict Arnold's Masonic connections are mired down in confusion and the bitterness regarding his defection.

According to The Most Worshipful Grand Lodge of Ancient Free and Accepted Masons of the State of Connecticut, Arnold was already a Mason when he was introduced by Nathan Whiting, and therefore considered a "visiting brother." Where he received his initial membership is not known, but he definitely was a member when attending the Hiram Lodge (1) in New Haven, on April 10, 1765. A transcription of the minutes of that meeting read: "Br. Benedict Arnold is by R. W. Nathan Whiting, Master, proposed to be made a member of this R. W. Lodge of Free and Accepted Masons accordingly was Ballotted for and accepted and is accordingly made a member in this Lodge."[1]

There is also a record of his attendance at a meeting of the Solomon Lodge (1), in Poughkeepsie, New York, on June 12, 1771. On May 16, 1781, minutes of this lodge read: "Ordered that the name of Benedict Arnold be considered as obliterated from the Minutes of this lodge, a Traitor." His name is crossed out of the records.

An interesting letter of Benjamin Stevens, retired quartermaster of the 1st Regiment, Connecticut Line, survives, written June 25, 1830, to his brother and sister, wherein he reminisces regarding his experiences while stationed in Morristown the winter of 1779–80:

The Masons boast very much of General Washington being a Mason but deny that General Arnold was a Mason. When we lay in the wood at Morristown when the Masons kept St. John's Day the 14th of December Mr. David Judson who was a Mason and attended the Lodge that day told me that General Washington walked at the LEFT hand of General Arnold as Arnold ranked above him in Masonry.[2]

According to Masonic Magazine, October 1, 1867, Benedict Arnold's name was struck from the rolls of Hiram Lodge, yet in an interesting lecture of W. G. George Hall, Masonic historian, given on June 3, 1937, we read:

As I have failed to find and have never heard or read of Benedict Arnold being either expelled or suspended from the rights, benefits and privileges of Masonry, I have every reason to believe that he died a Mason in good standing and a member of this lodge. If any action was taken looking toward his suspension or expulsion from Masonry, the place for such action was this lodge. The records of Hiram Lodge disclose nothing that would hint or suggest that such action was ever contemplated.[3]

One more note: it is interesting to find that the Hiram Lodge (1) in New Haven planned the observance of the 239th anniversary of the lodge in 1989, at which time a considerable exhibit of memorabilia regarding Benedict Arnold was shown.

Around the time Arnold was being accepted in the Masonic Lodge in New Haven, this newly arrived gentleman of certain means was also accepted as a desirable suitor for the hand of the daughter of Samuel Mansfield, High Sheriff of the County. In 1767, he married the young lady, Margaret, in her father's house.

Life settled down to one of both domesticity and profit from the stores, along with trading ventures. Ships, of which he was a co-owner with Adam Babcock, included the *Sally*, of 30 tons, the *Three Brothers*, of 28 tons, and a sloop, *Charming Sally*. Trade had extended to include the acquisition, in Quebec, of horses, pork, wheat and barrel staves, which he transported down to the West

Indies in exchange for molasses and rum. Arnold had become a success at age twenty-six. By the next year he had also become the father of a son, another Benedict. There followed, in rather quick succession, two more sons, Richard and Henry. The enlargement of family meant the need for larger quarters, so a house was built on Water Street, just below Olive Street, on property purchased from his father-in-law.

The house was not only large, but also very handsome, classically proportioned with a fan-light over the front entrance, shuttered windows (equipped with newly innovative counterbalanced sash), mantels of polished marble, and spacious closets. There were also stables as well as warehouses and wharves, a large garden with walks and clipped shrubs, and an orchard.[4] All of this with a clear view out over the harbor and Long Island Sound.

In the midst of this thriving existence began the stirrings of unrest. Great Britain decided to exert the pressures on the American Colonies, which would very shortly erupt into a full-scale revolution.

The raising of taxes (supposedly to coerce the Colonies to help defray the cost of the late war with the French), plus the restrictions regarding trade, were causing rumbles.

To help pay for military protection during the war was surely not an unreasonable claim, but confining trade with British ports only was unfair and lowered profits drastically. Smuggling became rampant, despite the fact that discovery meant severe fines, or, what was worse, confiscation of not only the cargo, but the vessel itself. One's means of livelihood could be taken away in an instant.

Taxing and restricting the Colonists, without allowing them representation in Parliament, in order to voice their complaints, was regarded as wrong, and the rumbles began to resemble a roar.

Arnold, only one of many concerned, became involved in the gathering of radicals, openly voicing his opinions. The magic of his magnetic personality, and qualities of leadership, soon to be demonstrated so spectacularly on the field of battle, rallied friends and acquaintances equally concerned and affected. Of course, this was considered seditious and contributory to open rebellion. The pot was coming to the boil!

# Chapter III
## Off to War, 1775–1776

News of the Boston Massacre reached Arnold in the West Indies, and he voiced his indignation. It is not surprising to find him, upon his return, deep into the excitement.

He rallied together a group and petitioned the General Assembly for permission to form a 2nd Company of the Governor's Foot Guards. A charter was granted and soon thereafter Arnold was appointed their captain. He not only designed their uniforms, still in use today, but diligently trained the corps.

When news of the Battle of Lexington reached New Haven, Arnold forced the release of arms for his company from the arsenal, and marched off to Cambridge, Massachusetts, General Putnam joining them en route. He left his business in New Haven in the hands of his wife and sister, Hannah, as he became committed to the rebellion.

When Arnold and his small corps of smartly comparisoned troops arrived in the camp at Cambridge, he placed a plan before the Massachusetts Committee, suggesting an attempt to capture Fort Ticonderoga.[1] There was an urgent need for arms, not just rifles and muskets, but the heavier sort—namely, cannon. There was also a need, and perhaps this was the most urgent of all, to close the "back door" (the route down from Canada, which the British could use to great effect if they chose to stop this budding rebellion). Fort Ticonderoga not only maintained the vantage point to quell any such move, it also contained a number of cannon which could keep the British neatly penned up in Boston, if only they could be captured and moved there. That Fort

Ticonderoga happened to be occupied by British troops didn't seem to deter the decision to capture it.

The distinction of being the first to suggest such a plan must be credited to Benedict Arnold. Colonel Samuel H. Parsons, of the Connecticut Assembly, returning from Massachusetts to Hartford, had met Arnold on his way to the camp at Cambridge. During this meeting the plan to "surprise Ticonderoga was suggested."[2] Colonel Parsons wrote Joseph Trumbull on April 26, 1775, telling him of this meeting, and that Arnold told him "a great number of cannon were there."[3] Governor Hall of Vermont repeated Parsons's information and said that Arnold accentuated "the importance and feasibility of its [Ticonderoga] capture and his desire to attempt it."[4] Arnold also shared his hopes regarding the capture of Ticonderoga with Dr. Joseph Warren, a member of the Massachusetts Committee. Warren was of the same opinion, and pressed the scheme before the Committee.[5] A warm friendship developed between the two men and Arnold was able to return the favor when he acted, after Warren's death at Bunker Hill, to aid the orphaned children of his friend. It does not seem strange that Arnold would have knowledge of the fort, when one remembers that he had had some experience in the area as a boy. He had also been involved for some time, before the outbreak of hostilities, in trading with Canada.

Following the assignment of his commission May 3, Arnold rode west, stopping in Concord, Shrewsbury, and Deerfield, to arrange for cattle to be transported and men to be enlisted. Reaching Williamstown the sixth, he lodged at the tavern of Nehemiah Smedley, finding disturbing news. A similar expedition was already begun. Not waiting for the arrival of his troops, he dashed off, overtaking a small detachment from Connecticut and a party of Green Mountain Boys, commanded by Ethan Allen. On their way through Pittsfield, the group had been joined by a band of Massachusetts men under the leadership of Colonel James Easton and Major John Brown, two who would begin, during this expedition, to make trouble for Arnold. Now they sided with Allen. We will meet them again in Canada.

When Arnold produced his commission to lead such an expedition, he was met with stony stares. No doubt his style of delivery was strong and to the point — he didn't always exhibit tact — and his temper would not have been appeased by refusal. Actually, he was in the right, as the only commissioned officer, even if Allen's men would not acknowledge a leader other than their own.

After strong exchanges from both sides, Arnold realized he would have to defer to Allen, at least for the present. If he joined the group, he could at least hope to maintain some sort of order.

Early in the morning of May 10, the party reached the shore of Lake George, and the disappointing discovery that there were not enough boats available for transport across to the fort. Since surprise was of the utmost importance, and their only hope of success, a small group crossed, with Allen and Arnold at its head. A sally port gave no resistance and the fort was quickly taken. The supplies they had hoped to find were more plentiful than expected. Along with artillery were small arms, ammunition, pork, flour, and rum! The last was quickly distributed among the men and any sense of order was gone. Arnold's protests and attempts at discipline went unheeded, or openly flouted with several random shots fired in his direction, luckily not on target.

Arnold's insistence on assuming command continued to be unsuccessful. His status as the commissioned officer delegated by the Massachusetts Committee was simply not recognized, despite Warren's advice to the Connecticut authorities, on May 17, to appoint "Colonel Arnold to take charge of them [the arms, etc.] and bring them down in all possible haste." This, Warren suggests, "may be the means of settling any dispute which may have arisen between him and some other officers which we are always desirous to avoid, and now especially, at a time when, our common danger ought to unite us in the strongest bonds of amity and affection."[6]

The Connecticut Committee not only refused the suggestion, but appointed Ethan Allen commander of Ticonderoga until further orders from that state, or from the Continental Congress. Thus Benedict Arnold became embroiled for the first of many times in the squabbles between individual local authorities, which seemed to exist throughout the rebellion.

Arnold's detachment reached Ticonderoga four days after capture of the fort, bringing with them a schooner belonging to Major Philip Skene, a Loyalist, which they had appropriated at Skenesborough. Acting quickly, Arnold manned the ship and sailed down Lake Champlain to St. Johns, where he overwhelmed the garrison and captured valuable stores, plus a sloop and a number of bateaux. Loading the supplies on board, he moved up the lake, passing — of all people — Ethan Allen, bound on the same mission!

The British were quick to reinforce the garrison at St. Johns, and make plans to re-capture the forts, and Arnold, at last informed by the Congress of Massachusetts that he was indeed commander, prepared to defend his position. While he sent frequent reports to Congress, sought information regarding the feelings of the Canadians, planning an invasion, if possible, of Canada, his enemies were not idle. They wrote Massachusetts concerning his faults and conduct, resulting in a delegation being sent to investigate the situation, and inform Arnold that he would, in the future, be subordinate to a new commander, Colonel Moses Hinman, a Connecticut man. Arnold met this affront with fury! The squabbles with civil authorities and fellow officers turned him so sour that he decided to resign. Reaching Albany, he received an added blow when he was informed that his wife had died. He returned to Connecticut.

His sister, Hannah, had assumed the care of the three young boys, as she was shortly to take complete charge of his business affairs, but there was much personal business to attend to as well. To add to his misery, he suffered a recurrence of gout, which was to plague him throughout his life.

While he sorted out cargoes waiting to be dispersed, and arranged to send others on their way, he restlessly awaited news·

of his still unsettled accounts for monies due him from the Fort Ticonderoga venture. Only after the intercession of his friend, Silas Deane, was he finally reimbursed.

Plans were submitted from several sources for an expedition to Canada. They outlined two separate campaigns, one to move down Lake Champlain, take St. Johns, Chambly, and Montreal, then to join another at Quebec, which would have followed a route up the Kennebec, Dead, and Chaudiere Rivers. Arnold's offer to lead the expedition through Maine appealed to Washington. The two men had finally met in camp at Cambridge, and there seems to have been an instant rapport, which continued throughout the war, ending only with Arnold's defection. Moreover, Washington was sympathetic towards Arnold's recent troubles, and knowing that Arnold and Schuyler were friends and worked well together, decided to appoint Philip Schuyler to one spur of the Canadian venture, Arnold to the other.

The plan was in action. Time was crucial if the expeditions were to be effective before the onslaught of winter. Two hundred bateaux were needed on the Kennebec, provisions had to be gathered and men enlisted. It seemed almost impossible that everything could be accomplished in time. The route had to be checked out with Indians familiar with the wilderness and who might have information concerning the garrison at Quebec.

Finally, early in September, Schuyler agreed to lead the route down the lakes to Canada, and moved north to besiege St. Johns. Almost immediately he had to return to Ticonderoga due to illness, and Brigadier General Richard Montgomery, originally of the British army and now with the Continental army, replaced him. Montgomery was successful in the capture of Chambly in October and pressed on to take St. Johns and Montreal early in November.

Meanwhile Arnold was a dynamo of action. Ten companies of New Englanders were enlisted, led by Lieutenant Colonel Roger Enos of Vermont, Major Return Jonathan Meigs of Connecticut, Colonel Christopher Greene of Rhode Island, and Major Timothy

Bigelow of Massachusetts. These units were joined by three companies of frontiersmen, two from Pennsylvania and one from Virginia, and eight companies of riflemen. These last were soon to make their worth very evident. Their leader was Captain Daniel Morgan of Virginia. The entire expedition numbered 1,050, including two women (wives of Pennsylvania riflemen), a couple of Princeton College boys (Aaron Burr was one) and Eleazer Oswald, who served as Arnold's private secretary. Despite numerous delays, the men marched to Newburyport where they embarked for Gardiner, Arnold joining them as they sailed Tuesday, September 19.

Five days later they anchored on the Kennebec, off Colburn's shipyard at Gardiner where Arnold found a serious problem awaiting him. This would be just one of many to test his never copious patience.

Reuben Colburn had been given a nearly impossible task — to build two hundred bateaux in eighteen days, and what he had accomplished were poorly constructed. Why bateaux were suggested in the first place is not known; a heavier, more unwieldy craft can't be imagined, especially for the conditions they were to face. Canoes would have been ideal, as the few they used soon proved.

Despite the gloomy news brought back by scouts that General Guy Carleton, governor of the province, was expecting an invasion from New England, and that spies were posted on the route they hoped to travel, Arnold's indomitable confidence held firm. He had the journal and map of the British army engineer, Lieutenant John Montresor, drawn in 1761, a number of St. Francis Indians, who would act as guides, along with a deep conviction that they would be successful, so he moved his army up the Kennebec to Fort Western, near Augusta. Here, he drew up his campaign plan and deployed his forces into four divisions, with Morgan, Greene, Meigs, and Enos to lead them. Morgan, with his riflemen, was delegated to cut a road across the Great Carrying Place between the Kennebec and Dead Rivers, and so was the first detachment to get under way. They were followed by the other divisions, a day or so apart. Arnold was detained briefly at Fort Western, but followed rapidly, via canoe, and was soon at the head of the expedition. His optimism never shone brighter than when he wrote Washington, on September 25, that "we shall be able to perform the march in twenty days."[7] However, between September 25 and October 9, he was to encounter difficulties which seemed insurmountable: falls where the bateaux had to be emptied, lifted up and repacked; a swift change in the weather to freezing conditions; the discovery that the bateaux, built so hastily, needed repairs to hold them together; and that many of the provisions had been ruined as a result of being soaked in the leaky boats, and therefore had to be discarded.

The route grew more difficult as the forest gathered around them and the sparse settlements dwindled. The men were able to augment their supplies with the occasional luck of a hunting or fishing party, but there never seemed enough to go around such a large complement of men.

On October 11, Arnold reached the Great Carrying Place and received the news from a reconnaissance crew that the route ahead of them was even worse, but that at least there weren't any hostile Indians along the Chaudiere as they had feared. The marshy conditions, resulting from heavy rains, made the area a nightmare. Transporting heavy bateaux, provisions and equipment, while struggling for one's own footing, was a Herculean feat, which wasn't made easier by the onslaught of nausea and diarrhea brought on by the men drinking brackish water.

On October 13 Arnold wrote several letters, which would threaten the entire expedition. Before the war he had traded with Canada, and in due course made many friends and business contacts. One of these was John Manir, actually John Dyer Mercier, a merchant in Quebec. One of Arnold's letters was to this gentleman, asking him for information concerning the strength of the garrison at Quebec, and the general feeling of the Canadians concerning this attempt to set them free to join the rebellion. Another of the letters was to Schuyler, which was to be delivered to Montgomery. Needless to say, the letters were very informative, detailing the expedition's route as they struggled north through the wilderness. He had entrusted these letters to Eneas, an Indian he thought he could trust. Unfortunately, they were handed over to the commander of the garrison, Hentor Cramahé, who promptly arrested Mercier, placed the city on constant alert, and moved boats of any kind that could be used to transport enemy troops across from the Point Levis side of the St. Lawrence. Although Arnold still had a considerable distance to travel, with added trials to encounter, Quebec was ready for his arrival.

Torrential rains, with hurricane-like force, caused flooding of the Dead River, making a crossing hazardous and causing confusion and loss of direction of the men. More of their meager provisions were lost; the situation appeared so hopeless that Arnold called a council of war. He told his officers the true situation, holding nothing back. After a brief hesitation they agreed to continue.

Captain Oliver Hanchet, with a small party, was to go ahead in an attempt to reach the French settlements, obtain supplies and get them back to the suffering troops. The sick were to be sent back to the rear divisions, and Greene and Enos were to proceed with all possible speed to join Arnold in the van.

When Enos received his orders and learned what lay ahead, he determined to return to Cambridge, and promptly did so, taking with him a large supply of provisions. In doing so, he wantonly abandoned the expedition to its fate.

When Arnold learned of Enos's return, he was furious, as was Washington, who ordered Enos arrested and tried for refusal to obey his commander's orders. At about the same time this information reached Arnold, he also learned what had happened to his letters. Coupled with his current problems was the knowledge of the loss of secrecy upon which success of the expedition depended.

Arnold's conduct, through all these adversities, had won him the admiration of his men. John Joseph Henry, though not an Arnold fan generally, writes of his commander's kindness to him when he discovered the young man so ill he was unable to stand. Arnold quickly sought out a nearby settler, arranged for Henry to be taken to his cabin to be cared for, and also gave Henry two silver dollars out of his own pocket.[8]

The heroism of those who continued the journey was phenomenal. Tales of marching in bare feet, wading in water up to their waists, boiling torn, useless moccasins to provide some nourishment, killing dogs in the party for food, fighting illness and weakness, create the horror which existed. One of the women who had accompanied her husband, buried him herself when he died along the trail, then rejoined the expedition.

Hanchet's small party went astray, and Arnold headed another to search ahead for supplies. They reached the Chaudiere and only luck saved the whole army from going over falls down the river. Another portage was required before they could again enter the river. At last the settlements of the Canadians were reached, and the people proved sympathetic to the ragged, starving men emerging from the wilderness. Supplies were dispatched back to the divisions still struggling along the trail. Oatmeal, flour, cattle, and mutton were welcome sights and soon restored the optimism of men who had reached the point of hopelessness. In a letter of November 8 to Washington, Arnold speaks of the horrendous conditions, Montgomery's capture of Chambly, and dated news of conditions at Quebec, which account for the general buoyancy of his mood. The virtually indestructible drive of the man must have been incredible. Here the surviving remnant of his army are not yet steady on their feet—the assault upon a fortified city still before them—and his confidence is unshakeable!

It appears that even Henry's feelings (perhaps because of his rescue due to Arnold's personal intervention) changed, since he writes from near Quebec: "Our commander is a gentleman worthy of the trust reposed in him; a man, I believe, of invincible courage, of great prudence; ever serene, he defies the greatest danger to affect him, or difficulties to alter his temper; in fine, you will ever find him the intrepid hero and the unruffled Christian."[9]

Still, there was the St. Lawrence to cross and it was too high — impossible for canoes (the only transport available) to navigate. Another frustrating delay, and one which allowed British reinforcements to reach Quebec from England.

Finally, the river was crossed and the initial party discovered, but they managed to gain the heights of the Plains of Abraham and dig in. A flag of truce, demanding surrender of the garrison, was insultingly fired upon, and all attempts to lure the men from the safety of the city unsuccessful. A siege was the only answer, and this would be impossible with supplies of the besiegers dangerously low. Arnold decided to await the arrival of Montgomery and withdrew twenty miles up the river to Pointe-aux- Trembles. Provisions were found, and the men were billeted amongst the inhabitants.

Their spirits were revived when news reached them of the fall of Montreal, and a supply of clothing, guns, and ammunition captured by Montgomery arrived, closely followed by Montgomery himself. This very personable former British officer was impressed with Arnold's ragged corps, finding them "an exceedingly fine one. There is a style of discipline among them, much superior to what I have been used to see in this campaign."[10]

After some unpleasantness with Captain Hanchet, who became truculent and uncooperative once again, Montgomery and Arnold finally returned to Quebec. Now, however, they had Carleton to contend with. He had escaped from Montreal and reached Quebec, obdurate and determined to lose no more of Canada to the rebels.

The only possible solution was to attack the city before the enlistments of the men ran out on January 1, but now there was further dissension among the officers, no doubt instigated by Major John Brown, Arnold's old enemy, aided and abetted by

Captain Hanchet. A near mutiny was only avoided by the diplomacy of Montgomery, and at last luck turned their way in the form of the weather — it began to snow on December 30! By the next day, blizzard conditions existed, as did plans for an attack that night. Dividing their forces into four separate divisions to attack at different locations, they hoped for the element of surprise. Unfortunately, they were to be deprived once again of this so necessary feature. Due to an informant their plans were known by the British.

In the assault, the brave Montgomery was killed, and Arnold wounded, both brought down at the head of their troops. Arnold was the victim of an apparent ricocheting bullet, according to Dr. Isaac Senter: "two-thirds of the ball entered the outer side of the [left] leg, about midway, and in an oblique course between the tibia and the fibula, and lodged in the gastroennemea muscle at the rise of the tendon Achilles, where upon examination I easily discovered and extracted it."[11] Morgan's corps, using scaling ladders, surmounted the first barrier, but due to hesitation further on, were surrounded and had to surrender. The Americans lost 48 killed, 34 wounded, and 372 captured.

Arnold, now in command, sent an urgent message from his bed in the General Hospital to General David Wooster at Montreal, asking for help; though he would not be moved to a safer position he was determined to give a good account of himself if Carleton advanced. "We entreated General Arnold," says Dr. Senter, who had accompanied the expedition as surgeon, "for his own safety to be carried back into the country, where they could not readily find him, but to no purpose. He would neither be removed nor suffer a man from the hospital to retreat. He ordered his pistols loaded, with a sword on his bed, adding, he was determined to kill as many as possible, if they came into the room."[12] This in the midst of a wide-scale desertion of troops running for the comparative safety of Montreal!

Arnold's courage was certainly admirable, as he fiercely tried to move the sluggish Wooster: "For God's sake, order as many men down as you can possibly spare, consistent with the safety of Montreal, and all the mortars, howitzers, and shells that you can possibly bring. I hope you can stop every rascal who has deserted from us, and bring him back again."[13]

Arnold might be out of the fray, but he was far from being out of action. He continuously besieged Wooster, who managed to procrastinate maddeningly, sending only a token support. The only balm Arnold received at this time was the news of his promotion to brigadier general.

The accolades poured in from every hand and were no doubt much appreciated, but they could only distract his attention briefly. The American current position was perilous in the extreme. While they continued to blockade the city of Quebec, hunger and an epidemic of smallpox settled in amongst them. Furthermore, Major John Brown once again began to plague Arnold.

It is evident that this man loathed Benedict Arnold for some reason. He'd known him before the war because of his marriage into the Arnold family and whether it was due to some prior disagreement, a personal distaste, or just plain jealously, we shall never know. Whatever the reason, he used every opportunity to malign Arnold and cause trouble for him. (A thorough examination of this situation is covered in appendix 3)

Now Brown argued that Montgomery had promised him a promotion to the grade of colonel, which Arnold knew to be true, since he'd been a witness. But, since Brown, along with Easton, was currently in disgrace because of being apprehended plundering the enemy officers' baggage, Arnold felt no promotion was in order. What's more, he clearly stated so in a letter to the president of Congress. As would be expected, Brown was furious. The bickering continued for months.

By the time Wooster finally arrived on April 1 to assume command, Arnold was able to move around, if painfully. The personalities of the two men, so vastly divided in temperament as well as age, did not augur a peaceful situation. Arnold was finally given the opportunity to extricate himself, due to the aggravation of his wound when his horse slipped and fell on the ice. It was better that the two men separated at this time. An open confrontation could only have belittled them both.

Arnold settled into the headquarters in Montreal, at the Chateau de Ramezay, where in April he soon had the not unpleasant duty of receiving and entertaining the Congressional Commission, sent to survey the situation and hoping to win favor with the Canadians so they would unite with the American cause. It was clearly a case of "putting the cart before the horse," since the Canadians were at that point disenchanted by the whole idea and had no faith in the success of the rebellion because of the debacle at Quebec, which was so soon to be raised by General John Thomas, Wooster's replacement.

The commissioners were three in number, all members of Congress: Benjamin Franklin, Samuel Chase, and Charles Carroll of Carrollton. Also persuaded to join the party was the Reverend John Carroll, a Jesuit priest, and cousin of Charles. It was thought he would be helpful because he not only spoke French fluently, but would also be able to offset the many American denunciations of Catholicism, which had made the French-Canadians wary of joining in the rebellion.

With his usual aplomb, Benedict Arnold made ready to receive the dignitaries. "We were received by General Arnold on our landing in the most polite and friendly manner, conducted to headquarters where a genteel company of ladies and gentlemen was assembled to welcome our arrival. As we went from the landing place to the General's house, the cannon of the citadel fired in compliment to us as the Commissioners of Congress. We supped at the General's, and after supper were conducted by the General and other gentlemen to our lodgings, the house of Mr. Thomas Walker, the best built and perhaps the best furnished in this town."[14]

The commissioners found deplorable conditions rampant in the army. Disease and apathetic conduct were everywhere. The

Canadians were refusing to provide sustenance because they were aware of the fact that no funds were available for payment. Creditors were constantly clamoring for payment for goods already delivered.

In the midst of this maddening situation, Arnold was burdened with further vexation. Before the commissioners left Canada, they had instructed him, because of the dire need of the men, to confiscate such merchandise as he required from the merchants in Montreal, and distribute them amongst the men. He was to issue certificates to the merchants, promising future payment. He did this and directed Major Scott to deliver the supplies to Moses Hazen at Chambly. Hazen, still angry because of a tongue-lashing he had received from Arnold at a strategy session, refused to accept the supplies, or even ensure their safety. Instead, he left them on the riverbank where they soon fell prey to thieving soldiers. Out of this aggravating situation a nasty exchange ensued, resulting in Arnold ordering a court-martial for Hazen. The evidence of Major Scott surprisingly was not accepted by the Court, and because Arnold protested, he was accused of "ungentlemanly conduct," rather a strong interpretation of his words which indicated that he thought the refusal to accept Scott's evidence "unprecedented and unjust."[15]

When the Court appealed to General Gates, he took the easy way out and dissolved the Court, sending an explanation of his action to Congress. Arnold had been following orders and openly confided in the commissioners, as well as Generals Schuyler and John Sullivan. He certainly didn't act very secretively.

During the spring of 1776, a position approximately thirty-six miles above Montreal, called "The Cedars," was being held by Colonel Timothy Bedell, under orders of General Arnold. When, in May, a party of British, Canadians, and Indians began to move against this outpost, Colonel Bedell made a dash to Montreal to obtain help. The post was left under the command of Major Isaac Butterfield, who panicked at the presence of the Indians, and without even attempting a defense, surrendered.

Arnold sent Major Henry Sherburne, with 140 men to strengthen the post, and intended to follow as soon as he could, not knowing that it had already surrendered. Unfortunately, Major Sherburne walked straight into an ambush, and after a fierce fight was captured. Arnold was livid at Butterfield for not making any attempt to defend the post, which might have been successfully held until Major Sherburne could arrive. The loss of life was extremely heavy and particularly brutal, many men being slaughtered even after they had stopped fighting.

Arnold rushed out in an attempt to re-take the post and rescue the prisoners, but the Indians had moved quickly to place their captives beyond his reach. His attempt to negotiate via a friendly Indian brought no solution, only an answering threat that all captives would be put to death instantly if any attempt was made to free them.

Finally, the British sent a flag of truce with a proposition: the captives would be freed if an equal number of British prisoners were exchanged. If the edict was turned down, all the prisoners would be killed by the Indians. Arnold signed the agreement. He could do nothing else. "Words cannot express my feelings," he wrote the Congressional Committee, "torn by conflicting passions of revenge, raging for action, urged me on, on one hand; and humanity for five hundred unhappy wretches, who were on the point of being sacrificed if our vengeance was not delayed, plead strongly on the other."[16]

The matter continued to be tossed back and forth, Congress refusing to sanction any agreement, and Washington writing to the British concerning the case.

Arnold returned to Montreal, and now it became evident that the long attempt to join Canada to the rebellion must be abandoned. The army, brought to despair by disease and lack of pay, could not continue amidst the news that reinforcements of 13,000 men were pouring into the British camp, determined to force the Americans out of Canada. All the suffering and loss of life had brought nothing but defeat in the end. General John Thomas, who

had replaced Wooster, had died of the smallpox, and the command was now in the hands of General John Sullivan, a New
Hampshire lawyer and politician. The choice was not a wise one,
which soon became evident when he was defeated in an engagement at Three Rivers, early in June. Arnold wrote Sullivan that
they must evacuate the men. He would hold Montreal until they
could be brought out, and then retreat to St. Johns. When Sullivan
abandoned Sorel, Arnold had to leave Montreal in a hurry and
move to St. Johns.

On June 18, Benedict Arnold and the young Captain James
Wilkinson were the last to step into the boats from the waterfront
at St. Johns. Everything had been done to destroy whatever could
be of use to the British who were hot on their heels. Removing
the saddles from their horses, they shot the animals, and stepped
into a boat, Wilkinson first. True to his promise, Arnold was the
last to leave Canada.

There are so many "ifs" concerning this expedition: "if" it
had not taken so long to get there; "if" conditions had been kinder
along the wilderness trail; "if" Arnold's messengers had not betrayed him, alerting the garrison at Quebec; "if" he had not been
delayed in crossing the St. Lawrence; "if" he had not been hampered by the imminent expiration of many of his men's enlistments; "if" Montgomery had not been killed; "if" Arnold had
not been wounded. They go on and on. The only explanation,
when one looks back upon their number, is that fate decreed
otherwise.

Arnold's understanding and tolerance of military duties,
which must prevail equally among the men, as well as officers,
is illustrated by a predicament he found himself in at one point
during the siege of Quebec. The anecdote was recorded in the
deposition of Josiah Sabin, when he applied for a pension following the war. Sabin, a Fairfield, Connecticut, man, was one
of Seth Warner's Green Mountain Boys and served in the unit

sent down Lake Champlain early in 1776 to assist Arnold in the capture of Quebec. When he filed his deposition in 1832, it was evident that the incident remained clearly in his memory:

> General Arnold, who had been out woman hunting be-
> yond the line of sentinels, late at night attempted to pass this
> declarant to come into quarters. This declarant ordered him
> to stand and to give the countersign. The latter he could not
> do, as he left his quarters before the countersign was given
> out. He was compelled to remain in this situation until the
> guard was relieved. General Arnold afterwards complimented
> this declarant for his faithful performance of duty.[17]

Embarrassing no doubt, perhaps even humorous, but nevertheless an illustration of Arnold's taking his clouts along with his men.

Much has been written concerning Arnold's incredible march through the tractless wilderness of Maine. That any of the original 1,050 who started out survived, is nothing short of a miracle. The various journals kept by men who were a part of this expedition have been gathered together into a single volume, *March to Quebec*, by the novelist Kenneth Roberts. He had ferreted out and studied each journal during his research for the novel *Arundel*. They make interesting reading, indeed. We find Arnold sharing the privations of his men, urging them on past the limits of endurance, establishing the camaraderie and devotion of those under his command, which would continue throughout his military career.

# Chapter IV
## Commodore to Major General, 1776–1777

By late June, Benedict Arnold had reached Albany disheartened and despondent over the lack of a victory, and harassed by the bickering and attacks of several subordinate officers, which added to the difficulties of rendering an accurate account of supplies, many of which he had provided for out of his own pocket. Arnold was deeply angered at the slander directed at him, accusing him of plundering supplies. "I cannot but think it extremely cruel," he wrote to Gates, "when I have sacrificed my ease, health, and a great part of my private property, in the cause of my country, to be calumniated as a robber and thief—at a time, too, when I have it not in my power to be heard in my own defense."[1] It was true he could have sought a court-martial, but again time played him a cruel trick. Late summer found him involved in building a mini-fleet and training crews for a stand against the expected British attempt to sail up Lake Champlain and split the Colonies.

On July 23, 1776, Benedict Arnold arrived in the small village of Skenesborough (Whitehall, New York), situated at the extreme southern end of Lake Champlain. Conditions in the shipyard were chaotic. The heat was unbearable, mosquitos were a torment, and malaria-type fevers rampant amongst the men. The remnants of a Loyalist shipyard with two sawmills and a forge had been re-activated. Timber was being felled and brought to the mills by men literally staggering with exhaustion and illness. Arnold plunged into the melee with his usual gusto, working with the men, dashing off letters far into the night begging supplies. Everything was needed: sailcloth, nails, rigging, cordage, axes, blocks, and oakum. The list grew longer by the hour. But needed most were ship carpenters. When finished and afloat, the ships would need sailors, not farmers, which was about all he had to work with. Confusion reigned.

He went down to Ticonderoga to supervise vessels building there and back again to Skenesborough. All the time the thought in his mind that plagued him most was what the British were doing at St. Johns, on the other end of the lake. He knew they would have a superior force, unlimited supplies and men, but hoped they would be delayed getting it all together.

By August 15, nearly all the mini-fleet was afloat, though still needing some finishing and rigging. There were three schooners, one sloop, two galleys, and eight gondolas (the latter two types designed to navigate in the shallow areas of the lake, and maneuvered by the use of sweeps). Arnold was ready to take command. Unfortunately, for the second time in his military career, he was beset with a squabble for leadership. This time it was not Ethan Allen, but he was caught between Horatio Gates and General Schuyler. Schuyler was still the commander of the Northern army, with Gates his assistant, though he would have preferred otherwise. Schuyler had appointed a Dutchman, Jacobus Wynkoop, as commander of the fleet when it was ready to sail. Gates appointed Arnold, who he felt was more experienced in nautical matters. After some unpleasantness, when Gates insisted on his choice, Wynkoop was dispatched to Albany, and Arnold remained undisputed commander of the fleet—commodore, indeed!

He immediately decided his men needed time to learn how to handle their ships, and the best way to do that was to take them onto the lake. They would also be able to learn more of what was transpiring at the enemy camp, if they could approach near enough to observe. They might even be able to cause some delaying action.

After several weeks of this, hampered by a storm, he was able, from a temporary anchorage off the Isle la Motte, to gain an all too clear picture of the activities in St. Johns. The news was not good. Against such a superior force as the British were building the only course was to make the enemy come to him.

Withdrawing further south, Arnold found the perfect spot, Valcour Island. Three miles long, two wide, and a bit less than a mile off the west shore of the lake, the island was relatively high, covered with a thick stand of pine. A small bluff on the west shore of the island overlooked the mainland. He could arrange his fleet in the bay, and the trees on the island would hide his masts from anyone on the lake. Presently joined by an additional three galleys, he transferred from the *Royal Savage* to one of them, the *Congress*, making it his flagship. All told, he had 800 men and 86 guns of rather small calibers.

As Arnold waited for the enemy to find him, he must have realized his position was precarious. Surprise was important, but if his ships were trapped in their present position, which could happen, there was no escape through the channel to the north. The wait must have been an uncomfortable one, and it would have been even more so if the Americans had known the exact strength of the enemy: ship *Inflexible*, schooners *Maria* and *Carleton*, the rideau *Thunderer*, one gondola, 20 gun boats, 4 longboats, an additional 24 longboats, loaded with provisions — all heavily manned, capable of throwing twice the weight of metal of Arnold's ships. The ordnance of the British fleet was far greater in fire power. The *Inflexible* alone could have blasted Arnold's fleet out of the water. The one advantage he had, outside of surprise, was the southerly breeze which would bring the British past the island before his fleet could be spotted, and then make it difficult for them to come about to attack.

On October 11, at eleven o'clock in the morning, they finally came, passing Valcour Island by some two miles before sighting Arnold's fleet, which he had arranged in a crescent in the bay, with *Congress* in dead center. It was now Benedict Arnold against

Sir Guy Carleton, commander of the British force, which at that moment had hurriedly swung about to battle the stiff north wind. Their gunboats, aided by their oars, were able to make faster time, and they made haste to range in a line outside the bay, penning Arnold in. Before the larger vessels could establish a position, Arnold weighed anchor and brought *Congress*, along with *Royal Savage* and two other galleys, out to attack the gunboats, hoping to put some of them out of commission before the *Carleton* could beat up within range. The gunboats, each armed with a field piece, and several with howitzers as well, had moved up to within musket shot, and proved too formidable. The *Carleton* joined them to inflict considerable damage to *Congress* and *Royal Savage*. In attempting to maneuver in the narrow channel, *Royal Savage* ran aground on the southern end of Valcour. The vessel was set afire by the enemy, and her crew had to abandon her.

*Congress*, back in position, kept up heavy fire, with Arnold personally having to aim his guns to concentrate on the *Carleton*. For nearly five hours the *Carleton* became the target of nearly every gun in Arnold's fleet, suffering heavy damage. The larger ships of the British fleet struggled to come to her aid, finally reaching her in the final hours of the battle, and managed to tow her to safety. Half of her crew were dead, or wounded, and she was rapidly taking in water. As the afternoon waned and dusk approached, the British pulled back, though continuing a long-range fire.

When darkness finally fell, firing from both sides ceased. The British felt confident that they had Arnold's fleet safely penned up in their bay and that when dawn came the next morning they could finish him off.

But, as so often happened, the enemy forgot to reckon with Benedict Arnold's ingenuity. He called a conference of his officers, and it was quickly agreed that to remain where they were and fight it out in the morning was pure suicide. Three-quarters of their ammunition was gone. Their only chance was to attempt to escape, a risky procedure if the watch aboard the enemy ships were alert.

About seven o'clock, when sufficient darkness had fallen, and a fortuitous fog had developed, Arnold began to move his fleet out of the bay, hoping to pass between the west end of the British line and the mainland.

The *Trumbull* hoisted sail first and began to move slowly, with the rest of the fleet following, one behind the other, with but a single shaded lantern hung aft of each ship, visible only to those directly behind.

Holding their breath, and no speaking permitted — sound carries well over water — within a few hours they had done the impossible. When enough distance had been gained, the crews broke out their sweeps to add speed to their escape.

All went well until dawn brought a wind from the south, making it very difficult for the crippled fleet to move with any speed. When they reached Schuyler's Island, some five miles south of Valcour, the damage incurred during the battle made it evident they would have to anchor to make hasty repairs and abandon the three gondolas, *Providence, New York,* and *Jersey,* which could go no further.

Meanwhile, this same dawn caused consternation amongst the British fleet when the light showed an empty bay at Valcour. Carleton, suddenly aware of what had transpired during the night, swiftly set sail in pursuit. The same south wind, which had impeded Arnold, slowed the British as well, but with more canvas available to them, they gained steadily on Arnold, whose crews rowed steadily the rest of that day and through the night.

The morning of October 13, the wind veered around to blow from the northeast, and the two fleets reached the shallows at Split Rock at about the same time. The battle was joined once again, with an almost immediate surrender of the galley *Washington.* Her damage from the first battle was too severe for her to continue. Arnold was then at the mercy of the British fleet and sustaining such damage to *Congress,* and the four gondolas which remained of his fleet, that he ordered them run ashore in a small bay on the Vermont shore, approximately five miles west of what is now Vergennes, and which is called, to this day, Arnold Bay. *Congress*, bringing up the rear of this action, continued firing to protect as much as possible the disembarkation of the smaller ships.

When Sir Guy Carleton saw that he had won, he ceased firing and watched as the small mangled ships were set afire by the Americans, *Congress* last, Benedict Arnold the last to leave her.

The ragged line of survivors started through the woods to Crown Point, which they reached that evening, escaping the Indians who were put ashore in pursuit.

The battle was lost. The ships so hastily built were gone, except *Trumbull, Revenge,* and *Enterprise*, which escaped to Crown Point, but in the midst of defeat there was a victory of sorts. Carleton had lost valuable time. Winter was nearly upon them. His hopes of capturing Fort Ticonderoga would have to be set aside. The American cause gained another year in which to gather the strength to sustain the campaign of John Burgoyne in 1777. The winter of 1776 brought silence from both sides, and respite to heal their wounds. The fight was still far from ended.[2]

This same winter of 1776–1777, found Benedict Arnold back in New England. Besides a brief visit with his family in New Haven, he had been delegated by Washington to report on the general threat to the New England area, now that the British had occupied Newport, Rhode Island. In this capacity he visited Boston, where he contacted old friends and was included in the general social scene, apparently mixing business with pleasure. Here he came under the spell of a certain young lady.

Elizabeth DeBlois, the sixteen-year-old daughter of Gilbert DeBlois, importer of hardwood and liquors, vestryman of King's Chapel, was a banished Loyalist. The young lady was a slender dark beauty with gray-blue eyes, an oval fair face and a luscious, shapely mouth, pleasantly curved at the corners in a slight smile. She had been very popular with the young British officers before the evacuation. Her family was wealthy, even if strained a bit at present due to the war. Arnold, now thirty-six, was captivated.

*Elizabeth DeBlois*

Photo Courtesy of *Yankee* Magazine;
Painting in possession of Stephen DeBlois

He took every opportunity to be in her presence, which was often, and was perhaps aided and abetted by Lucy, wife of General Henry Knox, which is indicated by a letter of March 4, 1777, concerning a trunk of gowns Arnold had acquired, and which he had delivered to Mrs. Knox, to be offered, hopefully, to Miss Betsey:

> Dear Madam:
>
> I have taken the liberty of inclosing a letter for the Heavenly Miss DeBlois, which beg the favor of your delivering, with the trunk of gowns, etc., which Mrs. Colburn promised me to send to your house. I hope she will make no objections against receiving them. I made no doubt you will soon have the pleasure of seeing the charming Mrs. Emery, and have it in your power to give me some favorable intelligence. I shall remain under the most anxious suspense until I have the favor of a line from you, who (if I may judge) will from your own experience, conceive the fond anxiety, the glowing hopes, and chilling fears, that alternately possess the breast of
>
> 
>
> Dear Madam,
>
> Your Obed't
>
> Most Humble Serv't,
>
> 
>
> Mrs. Knox, Boston                B. Arnold[3]

Whether Arnold's gift offended the young lady, or she just didn't take to her ardent suitor, or, which is most likely, her mother demurred, she turned him down.

At this point Arnold was having difficulties of another sort. Massachusetts continued to delay sending troops against the British in Rhode Island, and in February he received the news that Congress had appointed five major generals, all junior and inferior to Arnold. In its attempt to placate the individual states, Congress promoted five men who would eventually prove their lack of ability, over a man who was senior to them all and certainly more qualified. Resentment between Massachusetts and Connecticut (which already had two major generals) surely contributed to the decision. However, it was a grand slap in the face if ever there was one, and Arnold reacted as one might expect—he tendered his resignation, as did several others who also felt they had been slighted.

Washington was chagrined over the omission of Arnold and while advising him not to be too hasty, promised to investigate the matter. Fearing to lose the services of an officer he valued, Washington did make inquiries on his behalf, without success, and Arnold continued to plan his resignation.

The night of April 25, 1777, while Arnold was in New Haven with his family, two thousand British regulars landed at Compo Beach, Westport, Connecticut, just east of the present city of Norwalk. Their intention was to conduct what we would call today a "commando raid" on Danbury, approximately twenty-two miles north, where the patriots had collected stores of salt, meat, flour, and grain, as well as quartermaster's supplies of hay, tents, uniforms, powder, shot, muskets, and various hogsheads of rum. These items were all collected with great difficulty, bit by bit, to be used by Washington's army, but a spy had spread the word to Sir William Howe, and the British were anxious to destroy them, particularly the military items, before they could be distributed. With great dispatch the landing party, led by Major General William Tryon, ex-royal governor of New York and Brigadier Generals James Agnew and Sir William Erskine, were guided north by Ephraim de Forest, a Redding shoemaker, and two other Tories, Eli Benedict and Stephen Jarvis. They reached Danbury with virtually no opposition and commenced to wreak havoc in the town, destroying the supplies. Aided by the supply of rum they discovered, the troops were soon running wild, setting fires indiscriminately.

Meanwhile, the alarm was spread by the meager defenders at Danbury, who, realizing they were ill equipped to put up any defense, had retreated from the town. Brigadier General Gold Sellect Silliman, reached at his home in Fairfield, immediately gathered his four hundred militiamen and moved towards Danbury. At Redding he was joined by Brigadier General Benedict

Arnold, with a motley crew of farmers he'd gathered on the way. He was followed by General David Wooster and some two hundred men from the New Haven militia. All three detachments converged on Bethel where they spent the night, soaked to the skin by a sudden spring storm. Together they numbered about seven hundred men, of whom only a few were professional soldiers. Wooster was selected to command. A senior officer, he was then sixty-seven. He and Arnold were not exactly friends, after the campaign in Canada.

By dawn of April 27, the British were making a hasty exit of Danbury, their purpose accomplished. Alerted that there was a contingent of rebels between them and their ships at Compo Bay, they hastened south towards Ridgefield, destroying further stores at Isaac Keeler's mill on the way.

The British had overestimated the American strength at Bethel, perhaps because they were informed that the force included Benedict Arnold. William Tryon hoped to avoid "Mr." Arnold, who was well known to the British and considered a formidable adversary. Thomas Glyn, Ensign, noted that "he gave a great specimen during this War that tho ignorant of a Military Education and of all Military Science, yet by great resolution and a mind full of enterprise, he became a most excellent Partisan skillful in the management of Light Troops."[4] As they stopped to prepare a meal, they were caught off their guard by men led by General Wooster. The resulting confusion prevented an orderly defense, and Wooster was able to take prisoners and cause considerable damage. On the double, the raiders pressed on to Ridgefield, but Wooster came at them once again. During the resulting foray, Wooster received a mortal wound and confusion spread amongst the rebel forces, enabling the British to press forward to Ridgefield.

Silliman and Arnold had not been inactive during Wooster's harrying of the British rear, but were busily gathering men they encountered on the way to Ridgefield. Arnold's charisma and his already established popularity brought followers eager to serve with him. The small force reached the town and threw up a hasty barricade across the narrowest section of Main Street, quite the highest level of the town and the only spot to make any sort of stand.

Tryon's Dragoons went ahead, discovered the rude barricade of carts, barrels, and logs, and the small force waiting behind it. When this knowledge was reported to him, Tryon grouped his men into three columns, all seasoned regular troops, veterans of Lexington, Concord, and Bunker Hill. The 4th Royal Artillery added the further strength of six field pieces.

Behind the barricade the Americans watched, awed to silence at the strength of the British force advancing towards them. When they were finally within range, the Americans opened fire. The British retaliated, but the barricade held. Tryon quickly realized he wasn't going to breach the barricade as easily as he'd thought, so he sent a force to find out if a flanking operation was possible. General Agnew's men finally gained the advantage and the Americans were forced to retreat.

Mounted on his horse, Arnold, trying to organize an orderly withdrawal, was an attractive target. His horse fell to heavy fire, Arnold himself untouched. He managed to disentangle himself from his fallen mount's stirrups and escape the intentions of a soldier who dashed towards him, shouting: "Surrender! You are my prisoner." Arnold replied with a pistol shot, which felled his assailant and enabled him to escape.

The British were now in possession of the town, but after some random shooting and cannonading of the Keeler Tavern, they withdrew to make camp for the night. Early the next morning, they began a hasty run for their ships, harried by Arnold, who was joined by Colonel John Lamb, Colonel Eleazer Oswald, and Lieutenant Jabez Huntington, and the remnants of militiamen left from the stand on Main Street.

By the time the British reached Compo Bay, their supply of ammunition was sorely diminished and they determined to make a final charge with bayonets. The Americans were so demoralized by this horror that they refused to face the enemy again,

despite Arnold's efforts to rally the militia. There were no further advances and the British boarded their ships without another shot being fired.[5]

Once again Arnold had come to the aid of his country, and
for his actions was rewarded by Congress with another horse
"properly comparisoned," and promotion to major general! However, they withheld his seniority. The five promoted before him
remained his seniors. Thus Arnold became a pawn in the controversy between Congress and the military. They could not understand the niceties of rank and what the proper designation of
such could mean, considering it all a matter of "scrambling of
apes for nuts," as John Adams put it.[6]

While Washington wanted Arnold in Peekskill to take command of the Hudson, Arnold thought it best to go to Philadelphia to try and settle the matter of his rank and also his still
unresolved accounts left over from the Canadian venture. He
failed on both counts and decided, once again, in July, to resign.
Washington and Schuyler dissuaded him and so he joined the
northern army at Fort Edward, and with General Schuyler prepared to meet the challenge of Burgoyne's invasion, which had
already brought about the recapture of Fort Ticonderoga.

## Chapter V
## From Honor to Dishonor, 1777–1780

To consolidate the success of splitting the Colonies, with a hoped-for collapse of the rebellion, the British planned a three-part pincer movement: a force led by John Burgoyne to come south from Canada to Albany; a party led by Barry St. Leger to sail up the St. Lawrence River, enter the waters of Lake Ontario, land at Oswego, capture Fort Stanwix, and move through the Mohawk Valley to Albany; the third prong to be Sir William Howe moving up the Hudson Valley.

Finding John Burgoyne delegated to lead the invasion force from Canada, we must not come to the conclusion that General Carleton had fallen from grace, though he was disliked by Lord George Germain, Great Britain's war minister, and it was thought in certain circles that he had committed a grave error in allowing the American army to escape from Canada the previous year. It was more important to keep him in Canada to restore the strength of the government. This left Sir William Howe, senior to Burgoyne, not at all sure he should attach importance to the Hudson Valley at this time, when the New Jersey territory and Philadelphia could be acquired. Once Burgoyne and St. Leger had met at Albany, the Hudson Valley could easily be subdued. Much to everyone's consternation, Washington's included, Burgoyne moved his fleet of over 200 sail, 14,000 troops, artillery, horses, and equipment, south to menace Philadelphia!

The choice of Burgoyne, always a cavalryman, as a leader of an expedition that consisted entirely of infantry and artillery, was questionable. His patience for this type of warfare would be severely

44

tested long before Albany was reached. A cultured man, well liked, always good company, with a penchant for gambling and the theatre, he would change his opinions of American courage and ability on the field of battle before the campaign had ended.

In the beginning, despite the difficulties of terrain, there was no stopping him. Ticonderoga fell, and the Americans, routed at Hubbardton, were in full retreat south to Fort Anne. Then, that too was lost. Desperately, the Americans destroyed bridges and began felling great trees of the forest, piling them across the route the British had chosen on their march towards Fort Edward. At least it would cause them time-consuming delay. Burgoyne decided to rest awhile at Skenesborough, and this was part of his undoing. Had he continued his original rapid pace south and selected the route from Fort Ticonderoga, via Lake George, he would have reached Fort Edward in considerably less time, but he chose a period of revelry at Skenesborough, confident that he had the whole campaign in the bag.

Fort Edward, not much of a fortress, could not be held and was summarily abandoned by the American forces, a victory for Burgoyne without his having lifted a finger. At this point, Burgoyne's early employment of a strong contingent of Indians worked to his disadvantage. They could not be controlled, roaming the countryside, butchering Whigs and Tories alike. A young lady by the name of Jane McCrea was soon to illustrate this mistake vividly.

Jane McCrea was staying at Fort Edward in the house of a Mrs. McNeil, in the hopes of being reunited with her lover, David Jones, who was traveling as an officer with Burgoyne's camp. A party of Indians broke into Mrs. McNeil's house and forced the two women to accompany them to Burgoyne's camp. They were soon separated, with Mrs. McNeil arriving at the camp intact, if humiliated, while Jane was brutally killed and scalped by her escort. Jane was known for her fine length of hair which fell to her feet when unbound, and so her scalp was recognized with horror by Mrs. McNeil and David Jones, when it was exhibited in the British camp. Burgoyne, fearing to antagonize the Indians, was helpless to punish the killer. Jane's murder had an enormous effect upon everyone. Loyalists who would come into Burgoyne's camp were no safer than the Americans. Fear provided the stimulus needed for recruits to join the American forces, and bring an end to Burgoyne's invasion from the north. The recruits began coming into the American camp from everywhere. The danger must be kept from destroying their own families.

Washington, waiting near Philadelphia for news of Howe's intentions, felt that he could send from Trenton Morgan's crack regiment of riflemen, five hundred men strong, north, along with two Continental regiments of the New York line, stationed at Peekskill. At least they would provide some reenforcement to Schuyler trying desperately to contain Burgoyne.

Meanwhile, St. Leger had found Fort Stanwix manned much heavier than he'd expected. The Americans held out fiercely against his force of troops and Indians. Expecting a smaller force and a different terrain, he was rather short of artillery as well.

When news of St. Leger's attack on Fort Stanwix reached Schuyler at Stillwater, he decided to send a small relief force to aid General Nicholas Herkimer, who had made a valiant but unsuccessful stand at Oriskany, where he had been seriously wounded. Schuyler called a council of war to propose his plan, and was met with opposition and accused of weakening their present position with Burgoyne a mere twenty-four miles away. The risk was too great. Schuyler remained adamant. Someone must go to aid Stanwix. The Mohawk Valley could not be lost.

In the midst of stubborn silence, one man rose to his feet and volunteered — Benedict Arnold. He agreed with Schuyler that the situation involving the Mohawk Valley was critical. They could not risk an uprising of Tories bringing aid to St. Leger. Schuyler was well aware that the New Englanders were not overly fond of him, suspecting he was loyal to the king, but he accepted Arnold's offer, and with less than one thousand men and Brigadier General Ebenezer Learned, as second in command, Arnold departed, reaching Fort Dayton, German Flats, on August 20. There they were soon informed of the strength of St. Leger's force.

Benedict Arnold has been so often portrayed as "hare-brained," "impulsive to a fault," "rash," dashing off to do mad things, which he usually managed to accomplish, but this time he also exhibited his ability to be prudent when the situation demanded. He applied a clever ruse.

A German by the name of Hon Yost Schuyler, a recent captive and scheduled to be hanged for planning a Loyalist uprising in Tryon County, was considered a half-wit. The Indians held such unfortunates in some reverence, so Arnold offered him a pardon and his freedom if he would go to St. Leger's camp and tell the Indians there that General Arnold was coming to relieve the fort, with "as many men as there were leaves on the trees." To add credence to Hon Yost's story, his coat was removed and shot through several times, so that it would appear he'd escaped with his life from Arnold's camp.

The ruse worked. The Indians, with St. Leger, rioted and not only fled into the woods, but took with them supplies of liquor, food, and clothing. It was considered expedient for the remaining force to retreat to Oswego. When Hon Yost returned to Arnold with this news, the Americans pressed on to Fort Stanwix where they received a warm welcome from the garrison.

After twenty days' absence, Arnold returned to the main camp at Stillwater. The Mohawk Valley was closed to the British, and since Howe had abandoned the Hudson Valley, only Burgoyne remained a threat.[1]

When Benedict Arnold reached Stillwater, the first week in September, he was to receive both good and bad news. The good was a report of a victory by General John Stark at Bennington. The bad was the replacement of Schuyler as commander of the Northern army by General Horatio Gates.

Up until this time there had not been any noticeable conflict between the two men so different in temperament and actions. Gates had good reason to admire Arnold, having had sufficient opportunity to observe his abilities during the activities on Lake

Champlain the previous year. He might even have liked him somewhat. Arnold, in his turn, was used to serving as subordinate. He'd had no trouble with Montgomery or Schuyler, and never with Washington, whom he greatly admired. The only present difficulty was that Arnold and Schuyler were close friends, as well as comrades in arms, and Arnold, never comfortable when treated badly himself, would have commiserated with Schuyler in his present position. However, there is no indication of any disagreements between Arnold and Gates in the early days before the confrontation with Burgoyne. While Arnold and Kosciusko, a Polish engineer serving with the American army, selected the ridge known as Bemus Heights as the best vantage point for a stand, Gates remained in camp overseeing his command. Fortifications and entrenchments were begun, surrounding the Neilson farm buildings already situated there, and Arnold rode out on sorties, becoming involved in minor skirmishes.

On September 12, it was learned that Burgoyne had moved south from Fort Miller, crossed the Hudson, and was in the vicinity of Saratoga (present-day Schuylerville). Now that he was beginning to move, his route was no longer in doubt. He was heading straight for Albany where he was still hoping to meet with Howe and St. Leger. Only there could he hope to find shelter and provisions for his army through the winter. Gates' army was steadily increasing in numbers as news of Bennington and Fort Stanwix spread.

The morning of September 19, Gates received the news that Burgoyne had advanced along the river road, split his forces into three columns and had turned westward into the woods, where almost immediately the denseness of the trees made it impossible for them to maintain contact with each other, move their artillery with any speed, or discover just where the Americans were. While the Americans knew of the enemy's approach, they too were hampered by the conditions of the terrain.

Gates opted for the game of waiting behind his lines, and now began the differences of opinion between him and Arnold, which erupted into rage before the outcome of this engagement would be determined. Arnold felt that it was madness to follow such tactics, certain that it was a mistake not to go out to meet Burgoyne's advance. He felt that the conditions of the terrain were an advantage to the Americans, who had never adopted the formal traditional methods of the British, and profited from their wisdom. He also believed that Burgoyne would encounter difficulties moving his heavy equipment through the forest, and could be reduced to small arms fighting as a result, whereas if he were permitted to bring his artillery into a position where they could be directed at the American works, they would be overcome. There would be nowhere to retreat, and the road to Albany would be open for Burgoyne.

Gates finally agreed to send Daniel Morgan's riflemen and Henry Dearborn's light infantry out of the camp. Arnold's command, the American left wing, would lend them support. For hours there was no contact between the forces, due to the density of the trees, but then one of Morgan's detachments came into contact with Burgoyne's center column at the small clearing of Freeman's farm. Morgan's men were so exhilarated by their success that they dashed off after survivors and blundered into the main body of the British line. The only option open to the riflemen was to scatter into the cover of the woods. Morgan eventually rallied his men with his "turkey call," but the situation could have meant ruin for his entire corps.

Burgoyne pushed forward to the clearing at Freeman's farm, and drawn up in battle position offered a tempting target to the newly arrived New Hampshire Continentals, under command of Colonel Joseph Cilley, and Morgan who had regrouped under Arnold's orders. As still more American regiments began to arrive and the British were joined by German contingents, the fighting settled into a pendulum action for three to four hours, as first one side then the other gained ground, fell back, and then came on once again. The fire coming at the exposed troops in the open was deadly and the British suffered most severely, their officers being carefully picked off one by one by riflemen in the treetops. Artillery pieces were captured and recaptured, Americans lacking linstocks to fire the cannon, or horses to move them, and the British not able to close where their bayonets would have been most effective. Officers on both sides exposed themselves most courageously, rallying their men wherever possible.

Supplies of ammunition were diminishing at an alarming rate on both sides, yet the battle seemed a draw with neither side the victor. Arnold had returned to camp to ask for reinforcements, and Gates had responded with Learned's whole brigade. While Arnold was still with Gates, Colonel Morgan Lewis, quartermaster, rode in to report the stalemate situation. Arnold, always impetuous, snapped: "By God! I'll soon put an end to it!" and dashed off at a gallop. According to Wilkinson, Lewis suggested to Gates that he'd better order Arnold back before he could commit some rash act. Gates took the advice and sent Wilkinson after him. Receiving the order, Arnold returned to camp.[2]

As I have noted, this is Wilkinson's version, and his word has proved under examination most unreliable. However, not allowing Arnold to continue onto the field where the troops currently fought only under the leaders of units, Gates deprived the men of a superior officer. Under such leadership the tide could well have turned conclusively in favor of the Americans, who outnumbered the Germans nearly two to one, and the British, who were all but completely exhausted. The day could have provided a victory, which would have cancelled any need for the engagement of October 7. The descent of dusk called a general withdrawal of both sides.

Historians argue to this day as to whether or not Arnold was actually on the field September 19. (These arguments are examined in detail in appendix 4.) The whole argument is ridiculous when one considers Arnold's nature. Knowing he was responsible for the entire left wing, which was then engaged, one finds it utterly impossible to picture him languishing in camp.

Burgoyne decided to dig in and hope for the reinforcements he could not possibly know would never arrive. At the same time

Gates, too, was also quite content to remain where he was. Reinforcements were coming in each day to the American camp, and his lack of ammunition was being surmounted due to supplies being sent from Albany by Schuyler. The situation was quite different in Burgoyne's camp. Supplies were dwindling and sleep was scarce because of the nightly raids of the Americans and the howling of wolf packs which prowled the areas where the dead had been so hastily buried.

In the American camp there was disturbance of a different sort: the quarrel between Gates and Arnold. Gates's friendship with Arnold had begun to sour. Arnold's open loyalty to Schuyler, and finally his rage when he discovered that, in reporting details of the September 19 battle, Gates had not mentioned either him or the units of his division. Arnold's pride, always thin-skinned, rose and he informed Gates that he and his aides wished to leave for Philadelphia to join Washington. The argument grew heated from both sides, and only cooled temporarily by the drawing up of a petition signed by every general officer, except Gates and Benjamin Lincoln, asking Arnold to remain. He acquiesced, though deprived of a command.

The news that Arnold would remain in camp was received with an applause that rang throughout the camp, and was heard within the British lines. That Benedict Arnold was the idol of his men is clear from the wild enthusiasm of the men whenever he appeared to inspect the line. The shouts and cheers piqued Gates, never popular with the men, to the point that he issued orders to stop such demonstrations.[3]

On October 4, Burgoyne called a council of war. A decision had to be reached. The waiting game had about been played out. General William Phillips, the British artillery expert, was silent; General Baron von Riedesel, the Brunswicker, wanted to retreat; and General Simon Fraser, leader of the Grenadiers and Light Infantry, agreed. Burgoyne decided upon a reconnaissance mission to determine the strength of the enemy forces. Between 10 and 11 A.M., Tuesday, October 7, he moved cautiously forward.

The American outpost near Mill Creek alerted Gates and the beat to arms was heard. Morgan was dispatched "to begin the game." He was to turn the British right, General Enoch Poor to confront the left, and Learned to take on the center. At about two o'clock the forces clashed.

Arnold, always restless, had paced the camp, hating to be out of the fray. Finally, when he could contain himself no longer, he rode his sorrel mare onto the field, conspicuous in his buff and blue uniform. It was said he was well fortified with rum, but was he? Did he need spirits to fire his need for action, or was the old adrenalin set coursing through his veins by the genuine excitement of a battle to be fought? He could no more remain in camp this day than a starving man refrain from meat!

Gates sent an aide, Major John Armstrong, after Arnold to order him back to camp. Armstrong never caught up with him until it was too late. He was not to be denied his day of glory, nor were his men to be denied the thrill he could inspire amongst them. They greeted the sight of him galloping ahead of them with cheers, and broke into a run to follow the figure waving his sword above his head.

An interesting memoir exists regarding Arnold's rousing spirit that day, and how it inspired the reaction of his men. At the centennial celebration of the October 7 battle, in 1877, Senator L. F. S. Foster of Connecticut told of his father's experience as adjutant of a Connecticut regiment made up of men from New London and Norwich: "The earliest recollection of my boyhood was sitting on my father's knee and listening to the stories of the march, the camp and the battlefield. I well recollect my father say that Arnold came dashing along the line, the speed at which he rode leaving his aid far behind him, and as he came up to my father's regiment he called out, 'Whose regiment is this?' My father replied, 'Colonel Latimer's, sir.' 'Ah!' said Arnold, 'my old Norwich and New London friends. God bless you! I am glad to see you. Now come on, boys; if the day is long enough, we'll have them all in Hell before night.' General Arnold was a native of Norwich, and was born within fifty yards of my house in that town."[4]

Gallantry amongst the enemy was also very much in evidence in the person of Simon Fraser, who placed himself, conspicuously mounted on a large gray horse, at the head of his troops, continuously rallying them to hold firm.

Arnold, observing Fraser, directed Morgan to have some of his best marksmen bring him down—a necessary sacrifice. Timothy Murphy is generally credited with success, though heavy fire from other guns was directed against Fraser as well. He fell, mortally wounded; his line wavered and ran for shelter. Burgoyne, in the general retreat, also acted as bravely and conspicuously as Fraser had done, but with better luck.

The British were suffering heavy losses on all fronts, much greater than the Americans, and now that Arnold was on the field, excitement reached fever pitch. With Fraser down and Burgoyne on the run, Arnold decided to lead an assault on the Earl Balcarres' redoubt. Since it was defended by artillery, their approach was in the midst of extremely heavy fire, both musketry and grapeshot. Still the Americans stormed the abatis before Balcarres' lines and attempted the breastworks themselves, under Arnold's leadership. Some of the later accusations of Arnold's being drunk, mad, or both, no doubt came from his actions exhibited here. He was a moving target that somehow could not be destroyed.

However, when Arnold, never the one to sacrifice men needlessly, realized Balcarres' position could not be taken, he dashed off to the American left, galloping between them and the enemy, very like a figure in a moving shooting gallery, exposed to firing from both sides. His time was not then and he made for Breymann's Redoubt. The Hessian's position was sparsely manned. Learned's brigade was approaching, demolishing the nearby Canadians on the way. Arnold, at the head of some of Morgan's men, charged the redoubt. Breymann went down, supposedly sabred by one of his own men, in retaliation for his putting to the sword four others. Retreating, the Germans turned to deliver one last shot. Arnold and his mare clearing the works were a ready target and they crashed to the ground, a musket ball shattering Arnold's left thigh and killing the horse. One of Arnold's men moved to bayonet the Hessian who had fired the shot, but Arnold shouted: "He is a fine fellow, don't hurt him!"[5]

The collapse of this position imperiled Burgoyne's whole main position, but the advantage was not carried through. Dusk was upon them, exhaustion universal on both sides. Another ten days would see the end, and Burgoyne's surrender.

This was the end of the battle for Arnold whom John Armstrong caught up with at last and delivered Gates's order to return to camp. He was carried, on a makeshift stretcher, back to the field hospital. In actuality, it was the end of his career as a battlefield leader in the Continental army. In this final moment of glory, had he died, there would now be statues of Benedict Arnold in public squares of many cities in the United States. Fate had other plans—he was meant to live and die another day.

On October 29, Arnold's seniority was grudgingly restored by Congress, but he remained in hospital at Albany for months, only reaching New Haven and home, the following May, where he was given a warm welcome by the citizens of the city, who greeted him with a salute of thirteen guns, a parade, and speeches in his honor.[6]

For those who insist Arnold was not directly responsible for the victory at Saratoga, I refer them to Burgoyne's report to Parliament, upon his return to England. The interrogation of Captain Money makes very interesting reading:

> Q. Did you ever hear, in conversation with the rebel officers, that General Arnold, foreseeing that inconvenience, had marched out of his lines, and attacked, without orders from General Gates?
>
> A. I did hear that General Arnold had marched out on the 7th of October, without orders from General Gates. I did also hear that he advised the going out to meet General

Burgoyne on his march, and engaging him before he approached their lines; and the reason he gave was this: If General Burgoyne should ever come near enough their lines to be able to make use of his artillery, that he would certainly possess himself of their camp; that their troops in that case would never stand any where; but if, on the other hand, the rebels should be defeated in the woods, the troops would, after that, have confidence in their works, for which reason Arnold advised risking an action in the woods before General Burgoyne came near enough to see their works.[7]

The conclusive evidence is found in Burgoyne's own statement:

I have reason to believe my disappointment on that day proceeded from an uncommon circumstance in the conduct of the enemy. Mr. Gates, as I have been informed, had determined to receive the attack in his lines; Mr. Arnold, who commanded on the left, foreseeing the danger of being turned, advanced without consultation with his general, and gave, instead of receiving battle. The stroke might have been fatal on his part had he failed. But confident I am, upon minute examination of the ground since, that had the other idea been pursued, I should in a few hours have gained a position, that in spite of the enemy's numbers, would have put them in my power.[8]

At this point Arnold was at the crest of his popularity. His career should have been all uphill from then on. Unfortunately, it would not be.

In April of 1778, while recuperating from his wounds on the long tedious journey home, Arnold's thoughts strayed once more to romance. The dark beauty of Betsey DeBlois invaded his memories. Once again he raised the siege, and while staying in Middletown, Connecticut, at the home of his friend Comfort Sage, he went to great pains to compose a love letter:

April 8, 1778

Dear Madam,

Twenty times have I taken my pen to write to you, and as often has my trembling hand refused to obey the dictates of my heart. A heart which has often been calm and serene amidst the clashing of Arms, and all the din and horrors of war, trembles with diffidence and the fear of giving offense when it attempts to address you on a subject so important to its happiness. Long have I struggled to efface your heavenly image from it. Neither time, absence, misfortunes, nor your cruel indifference have been able to efface the deep impression your charms have made, and will you doom a heart so true, so faithful, to languish in despair? Shall I expect no returns to the most sincere, ardent, and disinterested passion? Dear Betsey, suffer that heavenly bosom (which surely cannot know itself the cause of misfortune without a sympathetic pang) to expand with friendship at last and let me know my fate. If a happy one no man will strive more to deserve it; if on the contrary I am doom'd to despair, my latest breath will be to implore the blessing of Heaven on the idol, and only wish of my soul.

Adieu,

Dear Madam and believe me most sincerely

Your devoted and humble servant

B. A.[9]

By the 26th of April he had apparently received an unfavorable response, but still he persisted:

Dear Betsey,

Had I imagined my letter would have occasioned you a moment's uneasiness, I never should forgive myself for writing it. You entreat me to solicit no further for your affections. Consider, Dear Madam, when you urge impossibilities I cannot obey; as well might you wish me to exist without breathing as cease to love you, and wish for a return of affection.

As your intreaty does not amount to a positive injunction and you have not forbid me to hope, how can I decline soliciting your particular affections, on which the whole happiness of my life depends.

A union of hearts I acknowledge is necessary to happiness, but give me leave to observe that true and permanent happiness is seldom the effect of an alliance form'd on a romantick passion when fancy governs more than judgement.

Friendship and esteem founded on the merit of the object is the most certain basis to build a lasting happiness upon, and when there is a tender and ardent passion on one side, and friendship and esteem on the other, the heart must be callous to every tender sentiment if the taper of love is not lighted up at the flame, which a series of reciprocal kindness and attention will never suffer to expire.

If fame allows me any share of merit, I am in a great measure indebted for it to the pure and exalted passion your charms have inspired me with, which cannot admit of an unworthy thought or action, a passion productive of good and injurious to no one you must approve, and suffer me to indulge.

Pardon me Dear Betsey if I called you cruel. If the eyes are an index to the heart, love and harmony must banish every irregular passion from your heavenly bosom.

Dear Betsey I have enclosed a letter to your Mama for your Papa and have presum'd to request his sanction to my addresses. May I hope for your approbation? Let me beg of you to suffer your heart if possible to expand with a sensation more tender than <u>friendship</u>. Consider the consequences before you determine. Consult your own happiness, and if incompatible with mine forget there is so unhappy a wretch, for let me perish if I would give you one moment's pain to procure the greatest felicity to myself. Whatever my fate may be my most ardent wish is for your happiness.

I hope a line in answer will not be deem'd the least infringement on the decorum due to your sex, which I wish you strictly to observe.

In the most anxious suspence

I am Dear Betsey unalterably yours,

B. Arnold[10]

It is not known whether he received any word from the fair Betsey's father, or even if that gentleman ever received Benedict's letter. However, it is a fact that Betsey's mother had firm desires concerning her daughter, which did not include the acquisition of a husband who would have taken the girl from her side. Betsey's further romantic ventures, this time with a young merchant, Martin Brimmer, came to an end when Ann Coffin DeBlois stormed into an attempted wedding ceremony at King's Chapel, and forbade it. Betsey never married, but lived to the ripe old age of 82: "a straight, tall, elegant woman."[11]

During the spring of 1778, while Arnold was recuperating at home he heard of the plight of General Warren's orphaned children and generously sent funds for their immediate use and petitioned Congress, in behalf of the children, for a pension to cover their care and education.

By mid-May, he had joined Washington at Valley Forge, where he took the oath of allegiance required of all officers of the Continental army. The document has been preserved and a facsimile appears in nearly every Arnold biography, implying that he either signed it under false pretenses — a traitor already — or, that his subsequent defection was the action of a man who would say one thing and think nothing of doing the direct opposite, a man not to be trusted at any time. But is this true? He'd proved his ability to be trusted over and over again, as he'd proved by his dedication and many risks his love of this country. It is said that uncommon bravery in perilous circumstances does not necessarily prove loyalty, but the unreasoning thoughts of a madman. Perhaps. To gallop a horse between battle lines in full fire, or storm a rampart on the back of a horse in clear view of desperate, panicking armed men, could be the actions of a madman—or, a drunkard. However, Benedict Arnold was not mad, nor was he a drunkard then, or at any other time.

When Arnold joined Washington he was still in no condition for active duty, and so he was appointed the military governor of Philadelphia in June, when the British evacuated the city. Surely no appointment was ever so ill conceived. No man was more unsuited for the diplomacy of politics. Washington's kindness in this instance was misdirected. For the first time in his life Benedict Arnold was given a commission which he could not have been more unable to perform. He lacked tact and patience, and the ability to compromise required in a political position. Almost immediately, he tangled with the Council of Pennsylvania and Congress, the two already at odds with each other for power and authority. Arnold was caught between. His orders to establish martial law until the chaos concerning properties and goods could be resolved, made him extremely unpopular. As the weeks and months passed, resentment grew as observers noted his opulent life style.

He was owed back pay, meager as it was because of falling currency rates and rising prices, and his trading business in New Haven, left in the hands of his sister, was not exactly thriving. Speculation in privateers and business deals were common amongst the military, but Arnold was singled out for an attack. Everything he did was wrong. If he entertained a company of Tories and Whigs alike, he was criticized, if not for a party preference, then for the opulence of his table.

In the midst of all these troubles one bright moment appeared. He met Miss Peggy Shippen at a social affair at "Cliveden," the home of the Chew family, and her blonde beauty must have captivated him enough to displace the dark loveliness of Betsey DeBlois. Peggy, a Philadelphia belle half Arnold's age, was the daughter of Judge Edward Shippen. The courting began. In September Arnold proposed, and after some hesitation on the part of the young lady, and also her father, he was accepted.

*"Cliveden," Mount Pleasant, Fairmont Park, Philadelphia, Pennsylvania*

But the troubles with the civil authorities in the city continued. "I think all the world are running mad. What demon has possessed the people with respect to General Arnold," wrote Elizabeth Tilghman to Betsy Burd, "he is certainly much abused; ungrateful monsters, to attack a character that has been looked up to, in more instances than one, since this war commenced."[12] Mrs. Tilghman wasn't far wrong in her assumption that the world had gone mad. It must have seemed that way to many, and in particular to Benedict Arnold. After all his efforts concerning the plight of his country, he was very much disillusioned by the treatment he was receiving, as is evident by part of a letter to Peggy, written while he traveled to see Schuyler and discuss a possible acquisition of some land for a development in New York State: "I daily discover so much baseness and ingratitude among mankind that I almost blush at being of the same species, and could quit the stage without regret was it not for some gentle, generous souls like my dear Peggy."[13]

Throughout the spring, enmeshed in the bickering of government, Arnold's enchantment with the Glorious Cause began to sour. He could see no possibility of success ahead. The country could only face ruin as things were. The British attempts at a peace settlement had been refused, and an alliance with France was being considered. God knew what was to follow. He made a tentative contact with the British at this time, though maintaining anonymity. He was considering throwing in the towel.

Believing himself vindicated of charges brought against him, he resigned as military governor on March 19, and turned to thoughts of domestic bliss. On April 8 he married Peggy Shippen. The estate of Mount Pleasant, just outside the city, which he had purchased as a wedding present for his bride, they were never to enjoy.

The attack against him was now in earnest. Eight charges were drawn up by the Council of Philadelphia and presented to Congress for action against Arnold. He was accused of issuing a pass for a ship without knowledge of the Pennsylvania authorities; shut up shops so no one could make purchases besides himself; imposed "menial offices" upon a member of the militia; purchased a suit concerning a ship, thereby delaying justice in the case; appropriated wagons of the state for the transportation of private property; wrote a letter allowing a person to cross into the enemy lines; refused to explain the use of the wagons; and showed favoritism between civil and military and other characters who had adhered to the cause of their country, with an entirely different conduct towards those of another character (Loyalists).

A committee of Congress, on tenterhooks about crossing the Council (the State of Pennsylvania was too large and powerful to be insulted), examined the charges and made recommendations as to which could be tried in civil court and which should be referred to military authority. The committee was not entirely satisfied by the lack of evidence concerning the various charges, but after three weeks of waiting for answers, they made their recommendations. They kept very carefully to a middle line, which gave Arnold some hope of eventually being cleared by Congress, to whom he made application for an early verdict.

Finally, it came — a charge to the commander in chief to appoint a court-martial to consider the first, second, third, and fifth charges. Congress had backed down, ignoring the report of its own committee. It was the old situation all over again: the insistence of the power of individual states against Congress, and over all, the fear of the possible power of the military over civil authorities.

Delay followed delay, until Arnold was practically climbing the wall. Washington did everything in his power to hasten the assignment of a date, but time dragged on, and it wasn't until December that the court-martial convened at Morristown, New Jersey.

Arnold, impressive as always, properly uniformed, and struggling to contain his humiliation and anger, acted as his own advocate. On January 26 a verdict was reached. Arnold was to receive a knuckle-rapping by Washington in the form of a reprimand concerning the disposition of the court regarding the first and last charges. The other charges were considered of no consequence. More delays followed and it was not until April that Washington finally issued his reprimand. Although he tempered his words somewhat, Arnold was deeply humiliated and hurt. He wrote, regarding the verdict, to his friend Silas Deane, that "I ought to receive a reprimand. For what? Not for doing wrong, but because I might have done wrong; or rather, because there was a possibility that evil might have followed the good I did."[14]

The result of the court-martial rather shocked the Council. They had instigated the whole matter, yet felt a bit guilty at the verdict and embarrassment it would cause Arnold. "We find his sufferings for, and series to, his country so deeply impressed upon our minds as to obliterate every opposing sentiment, and therefore beg leave to request that Congress will be pleased to dispense with the part of the sentence which imposes a public censure, and may most affect the feelings of a brave and gallant officer."[15] Kind sentiments which surely came rather late. Before the verdict was announced, Peggy presented her husband with a son, Edward, in March, the one bright spot in a year begun in the midst of trouble, and which would bring chaos before it ended.

The conspiracy with the British was firmly established now. He was fully committed. His original desire to defect immediately was turned aside by General Clinton and he was placed in the unenviable position of "spy," an unsavory position for anyone, and for Arnold, hateful.

He requested and received the appointment as commander of the post at West Point, chagrined that Washington had offered him command of the left wing of the army instead. Arnold pleaded his still completely unhealed wound, which made him unfit for active duty, and Washington agreed—West Point it would be. By August Arnold had moved into the Beverly Robinson house across from the Point and established his headquarters.

The pace quickened. Arnold's anxiety regarding reimbursement for loss of property and the risk he was taking, should he be apprehended, remained to be settled, as well as pertinent details the British would require concerning the defenses of West Point. An intermediary was decided upon, and Major John André, adjutant to General Clinton, volunteered, though it certainly would have been advisable for a subordinate to handle the meeting, rather than the chief contact in the plot, which André had become through his correspondence with Arnold.

Meanwhile, Arnold asked Peggy to join him and she arrived with their infant son, on September 15. It was a rather crowded house now, with Arnold's two aides, David Franks and Richard Varick, as well as servants, sharing the space; so crowded that it seems unbelievable the two aides, acting in secretarial capacities, did not suspect something covert. There must have been couriers summoned to carry missives for Arnold that had bypassed their desks. However, they maintained their innocence, as did Arnold, when the plot was discovered.

There is evidence that at least one of Arnold's staff had suspicions. Colonel Nathaniel Wade, of Massachusetts, was stationed at the garrison of West Point, arriving there on August 4, 1780, just before Benedict Arnold assumed command of the post. On September 17, Colonel Wade sat down to dinner with other staff officers at Arnold's headquarters in the Robinson house. It was during this dinner party that Arnold received papers from the *Vulture*, concerning his eventual meeting with Major André. Of course, this information was not shared with the other diners, and Wade did not attach any significance to the event at the time, but he did remember, with great clarity, many years later, an incident which happened after dinner as he walked down the path to the boat which would return him to the garrison across the river. One of Arnold's aides, a major, accompanied him, whose name he could not remember in the later years. Was it perhaps Major David Franks?

During their walk, the aide said: "Col. Wade, there is something going on here that I do not understand and cannot find out. I say this to put you on your guard at the Fort. I fear there is something brewing about us, and all I can say is look out for!" With these mysterious words, the young man turned on his heel and walked back up the path. His suspicions had evidently been aroused by the secret communications written by Arnold in private, and the great care he gave to certain papers hidden from his staff.[16]

André came ashore from the *Vulture*, a British sloop-of-war, anchored in the river below Stony Point, where he and Arnold had a brief meeting. It was decided that they withdraw to the house of Joshua Smith, who had accompanied them, in Haverstraw, on the New Jersey side of the river, to spend the night. Before André could return to the ship the next morning, however, cannon on Tellers Point fired on the *Vulture* and she had to drop down the river. This complicated matters and it was determined André would have to make his way back to the British lines via an overland route. This proved his undoing, as he was apprehended and made prisoner.

News of his capture reached Arnold at breakfast, where his military family had been joined by some of Washington's staff, which had preceded him in his journey from Hartford, Connecticut.

Arnold hastily excused himself on the grounds that a matter at the fort required his attention, spent a few minutes with Peggy, who had not yet joined the guests at table, and dashed off on his horse, down to the river where a boat and crew were kept in readiness for his use between the fort and headquarters. When he reached them, he informed the crew that they were to row him not to the fort, but to the *Vulture*, which had returned to her original anchorage. So ended the career in the Continental army, of perhaps their most illustrious officer.

On board the *Vulture*, Arnold wrote to his former commander in chief:

> Sir:
>
> The heart which is conscious of its own rectitude, cannot attempt to palliate a step which the world may censure as wrong; I have ever acted from a principle of love to my country, since the commencement of the present unhappy contest between Great Britain and the Colonies; the same principle of love to my country actuates my present conduct, however it may appear inconsistent to the world, who very seldom judge right of any man's actions.[17]

## Chapter VI
## A Red Coat for a Blue

Historians have generally indicated that no one followed Benedict Arnold into the camp of the British in New York City. He was supposed to have been shunned by all—his defection an isolated event. Historian Howard H. Peckham is specific: "exactly 28 men deserted to the American Legion Arnold was forming."[1]

Shortly after his arrival in the British camp, Arnold issued a proclamation "To the Officers and Soldiers of the Continental Army who have the real interests of their Country at heart and who are determined to be no longer the dupes of Congress or of France." He outlined his plan to raise a corps of cavalry and infantry, and promised recognition and attractive steady pay, which would surely appeal to men who had long gone without either.[2]

It has always seemed strange to me that a man of Arnold's acknowledged charisma could have lacked followers after his defection. What of the men who had trudged painfully behind him into battle? Was there not one amongst them who would still feel the magnetic spell of the man? Evidently he did not remain long alone.

Benjamin Gilbert was a Revolutionary War officer in the Massachusetts Line. A native of Brookfield, Massachusetts, he was serving in upper New Jersey the fall of 1780, subsequently spending the winter of that year at West Point. In February of 1781, he accompanied Marquis de Lafayette south in pursuit of the army of Phillips and Arnold. He was also with Lafayette at Yorktown. In his letter book, which covers 1780–1783, he writes:

Arnold is appointed a General in the British Army and publicly declares that he will have a Brigade of the Continental troops with him before spring. He has sent out handbills offering ten Guineas bounty to any American that will come and join him....it has so much influence that many have deserted and daily are deserting. I fear the consequences.[3]

Another source indicative of Arnold's success in attracting followers exists in a letter written home by a Scottish lieutenant, Will Pagett, stationed with the British army in occupied New York City, in October of 1780. The letter recounts the tale of André's capture and then states:

The scheme was no less than the surprise and probably dispersion of the Rebel Army which there is little doubt but for the above accident [André's capture] would have succeeded...and great part of them have come over with Arnold, as there is a general diffidence and discontent reigning among them....nothing but Washington keeps them together....[4]

It is interesting to note that these same men, who joined Arnold and became part of his American Legion, accompanied him on his expeditions against Virginia, and also New London, Connecticut, and also re-joined Arnold when he returned to Canada in 1785. Captain Nathan Frink, former aide de camp to Arnold, lived in Saint John for a while, before moving elsewhere in the Province of New Brunswick. Lieutenant Andrew Phair, adjutant of the corps, settled in Fredericton, where he was postmaster for years. Lieutenant George Bull settled in Woodstock, New Brunswick.

From the outset of the war a natural disenchantment surfaced from time to time amongst civilians and members of the militia. The hardships of separation from families, and perhaps more important, knowledge of the neglect their homesteads and crops were suffering, preyed upon the minds of men who had been fired by the excitement of the rebellion in its early days, but quickly found they had little stomach for the privations and dangers of war.

The short periods of conscription in the militia meant a constantly fluctuating complement of men. The ranks would swell and diminish as tours of duty came to an end. This was maddening to officers who were never quite sure of how many men they could depend upon as any action presented itself. Military action was seasonal and came to an abrupt halt with the commencement of the winter months, and with the return of spring was particularly sluggish as men were not anxious to sign up again before fields could be cleared, plowed, and seeded.

From 1778 onwards it appears a general miasma began to develop amongst the officers of the Continental army as well. Weariness, a lack of confidence in the outcome of the war, and a growing distrust of Congress, rose from the ranks to infiltrate the high command, already rankled at the preference shown by Congress to foreigners who flocked to America, some genuinely interested in the cause, others seeking advancement which would enhance their image at home in the future. Congress, which had always distrusted and feared the military leaders they were forced to enlist, grew more unreasonable. The war began to be called "calamitous," "tragic," "costly," and "ruinous."

General Philip Schuyler voiced his feelings to John André during a meeting in Albany as André made his way south following his capture earlier in the war. Schuyler hoped for a reconciliation which would end the war.

Major John Acland, captured at Saratoga, states that Schuyler spoke to him of his "aversion" to independence and "assured" him that "many of his friends and relations [naming them, and they were of the first influence] felt as he did."[5]

Desertions of the common soldier continued at a normal rate during the disastrous winter of encampment at Valley Forge. Added to this were the resignations of officers in such numbers as to alarm Washington. The squabbles amongst officers, both American and French, which erupted in the notorious Conway cabal added to the general confusion and name-calling.

Benedict Arnold, writing to Nathaniel Greene, November 10, 1778, paints a very gloomy picture:

> Our affairs both at home and abroad are in so deplorable a situation as forms a picture too horrid to dwell upon, and must give pain to every man who is interested in the safety of his country; which in my opinion was never in a more critical situation than at present. The great Council of the Nation distracted and torn with party, and faction, the public credit lost and debt accumulated to an amasing an incredible sum, the currency daily depreciating, and Congress if possible depreciating still faster, having lost the confidence of the Army, and public in general, and abused or neglected their most faithful servants, these are the outlines of the picture — for the rest of your knowledge of matters will supply, from impending ruin may God defend us.[6]

When one examines all this confusion and dissatisfaction within the ranks, one begins to see what could have influenced Arnold's decision to go over to the British and hopefully end the war.

While he has left no written record to serve as evidence that he never believed in, nor wanted, total separation from Great Britain, we cannot assume that therefore he did not have any such misgivings. We cannot believe that his motives, as he fought so valiantly all through the war, were entirely selfish.

As to distrust or hatred of the French, here again, we have no documented evidence to prove this. The tale of his anger concerning the romantic attachment of his sister, Hannah, to a young French suitor, years before the war, and his subsequent emphatic termination of that connection, might well have had nothing to do with any feelings concerning the French specifically. He could have objected to the young man on other grounds entirely, e.g., his lack of position or financial prospects.

The threat of French dominance, which would have meant, should they have been successful in taking over the Colonies from the British, the certain introduction of the Roman Catholic faith, could have caused him apprehension. Arnold, as a New England Presbyterian, could have found this abhorrent — but did he? Once again, we have no evidence that he was overly religious. His mother was extremely devout, as we find in several of her letters addressed to her son as a child, when he was away from home at school. His views are unknown, outside of various references amongst his letters, to a "Divine Providence," or "God," which he apparently did believe. His easy transition from the church of his youth to that of the Episcopalian faith of his second wife, Peggy Shippen, indicates religious convictions which were not overly potent.

Benedict Arnold's views on so many subjects are unknown to us — he was not a diarist — and so we should take care with supposition in judging him. We cannot know now what he might have spoken to his contemporaries, nor can we venture to guess at the wealth of information lost to us when his wife destroyed all his personal papers after his death.

Historians like to believe that Benedict Arnold went quite literally from the frying pan into the fire when he defected to the British side. His troubles with Congress and his fellow officers, which enmeshed him in court-martial trials and constant unpleasantness during his career as an officer in the Continental army, were assumed to be nothing compared to the abuse he suffered in the British army. This opinion is not fully supported by facts.

He did encounter a certain amount of detachment amongst the officers who would have been disdainful of his mercantile background. The aristocracy — and the highest rated professional officers were of this class — would always look down upon anyone considered a tradesman. This would have been natural and expected by Arnold himself. He would also have been made aware of the discomfort felt by certain officers who had been close friends of John André. He, too, would have felt discomfort because of André's death. He was not a man who lacked feeling, and did not deserve Washington's angry accusation, following

André's death: "But I am mistaken if at <u>this time</u>, Arnold is undergoing the torments of a mental Hell. He wants feeling!"[7] William Smith, who witnessed Arnold's reaction at the news of André's death, thought him "vastly disconcerted and retires on the chariot coming for him from General Robertson."[8] There is also strong evidence, which surfaced in 1782, and which is dealt with in detail in chapter 7, that Arnold had offered himself in exchange for André's release, but that Clinton had declined.

However, there would also have been the frank admiration of the officers who had encountered Arnold in the field. He was considered by the British the most brilliant field officer in the Continental army. His bravery, audacity, and uncanny strategic ability could not be denied. The fact that he had betrayed his old commission would certainly create discomfiture in any military encampment. As happy as they were that he was now on their side, there would always be that measure of disappointment that he had finally broken and come over to them. Any fair man will admire a spectacular enemy, but if he defects it is an act against honor, and leaves a sour taste in the mouth.

Lieutenant Colonel Thomas Dundas best described the situation when he wrote to Clinton: "It is my duty to wish that General Phillips may command [in Virginia], or some other officer. Neither can I or, I fear, any other officer in this army serve with pleasure under our present Chief [Arnold]; I have no confidence in his capacity."[9] Clinton, however, had the greatest respect for Arnold, and a firm confidence in his abilities.

Then we come to Vice Admiral Marriot Arbuthnot, commander of the British Fleet, who was not on the best of terms with Clinton. In fact, it appears as though it was difficult for anyone to be on comfortable terms with Arbuthnot. He was a coarse, blustering, foulmouthed bully, not hesitating to use the most abusive language to one and all, alienating nearly everyone with whom he came in contact. He had crossed Clinton by insisting on awaiting naval reinforcement in Rhode Island, which was in danger of being taken by the French fleet.

However, this irascible gentleman could on occasion act the gentleman, as evidenced in his warm letter of November 2, 1780, to Arnold:

> Sir,
>
> Having been employed, since the middle of July, in hopes of falling in with Mr. Tierney, if he leaves these parts, this winter, I did not until very lately, know of your arrival at New York, or I should have been earlier in my congratulations.
>
> Permit me, Sir, to felicitate our country upon so important an event, it cannot but [be] conducive of the utmost consequence tending to the happiness of the whole community and I have the most sanguin hopes, by your success, to open the eyes of those deluded people and restore to them the liberty they once enjoyed, and which they have been a long time sighing after in vain. So soon as my duty will permit me to return with propriety to New York I will immediately say in person that I am most sincerely
>
> Sir,<br>Your most Obedient & most<br>humble Servant<br>Marriot Arbuthnot

Royal Oak, Gardners Bay, Nov. the 2nd, 1780[10]

Admiral Sir George B. Rodney, who had his moments with Arbuthnot, although he professed, "I really love him as a Man, but as an officer, I cannot possibly approve his Conduct,"[11] writes of Arnold: "What a situation would Arbuthnot have been in, had that Squadron joined Ternay and I not have come. I leave you to judge. Washington's army would have been increased to Thirty Thousand at least and the best General the Rebels had, would have remained an Enemy instead of becoming a Friend. Arnold openly avows it, and declares it has done more towards bringing the Americans to their senses, than any act whatever since the commencement of hostilitys."[12]

According to these gentlemen there was not the ostracism we have been led to believe. Bonds of friendship were formed between former enemies, due either to admiration for a talented man, or possibly a genuine liking for a man they found to be a most pleasant companion.

Even Clinton's extreme affection for John André did not alter his friendship and regard for Arnold (though James Flexner would have us believe otherwise). He "assumes" Clinton felt something "close to hatred."[13] But then, Flexner "assumes" many things when he writes of Benedict Arnold.

Charles Cornwallis remained a close friend and was most helpful to Arnold's family in later years. There had to be frank admiration, and a liking for Benedict Arnold, amongst the British, his former enemies, or else the many favors done for him and his family would never have been offered, much less come to pass. Cornwallis was most helpful in securing a cadetship to India for Arnold's son George. When Arnold wrote Cornwallis regarding this commission, he referred to other favors shown: "Nothing but my very great confidence in your Lordship's goodness, which I have experienced on so many occasions..."[14] Perhaps one of these occasions to which Arnold referred would have been the appointment of James Robertson Arnold, second son of Benedict Arnold and Peggy Shippen, to the position of a gentleman cadet in the Royal Regiment of Artillery under the command of Charles Marquis Cornwallis, in 1796, when he was general of His Majesty's Forces, and master general of the ordnance.[15]

Following Benedict Arnold's defection, and while he was still stationed in New York City, Benjamin Tallmadge, dreaming hopefully of retribution, wrote to Barnabas Deane:

> We have so many reports respecting the infamous Arnold, since he basely deserted our cause, that I hardly know what to tell you respecting him. This much I am informed from good authority, that he has been introduced by General Clinton to the officers of the British Army, on parade, as <u>General Arnold</u>.

I wish he may command the refugees on the lines, as is reported, and I think I would venture to warrant him killed or taken before the campaign is over. I am perfectly acquainted with the villainous principles of many of the refugees, that a promise of a pardon and a few yellow boys would induce them to bring off any officer in their command. Had M. Delancey been the best man we could have wished at the head of that corps in Westchester, we should have welcomed him at our quarters long 'ere this. But this must not be too freely talked of — Arnold's rashness, I think, would give us a great opportunity to catch him if he was on the lines, and I am confident Sr. Henry Clinton would not be an object of such consequence to us, as Arnold.[16]

However, Tallmadge was merely ruminating. There were others who were formulating definite plans. Assassination was not the answer. Washington wanted Arnold alive! Major "Light Horse Harry" Lee came up with a plan which smacks of a James Bond plot.

A Sergeant John Champe, of Lee's cavalry, was to appear to desert from his unit and escape to the British in New York City. Once there, he was to try to join Arnold's newly formed American Legion. This would enable him to learn Arnold's habits and hopefully bring about his capture and transfer back to the American lines.

Champe duly deserted on October 20 and was questioned by the British Adjutant General's Office on the 23rd. He emerged from this interview successfully, and shortly thereafter joined Arnold's corps, as well as made contact with the American spy network currently operating in New York. He would need help with Arnold himself, not an easy man to overcome, and also the use of a boat to take him and his captive across the Hudson to Hoboken, where Lee would be waiting with a detail of dragoons.

During this time, Arnold's wife had encountered difficulties in Philadelphia where she had been staying with her family, following Arnold's defection, and was not very anxious to rejoin her husband and share in his precarious position. The civil authorities in Philadelphia, finding her presence bitterly resented by the inhabitants of the city, finally issued a decree ordering her to leave. After repeated attempts were made by her family to make it possible for her to stay with them had failed, she was escorted by her father to New York where she rejoined her husband on November 14.

Champe, by this time, had become familiar with Arnold's schedule and began to put his plan into action. He knew that Arnold returned to his home late at night and would visit the garden, probably to use the outdoor privy, before retiring. He knew this would be the only opportunity to find Arnold alone. He loosened part of the fencing around the garden and planned to overcome Arnold, gag him, and with the help of another man get him to the boat waiting at a wharf along the Hudson. Between them it would be made to appear that they were escorting a drunken soldier to the barracks guardhouse.

It seemed a foolproof plan, and a night was selected to carry it off, but once again Arnold's phenomenal luck saved him. On the December night planned to capture Arnold, Champe was ordered aboard a troop transport along with his unit, which was about to sail for the southern campaign.

On December 20, Arnold, ignorant of his close call, sailed from New York, bound for the Chesapeake. Lee and his dragoons had spent a chilly night for nothing.

Champe served with Arnold in Virginia until he could desert once again, this time to his own side, which could have proved a dangerous escapade in itself, should he be recognized by anyone who thought his original desertion to the British an authentic change of sides. In this, he experienced some luck of his own and made his way back to Lee.

When Benedict Arnold sailed, as commander of the southern expedition, there were accompanying him — besides the 1,600 men, half British regulars and Hessians, half Loyalists — Lieutenant Colonels Thomas Dundas and John Simcoe, who, Clinton informed Arnold, were officers of great experience and available for consultation and advice, should it be required. Actually, unknown to Arnold, they traveled under "sealed orders" issued by Clinton—a blank dormant commission which is only to be made use of in case of the death or incapacity of Brigadier General Arnold, to execute the duties of the Command which is entrusted to his direction. You are upon no account to make known that you are possessed of such a commission, or open the same, except in the cases above mentioned; and if this should not happen, you are to transmit this commission to me unopened."[17]

The expedition ran into difficulties when a winter gale set in soon after their departure, and they experienced high seas all the way to the Chesapeake Capes. Unfortunately, along with seasick troops, there was a serious loss of half of Simcoe's horses, due to injuries. Shortly after the first of the year they were finally able to get up the James River to Westover, where they could disembark the ill and injured, before Arnold led a contingent of eight hundred men towards Richmond. The march was accomplished with ease and they occupied the town with no resistance. He established his headquarters at the City Tavern on Main Street and issued a request for the surrender of stores, in exchange for which he would spare the town. This request was made to the governor, who happened to be Thomas Jefferson.

Jefferson refused the offer, leaving Arnold no choice but to set fire to whatever stores they did not need for their own use. Private property, as well as public buildings were destroyed. Simcoe conducted a similar raid on nearby Westham, where he razed the cannon foundry and emptied the powder magazine. Warehouses and mills at Chesterfield were also put to the torch, and Arnold moved on to Portsmouth, encountering little opposition as he laid waste to the countryside on his way.

Portsmouth, after being fortified, proved a bore to Arnold. Inaction was something he could not abide. Aside from this, he was placed in a rather hazardous situation with a small company of men. Though the British squadron on the coast offered some protection, the French fleet was a definite threat. Added to the situation was the fact that Jefferson had set a price of 5,000 Guineas on Arnold's head, which made him a tantalizing target—fair game for anyone with a rifle and a sharp eye. Washington, too, would have very much liked to capture Arnold, and ordered Lafayette into Virginia with 1,200 Continentals and instructions to terminate Arnold. If captured, he was to be hanged.

Arnold's position grew even more perilous when Admiral René Destouches, after many delays, brought 1,200 regulars to the Chesapeake. Only the British navy could save Arnold, and Admiral Arbuthnot engaged Destouches on March 16, off Virginia, suffering great losses, but sending the French back to Rhode Island. Shortly after this engagement, transports arrived with 2,000 reinforcements and General William Phillips, who outranked Arnold, to assume command. Clinton sent along a letter:

> March 13, 1781
>
> I did imagine I should have had time to have written a long letter to you, but a northerly wind blows and I should be sorry to lose a moment of it. I therefore refer you to Major General Phillips whom I have sent with a reinforcement of 2,000 Men Elite. I suppose Mrs. Arnold sends you by this opportunity the letters from Lord George Germain. I think from what he writes me you will have reason to be satisfied with them.
>
> General Phillips seems pleased with the opportunity he will have of serving with you. When operations cease in that region (without we are obliged to carry them on the whole year there) I shall be glad of your assistance here.[18]

After Phillips's arrival, Arnold brought Cornwallis up to date:

> General Phillips is here in force to cooperate agreeable to your Lordships wishes. The Marquis la Fayette is on the opposite shore with, as is said, fifteen hundred continental troops and some militia. General Phillips proposes waiting

here five or six days in expectation of having your Lordships orders or opportunity effectually to answer your purposes. From information received, we suppose your Lordship either at Halifax or on this side. Wayne has arrived or is on his way to Richmond with the Pennsylvania Line about hundred men. Reinforcement has been requested by General Phillips and it is said was to sail from New York the 4th Instant for Portsmouth.

B. Arnold

Petersburgh, 12 May 1781
to Earl Cornwallis[19]

As for Phillips, William Smith felt that Arnold's succession in the south had aroused "Envy among the redcoats"[20] in the camp in New York, and that he was the man for the job, not Phillips. "I have fears of Phillips; he is ostentatious and indolent, and must dread another Saratoga Convention. Yet he fights now with Arnold, and has reputation to recover."[21]

Lord Germain, too, felt that Arnold should continue in command.[22]

Although Phillips had a tendency to look askance at Arnold at first, "as a man who may be likely to hang back where he had not proposed himself," when he had time to observe Arnold, get to know him, and see how well he had managed the command, he changed his mind and wrote to Cornwallis of "the ability, activity, and zeal of Brigadier General Arnold, who with a small corps of troops affected a very essential service up James River, has sustained a rather weak post here and carried on a variety of objects with great success."[23]

Though subordinate to Phillips, Arnold joined in the destruction of stores. Phillips became ill in May and died shortly thereafter, leaving Arnold in command of the army once again.

Benedict Arnold had much trouble in attempting to enforce protection in the south because of jealousy between army and navy. This was also evident regarding prizes on land or on sea, and that it had been agreed the prizes would be equally divided between the army and navy regardless of who captured the prize.

Arnold's position remained perilous as we can see from a letter of Cornwallis to Lieutenant Colonel Tarleton:

Jones's Plantation

15 May 1781

Dear Tarleton

I am making all possible expedition, and hope to be at the Nottaway on Friday evening. I would have you proceed tomorrow to the Nottaway, and remain near Simcoe's Infantry; Arnold is ordered to march immediately to meet me on the Nottaway. Wayne's having joined La Fayette makes me rather uneasy for Arnold until we join. If you should hear of any movement of the enemy in force to disturb Arnold's march you will give him every assistance in your power, continue to let me hear from you.[24]

Cornwallis's concern is evident in his letter to Arnold, after he'd received news of the death of Phillips:

May 17, 1781

Sir

I have just received the favor of your letter of last night. The account of the death of my dear friend Phillips gives me the most sensible grief.

My reason for ordering you to march to the Nottaway was, as you supposed, to prevent the Marquis bringing you to action before I could join you, at present that consideration ceases; I am so unacquainted with the post at Portsmouth and the situation of your ships and boats that I cannot give immediate orders. I must therefore beg that you will let your Corps remain where this letter finds you, and that you will come yourself with the Cavalry to meet me at Butler's Bridge early tomorrow morning. I must likewise desire that you will send to Portsmouth to assure the Commanding Officer that I will

use every means in my power to succour him, if there should
be occasion.

Cornwallis.[25]

Once Cornwallis reached Virginia and assumed command,
Clinton requested that Arnold be returned to him in New York.
By June, he had arrived there, somewhat richer, due to captured
prizes in Virginia.

On April 24, Samuel Thatcher, sheriff, attached Arnold's
house in New Haven and it was subsequently sold. His sister,
Hannah, and the boys from his first marriage had no place to go.
Fortunately, the family of his old friend Comfort Sage gave them
shelter in Middletown, Connecticut. Arnold, himself, had spent
some weeks with the Sages while he was recuperating from his
Saratoga wound, and was slowly making his way home to New
Haven.

The two families had been close friends for many years and
the warm kindness of Mrs. Sage was shown to the exiles when
she shuttered her house so that the Arnold children would not
have to see the effigy of their father dragged through the streets
and finally burned. The fury of the mob, following the news of
Arnold's defection was intense, so intense that a violent mob
entered the cemetery in Norwich, Connecticut, and destroyed
the tombstone of Benedict's father, and that of the infant son,
who had been unfortunate enough to bear the name of "Benedict
Arnold." Even the dead were not to rest in peace!

In 1781, Benedict's uncle, Captain Oliver Arnold, died in
New Haven. He had been ill and disabled for years. By the time
he died, family funds were nearly gone. Though the family might
have looked askance at any help from the "black sheep" of the
family, his support could not be refused. This aid continued even
after Benedict went to England to live. His contributions to his
cousins made it possible for the oldest son to obtain a satisfac-
tory education.

The younger son did not feel the same, resenting any help
from Benedict, no matter how kindly intended, and joined the

U.S. Naval service, under John Paul Jones, hoping perhaps, to erase some of the disgrace Benedict's defection had brought to the family name. He was unsuccessful, however, having to leave the service because of ill health and died while still young.[26]

After Arnold arrived in New York, he was involved with administrative duties all summer. On August 27, Peggy was delivered of another son, James Robertson Arnold.

Following the sacking of the British merchant ship *Hannah*, causing the loss of a cargo worth $400,000, the British lost their patience and ordered an attack on New London, Connecticut, early in September of 1781. Benedict Arnold was given the command. Unfortunately, the raid developed into a fiasco.

It was originally intended as a "commando" sort of raid to destroy *only* the fortifications, Forts Trumbull and Griswold, public stores and shipping, and also to create a diversion of attention from Cornwallis, who was experiencing the beginnings of difficulties, which would end at Yorktown.

It has been said that Arnold should have refused to lead this expedition against his home state. New London was, in fact, very near his birthplace, Norwich. But could he have done so without placing himself suspect? His position with the British army still very tenuous, could he have refused *any* orders given him? It is not likely.

When Arnold's expedition arrived at the mouth of the Thames River, around 9 A.M., fate had already started the chain of events which were to provide such a tragic ending. The original plan for arrival at midnight had been delayed by unfavorable winds. One thing followed another.

Arnold had split his troops into two divisions. One, on the New London side of the river was to be his, made up of the 38th Regiment; Arnold's own regiment, the American Legion; and a small detachment of Hessian Light Infantry. On the Groton side of the river, under the command of Lieutenant Colonel Edmund Eyre, were troops of the 40th and 54th Regiments, a battalion of

New Jersey Volunteers, a company of Hessians, and a battery of artillery. Lieutenant Colonel Eyre was to take Fort Griswold, thought to be lightly garrisoned, therefore making impossible the escape of shipping they had come to destroy.

At first, the operation appeared to be proceeding according to plan. Fort Trumbull fell to Arnold and he quickly gained the town. When he had the chance to reach a position which over-looked the situation, he quickly realized that the information given him by Loyalists in the area, regarding Fort Griswold, was very wrong. The fort was, in fact, strong and had received additional strength from men who had escaped the attack on Fort Trumbull, and crossed the river to the Groton side. Since the main objective was destruction of supplies and shipping, Arnold decided to pull Eyre out of the action, even though he outnumbered the forces within the fort. He quickly dispatched an officer to countermand his original orders. Unfortunately, the message was not received in time. The attack had already begun.

Before the confrontation was over, Eyre had fallen, along with a large number of his men; the fort was carried by the British, and the valiant Colonel Ledyard, commander of Fort Griswold, was slain as he presented his sword in surrender. This unforgivable action triggered a general massacre before officers could gain control of their men.

On the other side of the river, Arnold was having his own problems. At first, it seems events moved in an orderly fashion, so much so that Arnold was able to dine with some old shipping friends, obviously of Tory leanings. No ladies were present. But then, the frenzy of Arnold's troops, plundering and burning warehouses, got out of hand. In their haste, ships were not hauled far enough away from the docks before being set afire, and as a result a wind shift ignited the city. Before it ended, 140 houses in New London and Groton were destroyed.

A "lady" later accused Arnold of deliberately ordering the house where he had dined earlier to be set afire. The house was actually that of James Tilley, a Loyalist, and while it is true that the house did burn, due to the spread of flames from another quarter, it was not by Arnold's order.[27]

New London survives as a "blot" on Arnold's career. While the general destruction of fortifications and stores, the original intention of the attack, pleased his superiors, there were mumblings amongst the military staff concerning the heavy loss of life involved. By early December, Arnold had received permission to leave for England. He still hoped to present his ideas to the king and somehow reverse the direction of the war, which was all too apparent, moving towards total separation from Britain.

## Chapter VII
## Arrival in London, 1782

Late in January 1782, after a stormy winter crossing, landfall would have been made just off the Isles of Scilly, west of the coast of Cornwall, which have proved the graveyard for so many ships coming to England from across the Atlantic. Then, the ragged cliffs of the Cornish coast at Land's End, past Mount's Bay and Penzance, around the Lizard and finally into Falmouth.

Entrance from the sea into Falmouth Harbor is imposing. On the west the promontory of Pendennis, crowned with Pendennis Castle, on the east St. Anthony's Head, and just beyond the pretty estuary of the Percuil River, St. Mawes and its castle.

The ships were at last in the Carrick Roads, where the largest of vessels afloat could always find a deep and safe anchorage at all states of the tide. The Arnolds had arrived in England. Who was the first to land is not recorded, but the convoy would not have been very scattered at that point, with the menace of enemy ships in the Channel. The mild weather, usual in Falmouth, would have been a welcome respite to the travelers.

After a brief rest, the journey up to London would begin, posting up by coach. Another arduous journey, considering the roads and the infants aboard, but it was considered safer to land at Falmouth, avoiding the risk of a confrontation with French ships in the Channel.

To Peggy, London would have been a delight. Philadelphia, while certainly a considerable city, was provincial compared with London. The shops that dominated the West End, with their immense signs, some of copper, some of pewter, or wood, painted and gilded, suspended above their doors, were fascinating. The principal thoroughfares—the Strand, Fleet Street, Cheapside, and Cornhill—teemed with the traffic of coaches, horsemen, and sedan chairs. Most roads were paved with large uneven stones which caused an uneven ride to say the least, in coaches and all sorts of vehicles, innocent of springs or tires, adding to the unlievable clamor of the street vendors crying their wares, itinerant musicians, and knife grinders.

Leadenhall Market and Billingsgate were only two of the markets where produce of every kind was available. Tailors' and milliners' shops abounded, along with taverns and the Coffee houses, some serving as subscription houses for merchants trading in the Indies and elsewhere, others the haunts of dandies, politicians, scholars, and wits.

At night, streets were well lighted by lanterns or large globes of glass, inside of which was placed a lamp. They were set up at every tenth house and were lighted, beginning at Michaelmas, and continuing until Lady Day, burning from dusk until midnight.

This was the London the Arnolds would have found. At first they stayed with friends, Loyalists who had preceded them to England, but eventually they found a house in Portman Square.

It has always been believed that when the Arnolds arrived in London, they were shunned by everyone. There have even been accounts (never authenticated) that they were hissed out of a theatre when it was discovered that they were in the audience.

The fact that they were presented to the king and the Prince of Wales is usually omitted. Apparently, the king was much taken with Peggy's beauty, and "the Queen was so interested in favor of Mrs. Arnold as to desire the ladies of the Court to pay much attention to her."[1] I it was generally agreed that she was lovely.

One Tory in England went on record to say: "I saw Mrs. Arnold a few days after her arrival in town...and was really pleased she looked so well, as general expectation was raised so high by the incessant puffers of the newspapers and the declaration of Colonel Tarleton that she was the handsomest woman in England. They have taken a house and set up a carriage and will, I suppose, be a good deal visited."[2]

Whether they eventually did much entertaining or not, Arnold was much consulted by Lord Germain and the Cabinet, had many private conferences with the king, and was seen leaning on the arm of Sir Guy Carleton, his former enemy at Quebec, and "walking with the Prince of Wales, and the King's brother in the public gardens."[3]

Arnold would have found George III a most approachable monarch. He loved to ride about his lands like a gentleman farmer, or to drive out to visit friends like a common gentleman on holiday with his family. However, the worst of the king's characteristics was his inveterate obstinacy. He always assured himself that he alone was right in all decisions. Perhaps this side of his nature was a bit like Arnold's own. He, too, was prone to be self-righteous very often, and it was part of his undoing, as it was also the king's.

The king had been so impressed with Arnold at their first meeting that he invited him to a high state conference. Arnold, always affable and loquacious, made quite an impression. He seemed a sensible man, fully experienced in the situation which existed concerning the Colonies. At least Lord George Germain found him so.

Benedict would have been familiar with London, even if it had been some years since he'd been there. As a young man of nineteen, in 1760, he had acted on behalf of his Lathrop uncles in acquiring a cargo of items required for their store in Norwich, and had been in London for some time carrying out their directions.

When the Arnolds reached London they found confusion. No one seemed to have any idea just how the war would continue. There was talk of changing the existing, and unsuccessful, tactics. A certain youngster, William Pitt, would soon emerge and the current regime would topple. The Whigs would gain the ascendancy, and when this happened, the tide of sympathy would swing from the Tories towards the Colonists, and Arnold would lose what little regard he'd gained. Parliament overruled the king who wanted to continue the fighting and called a cessation of arms on March 4, 1782.

Cornwallis, too, had arrived in London in January, and surprisingly received a hero's welcome. "No officer was ever so popular under misfortune as he," Jervis reported to Clinton. "The officers who served with him sound his praises beyond example, the Court flatters him, and John Bull is delighted with the blood spilt under his Lordship's auspices....General Grey is the only land officer I have met with who has not sacrificed to Lord Cornwallis's shrine. He had never varied in his opinion, which always pronounced that the loss of a whole army would finish his career."[4] However, Cornwallis was far from finished. The king would not hold the Earl to blame and accorded him honors instead. What's more, he invited him to accompany him hunting! Great favor, indeed. The public be damned, the king was on his side!

It was evident that the earl would be firmly positioned before Clinton could return to argue his point. Since the ministry was not in any hurry to bring this about, it appeared that he would be the likely candidate for the role of scapegoat. The current administration had to save itself somehow; heads would have to roll—either the American secretary, Lord George Germain, or the First Lord, Lord George. Germain it was, and Carleton was appointed to his office.

Arnold would have avoided the public controversies concerning Clinton and Cornwallis. He was in a difficult position himself and that would have decided his reluctance to become involved. He sent a message to Clinton that he was shocked at the very idea that he might "criminate the Commander-in-Chief," and that on the contrary "he owed the highest obligation to you, and that he looked up to your professional abilities with respect

and veneration."[5] Whether these were actually Arnold's sentiments concerning Cornwallis is doubtful. He had had his moments while serving under Clinton. Yet, this message was sent to
Clinton by a friend whom Clinton had asked to be kind to the
Americans, and who had invited them to an assembly at his home.
Since this, outside of their reception at court, was the Arnolds'
first introduction to London society, they were quite obviously
the center of attraction and curiosity. Peggy, coming from Philadelphia society would cause a stir when it was discovered she
did not appear to be as provincial as expected. Her husband
would share in the attention, for quite different reasons. Their
poise, equally unexpected, came as a surprise.

"She was well dressed and had an ease in her behavior which
astonished everybody," Bull told Clinton, "and novelty made
everybody desirous of being presented to them. He played at
high whist with the Duchess of Bedford, and 'twas observed how
little of the <u>mauvaise honte</u> he had about him. Indeed it was the
same at St. James's, for they both seemed quite at home when
they were presented. But I believe it is the American creed to
contemn rank, and to hold no superiors...."[6]

Lord Loughborough commented on Arnold: "A lively little
man, and more like a gentleman (whatever he may have been)
than nine out of ten general officers."[7] Lord Loughborough's aside
pertained to Arnold's earlier profession as a "tradesman." They
would never consider him as anything else. This occupation carried with it a strong stigma — the "self-made" man had not yet
arrived upon the scene. Even wealth acquired through trade allowed a man to rise socially just so far. He might gain a knight-
hood, or an Irish Peerage. Other fringe benefits would come along
with these, an estate and a chance to mingle — on the outer edge,
surely — with a more acceptable social crowd, but a "tradesman"
he would always remain in England. This was Arnold's introduction to the class distinctions rampant in England. There were
all sorts of "slots" into which one could fit, but one did not move
from one to the other — ever!

His defection from the rebel cause did not enter into their evaluation. Because of their bigoted opinions they lost the valuable counsel of a very talented man. A man completely familiar with the terrain of the country where he'd lived all his life, and — above all — familiar with the wishes of his fellow Americans. Tradesman he might have been, and always remained to some degree, but it was through his endeavors in this very same profession that he had acquired a knowledge of commerce and its importance to the newly emerging country. The injustices imposed upon the Colonists by the ministers of the British government were clearly etched in his mind. He had tried to reach Clinton, with no success at all. Oh, they listened to him. His formidable record with the Continental army could not be denied. He had been recognized early in the war for his remarkable ability, however it had been acquired. Burgoyne, in a letter to Clinton, and also in his address to the House of Commons in 1779, stressed that the sole person responsible for his defeat at Saratoga was Arnold.[8] In fact, this accounted for the distrust the British felt towards him when he first defected. How was it possible that the man who had exhibited so forcefully his dedication to the rebel cause, now have second thoughts and offer his sword to the enemy?

However, the round of invitations had begun. The Bulls soon brought the Arnolds to visit Clinton's family at Weybridge, Surrey.[9] There were outings in the pleasure gardens. Ranelagh and Vauxhall, masquerades, and the many theatres were most attractive and would have offered a welcome change to the Arnolds. They were not exactly poor, though at first had to take care not to live beyond their means.

In January of 1781, Arnold had invested the money he received from Clinton, in the new and Consolidated Annuities, with a broker in London. They would provide an additional income and provide a comfortable, if not tremendous, livelihood.

The actual sum Arnold had received always seems huge when mentioned since it is usually equated in terms of today's monetary values. In reality, it was a moderate £6,000. When Arnold began his negotiations with Clinton he was the owner of a considerable estate: The spacious house in New Haven, furnished lavishly; his horses and carriage; ships and cargo, including part ownership in others; and the newly acquired Mount Pleasant, just outside of Philadelphia, an estate of one hundred acres, which included a fine Georgian mansion and various outbuildings. Should he be apprehended, Benedict Arnold's losses would be considerable, in fact, over £16,000. His frequent and insistent requests to Clinton concerning a financial understanding were merely an effort to protect himself from the losses he would certainly suffer should he be apprehended. However, to his detractors this was just cause to damn him as being avaricious.

In March of 1782, Peggy received a pension of £500 per annum. Early this year, a controversy arose, provoked by a Welshman, Robert Morris, who was secretary of the Bill of Rights Society, and son-in-law of Lord Baltimore. Morris wrote a letter to the *General Advertiser* on February 9, attacking Arnold rather strongly on various points, but specifically, "that he made no offer of his own person to save that of André."[10] It rankled Morris that Arnold had been received at Court.

The accusation was answered in the *Morning Herald* by Captain James Battersby of the 29th Foot, an officer in Burgoyne's army in America. He, and other officers of Clinton's military family in New York, would concur that Arnold had actually offered to be exchanged for André. Clinton, of course, could not permit the gesture. Whether Battersby's information was, or was not, based entirely on rumor, it is strange that, in such a public exchange, no one came forward to refute the claim.

Such an offer would have been well within Arnold's character. He was always "touchy" on any matter concerning his honor. An offer to rescue André, who had not at first appeared to be in any mortal danger, would not have been surprising.

Whether the story had any credence or not has never been proved. However, the debate reached such heat, that Battersby issued a challenge to Morris. He would meet him on a field of honor with any weapon he chose. Morris apparently had second thoughts, and wisely retreated. Arnold remained silent.

The general furor at Arnold's favorable reception, helped on by writings of Benjamin Franklin, John Adams, and John Jay, stirred reaction amongst the Whig faction in England, only to be counteracted by the continued favor shown Arnold by the king, the Prince of Wales, and other notables.

Silas Deane, another gentleman under suspicion during his career, was also in London. Arnold extended a welcome. After all, they had been business associates and friends of long standing. Deane, attempting to salvage his reputation, tactfully retreated, or, at least he maintained that he did, either from general feelings of abhorrence, or embarrassment at turning aside from an old friend. He writes, in his correspondence, of going to great lengths to change his address and therefore avoid Arnold, and then contradicts himself by admitting that he had been a guest at Mrs. Arnold's.[11]

Also, in 1782, at His Majesty's request, Arnold drew up his "Thoughts of the American War," based partly on notes William Smith had provided, should he be asked for something of the sort. How much was "Smith" and how much actually "Arnold" cannot be determined.

The peace had not yet been signed when Peggy and Benedict arrived in England. When they'd left New York, Benedict's intentions were not only to settle his wife and children in England in relative safety, but also to set before the king his ideas of how an amicable settlement of the war could be reached. He did not believe, or did not want to believe, that all was lost. It was though, and he should have been aware of this.

At this point most people in America did not want to have a peace with England, which would leave them a Crown Colony. They had gone too far and the idea of a complete break with Britain had begun to appeal to them. Surely they would be able to make it on their own.

Arnold's eagerness to try for a settlement was probably due more to his desire to be able to return to his home, pick up where he'd left off, and get back to a normal life. In his heart he must have known that, should there be a complete separation from Britain, he could never return. Was it panic that activated his urgency to stop this? Did he really believe that he had a chance of bringing this about? Apparently, he did.

Arnold hoped that the plan he outlined would explain the many differences that kept the Colonies apart from Britain. Here, again, his timing was off. Had his suggestions been conveyed earlier, when the majority of the Colonists did not want total separation from the Mother Country, the war might have taken a very different turn. Reconciliation would possibly have been conceivable. Now it was too late. The Colonists would not consent to another peace commission, even one composed of, as he suggested "rather statesmen than soldiers," unless all military forces, both army and navy, were withdrawn from America. In 1782 it was doubtful that any settlement would have included any connection with Britain whatsoever. Absolute freedom was the aim, nothing else would suffice. The end of the argument came on September 3, 1783, when the final peace was signed.

It is ironic to see that Arnold's projections, on the whole, were highly intelligent, and had England acted upon them earlier in the war, an acceptable settlement very possibly would have been brought about. Even if some of Arnold's proposals had been given credence during his tour of duty in the British army; if some of the petty jealousies and distrust of his fellow officers had been set aside, matters might very well have gone in a different direction.

# Chapter VIII
## The Fallen God

"Limited in his nature, infinite in his desires, man is a fallen god who remembers the heavens."

— Alphonse de Lamartine

When I first began to read about Benedict Arnold, an aimless occupation which soon grew into a serious study of the man, I worked my way through the vast amount of material existing, the most easily available at first: Isaac N. Arnold's fine biography, written with such concern for fairness. Coupled with a natural hesitancy to speak up *for* a man held in such ill regard, yet prompted by a desire to present *both* sides, was the knowledge that he and Benedict Arnold shared a common ancestor three hundred years before—he would not be accused of bias. Willard Wallace's admirable *Traitorous Hero*, bringing to light more recent information and presenting a thorough examination of his life and career from a military point of view; and Malcolm Decker's profusely illustrated *Son of the Havens*, often peppered with inaccuracies, and lacking sufficient documentation.

Dr. Wallace's book, written after the close of World War II, seemed to carry the prevailing trauma of that time when the subject of treason was at an apex, due to the trial of Julius and Ethel Rosenberg, who were accused of handing over nuclear secrets to Russia and subsequently were executed for the crime. Treason had been rampant before that during the Civil War, or, if you prefer, the War Between the States, but at its close "traitors" were granted amnesty if they would swear allegiance to the United States. Many did, but it was thought that Robert E. Lee did not.

93

However, on February 19, 1974, the 93rd Congress, 2nd Session, S. J. Res. 189, declared a posthumous pardon for Lee, restoring him to full citizenship. It is interesting, because it is duly noted that when General Lee had requested such an action, on June 13, 1865, it was denied because there was no accompanying oath of allegiance, and that only recently it had been discovered that General Lee did in fact swear allegiance to the Constitution of the United States, on October 2, 1886. The resolution restoring his citizenship was passed. It does seem a bit strange that so much time had to elapse before this oath came to light, especially since it had been made during Lee's lifetime. It seems that recent efforts were made to pardon a man as guilty of treason as Benedict Arnold.

Treason, according to the Oxford Dictionary, is: "violation by a subject of his allegiance to his sovereign, or to the state." Webster's Dictionary agrees with this definition, but then goes one step further: "The Constitution of the United States (Article III, Sec. 3) declares: 'Treason against the United States shall consist only in levying war against them or adhering to their enemies, giving them aid and comfort.'" The last part of this definition nails *both* Arnold and Lee to the wall! They did levy war against the United States — Lee with the Confederate army, Arnold with the British army, and *both* led military assaults against areas of their homeland. Lee is pardoned for this. Arnold is still held in contempt for the same thing.

On May 30, 1778, Arnold had signed the customary "Oath of Allegiance" to the United States, required of all officers of the Continental army. This was a matter of form, and it is doubtful, given any particular consideration by Arnold at that time. He had just been appointed to the command of Philadelphia and was basking in the particular consideration of Washington, who was really very fond of Arnold, valued his military expertise, and wished to assuage ruffled feathers, brought about by the continued failure of Congress to accord him the recognition he deserved.

There is one difference in comparing Lee and Arnold, and that is that Arnold made no attempt to re-instate himself, because he was fully convinced that his actions were justified. He could not apologize for what he felt had been right. Whether or not he was, does not excuse the tendency by Americans to smooth over the actions of the Confederate army — a treasonous action — and yet hold Arnold's treason an unforgivable act that expunges his brilliant heroic acts before his defection. The reason for Arnold's disgrace, even to this day, can only be attributed to the bitterness which arose from the extreme disappointment of a very young nation in a man it had revered above many of his colleagues, a man who, had he died on the battlefield at Saratoga, would have been commemorated by heroic statues in every public square across the nation.

As my curiosity grew I located other books, not so familiar: the biographies of Sellers, Sullivan, etc. The list grew, some for, some against; with Tillotson, Flexner, Van Doren, and the more obscure Taylor, a gold mine of information concerning the last days of Arnold and his family; Neilson, Stone, and Nickerson. Last, but not least by any means, Lossing's *Field Book of the American Revolution*, so precisely compiled, in many cases from reports of still living eyewitnesses to this tumultuous time of our history.

One thing that was glaringly noticeable everywhere was the continuous references to the early biography by Jared Sparks, written in 1830, as one volume of a series called "The Library of American Biography." This was the first biography of Benedict Arnold.

Sparks's references intrigued me because they have been painstakingly noted and quoted in nearly every biography since. Sparks was the source for this story or that — all fascinating. I wanted to see for myself what he had to say. I wanted, more than anything, to know his references. Lossing meticulously listed his, not only by name, but often referring to their particular age at the time of his interview, and his reasons for acceptance of their reminiscences.

Finally, I found a copy of the Sparks *Benedict Arnold*, a rather small, slim, insignificant volume. This, then, was the source for so many of the original tales quoted by subsequent biographers. My eagerness was quickly replaced by consternation. Amazed, I read through the book. The "hearsay" and "it was a well known story of the time" stories were all there—every one I had read "quoted" by later Arnold biographers—but where had Sparks found them?

The fact that the book was published in 1830, well after Arnold's defection, and his death, gave everyone, apparently, more than enough time to "remember" all the blackest tales imaginable, so that this remarkable man would be forever enshrined in American history as the arch scoundrel of all time. After all, every story must have a villain—Arnold was assigned the part. I have found Sparks so interesting that I have dealt with him in detail, in an appendix at the end of this book.

There was never a plot so rich in histrionics as the American Revolutionary War. We have the thrilling ride of Paul Revere (but did he actually make it all the way? Most Americans believe he did), the magnificent gesture of George Washington refusing payment for his services during the war (when he submitted his expense account following the war—and he did submit one—he was paid not in virtually worthless Continental paper currency, but in gold specie, surely a much better arrangement) [1], etc. etc.

The stories of Arnold's childhood, naughty boy stories at best—all dredged up from the depths of the memories of former acquaintances, would be laughable under any other circumstances, or, about, any other man. Everyone remembers, when someone falls from favor, the story of the child who tore the wings from helpless captive flies. Perhaps this type of story was a more comfortable memory than the ones which surely must have haunted some of those same acquaintances. Memories of the man's dauntless spirit and unquestioned bravery shown on so many occasions when he didn't wait to be called upon to defend his country. Those memories would doubtless have caused hurt and confusion in many minds. Men who had followed him, fought beside him, had known his warm kindness and concern for them in moments of danger when he seemed to have no concern for his own peril, would have had difficulty in separating the man they'd known from the one who had left so precipitately following the apprehension of Major John André.

That such a heroic figure could have succumbed to greed, vengeance, or whatever, was unacceptable — is still unacceptable. In their hearts they could not believe it. When a hero falls it is such a long way down to the bottom!

In their confusion and shock there must have been a few who questioned his motives. Perhaps there were more than a few. In any case, they were outnumbered by those who had always envied him his brilliance, the esteem in which his men held him, his dashing success. Jealousy does queer things to the minds of men. The Roman Catholic Church lists it as a "Cardinal Sin," and with great justification. It can poison the minds of men.

The poison has spread down through the years until the name of Benedict Arnold is considered synonymous with treachery. It is seen in a humorous vein in comic strips; comedians use it freely, wherever a "heavy" is required in the script. It's easy to write him in, even acceptable, much to our shame. How sad that we have come to this state of affairs. How sad that for years past children have been brainwashed in their early formative years, to one fact — that Benedict Arnold was a traitor — the necessary answer on an exam which would ensure one mark of 100 percent. Nothing else was taught, except that he had tried to turn West Point over to the British, and therefore was the personification of evil. This concept would be very seriously maintained to this day by military personnel, who would consider the act of giving secrets to the enemy particularly odious and dishonorable. Nothing of Arnold's career in the army was taught for many years. Students were not told just why West Point was considered so important, or that Benedict Arnold had *stopped* two invasions of the British from the north, in their push south to New

York, which would have annihilated the poor stockade fortifications of West Point. Today few people know anything about him, other than the parrotlike answer: "Benedict Arnold was a traitor."

Little thought has been given to an explanation, other than the well-known accusation against his wife, who emerges as the Revolutionary War Mata Hari. That she was implicated cannot be denied, but this is not the answer. Such an explanation only contributes to the odium surrounding the man. It brands him as not only evil, but weak, led by the nose into treachery by a woman. Benedict Arnold was many things — you can take your pick — but one thing he was not, and that was "weak." Nor was he evil.

It has also been said that he was a vengeful man, eager to repay Congress for their shoddy treatment; eager to repay the gossiping enemies who formulated the conspiracies to try his patience, and wound his pride. It seems rather strange that this could be believed of a man who reacted quite differently to these slights. He didn't plot revenge, or even attempt it. He simply resigned — not once, but twice, anxious to return to his private life and take up the reins once more of his lucrative business. It was his friend, George Washington, also moved on occasion to cast aside the military life and retreat once more to a private one, who cajoled him into returning. Washington valued Arnold's talents, recognizing them from the beginning. He wasn't about to lose them.

So much is said of Arnold's lavish spending, i.e., that he maintained a coach and four in Philadelphia. Surely it was known that, due to his Saratoga wound, he could still not sit on a horse, and a coach therefore would be a necessity. As far as a "coach and four" was concerned, the military governor of Philadelphia surely could not be expected to ride in a wagon! His entertainment expenses would also be a necessary expenditure. Whether or not they were as lavish as rumored cannot be confirmed at this late date, but in all probability they were exaggerated by the puritanical Supreme Executive Council of Pennsylvania, who had only exchanged one military authority for another when the British evacuated the city and the Americans moved in, with Benedict Arnold in command. They had had quite enough of being subject to the military. Arnold's orders to close all shops until the contents and stores could be identified and inventoried, instructions he had been given and intended to enforce, were an unpopular move.

One thing that must be remembered is that Arnold had advanced considerable funds out of his own pocket and arranged for extended credit with merchants in Canada during the attempt to capture Quebec and its aftermath. When he became military governor of Philadelphia he had still not been reimbursed for these expenditures. He was also awaiting back pay for his military services.

When he made purchases, or entertained, it was with the expectancy of these funds being restored to him. The fact that he was finding himself in debt would naturally have prompted him to attempt an early settlement of his differences with Congress over his financial affairs.

Greed has been offered as the third reason for Arnold's defection. Examination of his correspondence with Clinton clearly defines Arnold's request to be reimbursed for property he would stand to lose should he be apprehended. This property was considerable: three stores in New Haven, as well as a large house, wharfs and ships, along with shipping interests. There was also the estate of Mount Pleasant, the lovely Georgian mansion on the bank of the Schuylkill River, just outside of Philadelphia, which he had purchased as a gift for his bride, Peggy Shippen, and in which they were never to reside.

It will be noticed that I have not used the word "enigma," a term often used when describing Arnold. I do not believe he was anything of the sort. Reading his letters and those of his contemporaries, as well as studying his actions, sifting through the early hysterical nonsense that was recorded and which nearly every biographer since seems to have copied with no attempt to verify, the man emerges as a "complex" personality very definitely, but not an "enigma."

He has been termed "erratic" because he ran away at an early age to join the British army and fight the French and Indians, but then "deserted" twice. The first time, he was a boy of fourteen, a highly spirited boy, inflamed by the excitement of his times. He did not desert. Through the efforts of the Reverend Dr. Lord, pastor of his mother's church, he was returned home.[2] The second time he was seventeen—this time a young man—and he did take an absence without leave. There is an explanation—his mother was dying.[3] When he rejoined the military the next year there was no action taken concerning his desertion.[4] Nor would there ever be any question of desertion by this man until September 25, 1780.

Between the ages of nineteen and thirty-nine there was never an instant of hesitation in the course of his career, whether it was before the walls of Quebec, or as he spurred his mare to take her fatal leap into Breymann's Redoubt at Saratoga.

There was also never a moment's hesitation when it was in his power to use his own funds, or credit, to procure the necessities of life for his men, as he did at the end of the march through the Maine wilderness, before the attack on Quebec.

He would be accused of "stealing" military funds, or of offering "inaccurate records" of his expenses, and he would also be accused of drinking heavily to gain courage before battle. The last is almost laughable, as he was known by his contemporaries (even though memories changed in later years) as a rather abstemious man due to the often-unpleasant experiences he suffered as a boy because his father was an alcoholic.[5]

He did have a temper. It cannot be denied, and that he indulged it often is quite true. He seemed to have the devil's own talent for saying exactly what he thought, regardless of the situation, and stepping on the wrong toes—the toes of those who had none of his brilliance, but who surpassed him with longer memories.

As Willard Wallace states in his *Traitorous Hero* biography of Arnold: "It is interesting indeed that with truly able leaders like Washington, Schuyler and Montgomery, men who understood and appreciated him, Arnold had no trouble. It was generally with the second-raters, officers who were often more interested in their promotions than their jobs, that Arnold encountered difficulty."[6]

The accusations that Benedict Arnold was arrogant and conceited are so numerous amongst writings about him that it would be impossible to document each one. Suffice it to say that the accusations were made *after* his defection, as were so many other charges. It is all too simple to visualize a man filled with his own importance — an obnoxious characteristic — an egocentric popinjay. This sort of a person rarely exhibits any humility, much less to a superior, so it is interesting to read Arnold's letter to his commander, George Washington, written from a camp before Quebec, on February 27, 1776:

> The severity of the climate, the troops very illy clad, and worse paid, the trouble of reconciling matters amongst the inhabitants, and lately an uneasiness among the New York and some other officers, who think themselves neglected in the new arrangement, while those who deserted the cause and went home last fall have been promoted; in short, the choice of difficulties I have had to encounter, has rendered it so very perplexing, that I have often been at a loss how to conduct matters.
>
> As General Schuyler's ill state of health will not permit his coming this way, I was in hopes General Lee, or some experienced officer, would have been sent to take the command here. The service requires a person of greater abilities and experience than I can pretend to. General Wooster writes me his intention of coming down here. I am afraid he will not be able to leave Montreal.[7]

The warmth and respect he felt for another of his superiors, Philip Schuyler, is very evident in the following letter, written

July 30, 1776, from Fort Ticonderoga. Surely not the writing of a swaggering braggart:

> I am sorry to hear your treaty with the Indians is so long retarded. You must have an infinite deal of trouble with them, which I am fearful will prejudice your health; and your presence is much wanted both at Skenesborough and this place. I intend to visit Skenesborough on Monday next. I shall be happy to accelerate the business all in my power, and to take as much trouble from off your hands as possible, as I am sensible you have more than your share.[8]

All through his story one sees glimpses of his deep sense of caring, whether it was for his men, or his family. It is a warm sense of caring, the kind that would be concerned about the welfare of a fallen comrade's family, a concern which would follow through with funds not once but several times. The children of his friend, General Warren, could attest to that.

Samuel Adams made the effort to see that provisions for the education of the eldest son were made, and Dr. John Warren, brother of the general, took charge of the eldest daughter. However, this left the two youngest children in a serious situation. Arnold wrote to Miss Mercy Scollay, the lady General Warren had intended to make his second wife, and with whom the children were living:

> About three months ago I was informed that my late worthy friend General Warren, left his affairs unsettled, and that, after paying his debts, a very small matter, if anything, would remain for the education of his children, who, to my great surprise, I find have been entirely neglected by the State. Permit me to beg your continuing your care of the daughter, and that you will at present take charge of the education of the son. I make no doubt that his relations will consent that he shall be under your care. My intention is to use my interest with Congress to provide for the family. If they decline it, I make no doubt, of a handsome collection by private

subscription. At all events, I will provide for them in a manner suitable to their birth, and the grateful sentiments I shall ever feel for the memory of my friend. I have sent to you by Mr. Hancock five hundred dollars for the present. I wish you to have Richard clothed handsomely, and sent to the best school in Boston. Any expense you are at, please call on me for, and it shall be paid with thanks.[9]

Arnold continued his efforts in support of the children, sending money, as he had promised, and beseeching Congress to attend to a pension for them. His letter to Miss Scollay, of February 19, 1779, is interesting, in that he waxes poetic and voices his belief in values he is not supposed to have possessed, let alone prized:

Dear Madam

Unfortunately I was at Camp when Mr. Bell was in town and had not the pleasure of your favor until a few days past. The two letters you mention came safe to hand. A hurry of business will apologize for my not answering them. I think myself very unfortunate in not seeing Mr. Bell as I have many inquiries to make concerning my dear little boy and girl, as such I shall esteem them and make no doubt of their making every possible improvement under the eye of so affectionate and tender a mistress, who I sure will think it a delightful task to rear the tender thoughts, to teach the young idea how to shoot...to pour the fresh instruction o'er the mind, to breathe the enlivening spirit, and to fix the generous purpose in the glowing breast.

To a generous mind there can be no greater reward than the agreeable reflection of having protected those innocents from the misfortunes of poverty, and rearing them up to usefulness, when deserted by their ungrateful country.

In my last letter I mentioned applying to Congress in their behalf. On my application a committee was appointed to consider of the matter and report to Congress. One of the members going out of town soon after, prevented the reports being made, which was agreed to, by two of them, "that the three youngest children of the late General Warren should be provided for and educated agreeable to his rank in life at the public expense, and that when of age, the sum of one thousand pounds should be given as a portion to each." This report has never been made to Congress, by reason of some one of the Committees being out of town, I hope soon to have it done. If I am disappointed in my expectation, I intend making a collection for them by private subscription, which I have no doubt will be very considerable. In the mean time I shall esteem and provide for them as my own.

I have sent you by Lieut. Peter Richard five hundred dollars for the present, when you have occasion for more please to draw on me or send. I have not the least doubt of your economy and when I have the pleasure of hearing from you again, which I hope to have often, I must request you will send the account of their board and all other expenses that I may know how to furnish you with money in time. With love to my dear little innocents my best wishes for you and their health and happiness, I am with sentiments of the most perfect esteem and respect very sincerely, dear Madam your friend and Most Obedient Humble Servant.

B. Arnold[10]

Arnold kept plugging away at Congress and they finally took action. General Warren had been dead for five years, when they finally decided that the children should receive the annual amount of a bit over thirteen hundred dollars, as half pay. A retroactive payment came to nearly £1,000 as a gift to each child when they came of age.

That Arnold was deeply concerned with the conflict in which his country was engaged is evident in his myriad military endeavors, despite a lack of pay for four years; the jealousy of many of his politically minded contemporaries; and the insulting treatment of a Congress so beset with their own ineptitude that it is amazing they could make any decisions at all.

It is also a fact that he spoke openly against total separation from England, and equally against accepting help from the Roman Catholic French.[11] That he recommended acceptance of the peace treaty made by the British is not so widely known. Many think he manufactured all these things as excuses for his actions *following his defection*. This is fallacy—Benedict Arnold did not make excuses, much less for himself.

However, the portrayal of a warm, exciting, brave, tempestuous, passionate, kind, attractive man does not explain that defection.

Benedict Arnold was a remarkable, multifaceted man, a man who exhibited a definite personality pattern throughout his life, highly predictable, always unwavering. These characteristics are so evident from letters which have survived, that it is impossible to believe he would have changed. Not that adverse conditions, and he suffered many, cannot dampen a person's ardor or constancy. They can never completely change a person's principles and beliefs.

He was no more avaricious than others of his time who wished to further themselves in this growing country. Everyone wanted to make it big. He wasn't the only one with interests in privateers. Washington, Knox, and Greene, to mention three, were also involved. He might have been disenchanted near the end, understandably—here, too, he wasn't alone. He was passed over for promotion in favor of others junior to him. This would have hurt a proud man. Benedict Arnold was a proud man. He also resigned on each occasion and was asked to return by men who recognized his worth—Schuyler and Washington, to name two. When the hoped-for promotion finally came about it carried an added insult in that his seniority was not restored, nor would it be restored until it was impossible not to do so—Saratoga could not be ignored.

Much has been made of the Tory sympathies of the Shippen family and that they were instrumental in undermining Benedict Arnold's faith in the American cause. However, it has been fairly well established that the Shippens of Philadelphia were not all Tories. Edward Shippen, Peggy's father, was more supportive to the American than the British cause.

After careful consideration of all the possible reasons there remains only one, one that is very difficult for most Americans to accept, or even admit as a possibility. Could Benedict Arnold have decided that the war must end? Could he have offered to defect, or conspire to bring about the only solution he found practical? Did he, in fact, believe that his country was facing ruin, or worse, as he indicated in his letter of November 10, 1778, to General Greene:

> Our affairs both at home and abroad are in so deplorable a situation as forms a picture too horrid to dwell upon, and which in my opinion was never in a more critical situation than at present. The great council of the nation distracted and torn with party, and faction, the publick credit lost and debt accumulated to an amazing and incredible sum—the currency daily depreciating, and Congress if possible depreciating still faster, having lost the confidence of the Army, and publick in general, and abused or neglected their most faithful servants. These are the outlines of the picture....[12]

Did he fear subjugation to the French? If we remember that as a young lad of fourteen Benedict Arnold had tried to enlist in the British army near the end of the French and Indian War, a war only recently ended, the idea is not all that far-fetched. Now these same Frenchmen were offering generous aid to the Colonies, in a vengeful attempt to drive a wedge between Britain and America, and thus begin the breakdown of the British Empire. Was their sympathy sincere, or devious, hoping to acquire the Colonies for their own? Would not total separation from Great Britain leave the American Colonies vulnerable to just such intent? Was this what Arnold feared? If so, this wildly impetuous man might well have made an incredible gamble, attempted to "play God," and as a result of his apprehension make the ultimate sacrifice for his country.

The foregoing idea is not as far-fetched as it might seem. England had long been the natural enemy of France. If the Americans were aided, and England lost the war, she would have been reduced to a second-class power. The loss of America could herald the eventual loss of India, and such a defeat would revenge the arrogance displayed toward France by Pitt.

If Britain subdued her American Colonies, France's possessions in the West Indies would be in jeopardy. There was no other course to follow for France, but to provide the Americans with the munitions of war. There could not be a reconciliation between America and Britain, paving the way towards their united stand against France. The decision to come to the aid of the Americans was a selfish one, designed to strengthen the position of France in the world.

Revolutionary sentiment was beginning to awaken in France, but it had not taken hold as yet in sufficient strength to be a threat to their dissolute monarchy. Members of Congress denounced the alliance with France because of her known tyranny at home. This was our old enemy. Even Washington was distrustful. It appears Benedict Arnold was not alone. Others saw a threat to the Protestant religion by Roman Catholic France. If Britain was defeated, and we lost the support of a Protestant mother country, would France impose a change of religion here, as well as other terms, in exchange for her aid? Would we, in fact, be exchanging one master for another — one who could be more of a menace than the one from whom we hoped to obtain our freedom?

Benedict Arnold, most often portrayed as a short, stocky, obnoxious man with an explosive temper, and a tendency to arrogance and conceit, stomping about screaming invectives at everyone, was perhaps at times, all of these things. What rarely is brought to our attention, are his more redeeming qualities: caring concern for his family, the men under his command, his Negro slave, the orphaned children of a friend; a delightful gentle sense of humor — a man with a magnetic charisma that appealed to women, as well as men; an ability to share in the rowdy camaraderie of shipmates at sea, or, the intimate conversation of a select salon.

Benedict Arnold was a "fighting general" who suffered the same hardships as his men during that unbelievable march to Quebec. He was afoot for most of the journey, suffering hunger with everyone else, sharing the same labor, often waist deep in freezing water, making every effort to encourage the men and hoping to cheer them on. As a result his men adored him.

It has been cited that General Gates, while remaining in camp during the battles of Saratoga, conducted himself properly as commander. It was not expected of him to be on the field. Surely this is a modern interpretation of warfare. In the eighteenth century other commanders found it imperative to be on the field with their men, if not in the thick of the fighting, at least in a position where they could observe the progress of the battle and be able to make the necessary decisions of command.

Therefore, it is interesting to note that this same Commander Gates was ready to retreat and had wagons loaded, ready to move. In fact, they were ordered several times to move. If Arnold's actions had not forced Gates's hand, Burgoyne would have had the advantage of fighting on his own terms. Saratoga could have been a British victory. It appears Gates's confidence, or shall we say, his belief in victory, was not equal to that of those officers who were actually on the field.

Another great military genius, Napoleon Bonaparte, believed in casual camaraderie with his men. He knew them personally, made a point in knowing them intimately, so that they could function as a team. He, too, cared for the needs of his men and saw that they had them. He cared deeply, and his men reacted with blind devotion. They knew he would be with them on the day of battle, sharing the same dangers.

The adulation accorded Arnold by his men, placed him on a God-like pedestal. When he defected, their God had fallen. In their confusion and disappointment they could not see that he might have had a reason, a reason just as strong as the one that led him into battle.

Samuel Downing, a native of Newburyport, Massachusetts, who served with Arnold in both the Mohawk Valley and at Saratoga, remembered, in his old age, that: "Arnold was our fighting general, and a bloody fellow he was. He didn't care for nothing; he'd ride right in. It was 'come on, boys!' 'twasn't 'Go, boys!' He was as brave a man as ever lived. He was dark-skinned, with black hair, of middling height. There wasn't any waste timber in him. He was a stern looking man, but kind to his soldiers. They didn't treat him right: he ought to have had Burgoyne's sword. But he ought to have been true."[13]

Another old comrade, Alexander Milliner, looked back in old age at those glorious hours he'd shared: "Arnold was a smart man; they didn't serve him quite right."[14]

And still another old comrade in arms, Daniel Morgan, often at odds with Arnold, though having professional respect for him, remembered the swarthy general as "my old friend."[15]

Apparently, even if the "God had fallen," the man he had been could not be forgotten.

# Chapter IX
## London Pales

In 1783 we find the Arnolds living on Holles Street, London. The year dawned as a not very propitious one, with the birth in January of a daughter, christened Margaret. The infant, delicate from birth, only lived until August. The hoped-for daughter was not to be.

On September 3, the peace treaty was finally signed between Great Britain and the United States. The war was over. The United States was free. Whatever Arnold's hopes had been for reconciliation, before a total separation could be brought about, were dashed.

Still another loss was suffered when a son, George, was born in March of 1784, to die soon thereafter. During this same month, Arnold applied for Batt and Forage money, since he was under the impression he was entitled to this. William Petty, 2nd Earl of Shelburne, was approached to act in his behalf.

> March 5, 1784, London
>
> My Lord
>
> In obedience to your Lordships desire to me, to state my claims in writing to be allowed Batt and Forage Money, and rations of Provision, I beg leave to say that it is founded upon your Lordships promise to me (when last in office) that my detention in England should not operate to my pecuniary disadvantage, and that it should make no difference in respect to pay, etc. I beg leave to remind your Lordship that the promise was made to me in consideration of my having incurred a very considerable expense in consequence

of the Kings Order to me, to prepare to return to America, which has been much greater (including the expense of my detention and waiting in London) than the sum which I claim for Batt and Forage money, and for rations which is only £654 Sterling and which sum with many other emoluments has been allowed officers of my rank in America, and as your Lordship was pleased to say this morning that you thought me entitled to it, and would recommend to Lord Sidney that it should be allowed to me. I have the request that your Lordship will have the goodness to favor me with a line to the Lords of the Treasury for that purpose.

I have the honor to be

My Lord
Your Lordships Most Obedient and
Most Humble Servant
B. Arnold[1]

The Earl of Shelburne

At about the same time, Arnold began to assemble his "Memorial,"[2] a detailed account of his services to the Crown, the risks he incurred in their pursuit, and the amount of property loss he had sustained. This was to be presented to the Commissions appointed by an act of Parliament to enquire into the losses and services of those who had been loyal to the Crown. Documents certifying his claims were submitted by Joseph Stanbury, who confirmed his knowledge of Arnold's business connections and valuable property before and during the war; Joshua Chandler, a counselor at law, and an attorney in the Colonies, who also was familiar with Arnold's holdings and business; and also Jeremiah Miller, another friend from Connecticut; with referrals to Sir Henry Clinton and Colonel Dundas for further substantiations.

Listed in this Memorial are the debts of the state of Connecticut, to make good the depreciation of money due Arnold for the years 1778 and 1779; prize money due him from Congress in 1776; expenditures he had advanced out of his own pocket during the campaign of 1775–1776; the value of properties confiscated upon his defection; the whole totaling £16,125.2. Sterling.

At this point, the Arnolds settled down to await the disposition of the commissioners. Peggy, delicate and not completely recovered from two pregnancies, made more difficult due to the loss of both infants, was nervous and despondent. Benedict took her to sample the waters at Cheltenham Spa, where they lingered awhile.

Before they had left London, they'd both visited Westminster Abbey to see the recently installed monument erected to honor John André. Their thoughts must have been somber, indeed; Peggy, with her memories of a brief romantic idyll; Benedict, with an even briefer furtive episode, and possibly regrets as to how different things would be now, had André handled his part in the conspiracy with more expertise.

An existence such as this would never appeal to Arnold. Always restive, eager to be actively engaged in some scheme or other, he began to formulate a plan which he hoped would prove successful.

Before the war he'd been actively engaged in trading with Canada, and so now his thoughts turned to that part of the world once again. This time, it was the new settlement of St. Johns (present-day Saint John), New Brunswick. In 1783, Loyalist refugees from the Colonies had established a town at the mouth of the St. Johns River, on the Bay of Fundy. The area seemed to offer the prospect of a lucrative supply of white oak, much in demand in the West Indies. In turn, St. Johns could soon become an ample market for rum, traded in return for the lumber. In any case, due to the planned development of Canada, St. Johns seemed the place to be.

In 1785, with this in mind, Arnold began to outfit a brig, *The Lord Middleton*, to ply between St. Johns and the West Indies and also the coastal ports.

In May of this year, Peggy directed her father to sell the estate of Mount Pleasant, which he had purchased after it had been confiscated following Arnold's defection, and held in his name.

A daughter, Sophia, arrived in July, and it was sometime after this event that Benedict sailed for Canada. It would have been out of the question for Peggy to accompany him so soon after the birth of the child, especially since conditions in St. Johns were unknown. She was not to see her husband until he returned to England in 1787, to bring her and the children back to their new home in Canada.

The marriage of Benedict Arnold to Peggy Shippen has been treated by historians in many different ways. When Arnold first met her, traditionally at "Cliveden," the home of her friends the Chews, in Philadelphia, she was just eighteen and according to most accounts a captivating young lady. Her pale blonde hair, blue-gray eyes, in a heart-shaped face bear evidence to this in the pastel portrait of her as the general's lady, with their firstborn son, Edward, which Sir Thomas Lawrence drew during a visit of the Arnolds to Bath in 1783–1784.

She was the youngest daughter of Judge Edward Shippen, the former attorney general of the province of Pennsylvania, a man deeply troubled by his beliefs in the law, loyalty to the king and sympathy for the American cause.

Peggy had grown up in the midst of wealth, her every whim indulged. She had been given an ample education, as well as training in the typical "ladies' arts" of the day: dancing, music, drawing, and needlework. She was her father's favorite and the baby of the five children. She adored her father, and a close bond continued between them, ending only upon her death.

When Benedict Arnold appeared upon the scene, Peggy was considered the "belle of Philadelphia," riding a crest of popularity begun during the British occupation of the city. Arnold, the hero of the moment, handsome and exciting, and also wounded, attracted her as she attracted him. He began to court the young lady. Evidently, her father had reservations about the match and tried to restrain Peggy by pointing out the nineteen years difference in their ages. He also felt that their temperaments did not suit. Arnold, with his quick temper, restless nature, and lack of patience; Peggy, with her history of hysterics and fainting spells, so easily brought on if she were upset or thwarted, a tendency which continued all through her life. Peggy, however, remained adamant, and it was with difficulty that Judge Shippen persuaded her to wait until the following spring.

Meanwhile, the whole of Philadelphia society conjectured as to the outcome of the romance. Elizabeth Tilghman wrote to Elizabeth Shippen Burd, on January 29, 1778: "All ye powers of love I had like to have forgot the gentle Arnold, where is he, how does he and when is he like to convert our little Peggy. They say she intends to surrender soon. I thought the fort could not hold out long. After all there is nothing like perseverance and a regular attack."[3]

On December 21, 1778, Judge Shippen wrote to his own father about Peggy's sister's nuptials to Major Edward "Neddy" Burd, and mentions: "My youngest daughter [Peggy] is much solicited by a certain general, on the same subject; whether this will take place or not, depends upon circumstances. If it should, I think it will not be until spring."[4]

Just what the "circumstances" might have been he does not clarify, but quite likely they pertained to his unease concerning the charges which had been brought against Arnold by the Pennsylvania Council. He went so far as to check into them, but in the end gave in to Peggy, who seemed to vacillate between "yes" and "no" at this point. Perhaps it was just the coy behavior of a very young girl. However, her new brother-in-law, Neddy, wrote to his own brother-in-law: "You mention a report of another wedding being likely to take place in the family. You may recollect my suspicion, when I last saw you notwithstanding the refusal [by the Judge, according to Shippen family tradition]. My expectations have been answered. I was almost sure it could not be otherwise. A lame leg is at present the only obstacle. But a lady who makes that the only objection, and is firmly persuaded it will soon be well can never retract, however expressly conditional an engagement may have been made. However we have every reason to hope it will be well again, tho' I am not so sanguine as he is with respect to the time; but the leg will be a couple of inches shorter than the other and disfigured."[5] All speculations came to an end finally, and on April 8, 1779, Peggy Shippen became the second Mrs. Benedict Arnold.

Whether Arnold had actually entered into a conspiracy with the British slightly before his marriage, or slightly after it, is pure conjecture. Just how much Peggy herself contributed to his change of mind, can only be presumed. It could not have been a great deal, because Arnold was already depressed by his treatment at the hands of Congress and the Pennsylvania Council, and was beginning to have a change of heart.

Charles Burr Todd, in his book *The Real Benedict Arnold*, practically makes Peggy a "Colonial Mata Hari," who was deeply involved in spying for the British, even before Benedict Arnold came onto the scene. Arnold, after their marriage, so completely enamored of her, supposedly is led (or seduced?) into the plot and his ultimate defection. It would not be the first time that a man came under the influence of a clever woman and persuaded to desert a cause, especially when that man was a very disappointed and unhappy one. The puzzle remains—was Arnold the type of a man who would have been susceptible to such a ploy? I find it doubtful.

Peggy's knowledge of and proven involvement in her husband's plan to defect was evident by her consternation when she heard, at a dinner party, that he had been offered the left wing of Washington's army, instead of the command at West Point. Her desires being quite the opposite, and her knowledge of the extent to which negotiations had progressed between her husband and the British, would certainly have caused her extreme panic, sufficient to bring on a fainting spell! Surely now, he would not change his mind!

To paint Peggy the instigator doesn't make much sense when one considers her conduct following Arnold's escape from the Robinson house following his discovery of the capture of André. If she had been such a spy, obviously preferring the British, would she not have joined her husband in New York immediately, instead of running home to her family in Philadelphia? She did have the choice! Instead, she remained with her family until it was no longer possible, despite their frantic efforts to make it so. The extent of their efforts can be seen from Neddy's letter to his father, November 10, 1780:

> You have doubtless heard of the unfortunate affair of Mrs. Arnold. We tried every means to prevail on the Council to permit her to stay among us, and not to compel her to go to that infernal villain her husband in New York. The Council seemed for a considerable time to favor our request, but at length have ordered her away. Yesterday was the day she was to have set off, and Mr. Shippen, intending to accompany her the greatest part of the way, could not be up at this Court. This circumstance has involved the whole family in the deepest distress. Mr. Shippen had promised the Council, and Mrs. Arnold had signed a writing to the same purpose, engaging not to write to Gen. Arnold any letters whatever, and to receive no letters without showing them to the Council, if she was permitted to stay.
>
> However, this did not answer the purpose we hoped for. If she could have staid Mr. Shippen would not have wished her ever to be united to him again. It makes me melancholy every time I think of the matter. I cannot bear the idea of her re-union. The sacrifice was an immense one at her being married to him at all. It is much more so to be obliged, against her will, to go to the arms of a man who appears to be so very black.[6]

What actually caused the change in Peggy's feelings towards her husband is difficult to surmise, but changed they apparently had. She, and her infant son, joined him at West Point a mere ten days before the plot was discovered, but was this reunion her idea, or at her husband's insistence?

Arnold, a virile, passionate man, was clearly anxious to have his wife at his side, as is evident by his letter to Major General Robert Howe, September 12, 1780:

Be assured, sir, no sensations can have a comparison with those arising from the reciprocity of concern and mutual felicity existing between a lady of sensibility and a fond husband. I myself had enjoyed a tolerable share of the dissipated joys of life, as well as the scenes of sensual gratification incident to a man of nervous constitution; but, when set in competition with those I have since felt and still enjoy, I consider the time of celibacy in some measure misspent.[7]

That there had been a mutual attraction and deep bond of affection is evident, but had it begun to wane for one of the partners?

Peggy surely was more comfortable in Philadelphia, near her family, than she could possibly be at West Point. She also seems to have been engaged in a bit of flirtation in her husband's absence, according to a letter written to Arnold by his sister Hannah:

As you have neither purling streams nor sighing swains at West Point, 'tis no place for me; nor do I think Mrs. Arnold will be long pleased with it, though I expect it may be rendered dear to her for a few hours by the presence of a certain chancellor; who, by the by, is a dangerous companion for a particular lady in the absence of her husband. [The chancellor being Robert R. Livingston, about whose attentions she continues] I could say more than prudence will permit. I could tell you of frequent private assignations and of numberless billets doux, if I had an inclination to make mischief. But as I am of a very peaceable temper I'll not mention a syllable of the matter."[8]

Aside from Peggy's frivolous behavior, it is evident there was no love lost between the two women.

When Peggy finally rejoined her husband in New York, it would have been very interesting to be present at their meeting. Apparently, much of Peggy's vivacity was now subdued, according to a letter of Mrs. Shoemaker to her daughter, January 8, 1781:

Peggy Arnold is not so much admired here for her beauty as one might have expected. All allow she has great sweetness in her countenance, but wants animation, sprightliness and that fire in her eyes which was so captivating in Capt. Loyd's wife. But notwithstanding she does not possess that life and animation that some do, they have met with every attention indeed, much more than they could have promised themselves, and the very genteel appointment which he [General Arnold] holds in this [the British] Service, joined to a very large present, (which I am told he has received), is fully sufficient for every demand in genteel life.

Speaking of Mrs. Arnold again, Mrs. Shoemaker writes that she attended a ball at headquarters in New York, and that

she [Peggy Arnold] appeared a star of the first magnitude, and had every attention paid her as if she had been Lady Clinton. Is not this fine encouragement for generals to follow Arnold's example?[9]

There is an interesting story concerning an adventure experienced by Peggy Arnold as she traveled from West Point to her home in Philadelphia, following her husband's escape. One of the stops on her journey was at the home of Mrs. Theodosia Prevost, the widow of a British officer, living at the time in Paramus, New Jersey.

Peggy is supposed to have told Mrs. Prevost, soon after her arrival, that she was tired of all the hysterics she had had to enact, and was relieved to be with someone to whom she could confide. She admitted knowledge of and collaboration in her husband's treasonous behavior.

The story came to light in Matthew L. Davis's *Memoirs of Aaron Burr*[10] and was subsequently used in Charles Burr Todd's biography of Arnold. Since the lady, Mrs. Prevost, eventually became the wife of Aaron Burr, the story would seem to have credence. Todd believed that Burr only spoke of the incident *after* both Benedict and Peggy were dead, because he had always believed his old commander had been "quite sinned against as much as sinning."

This kind remembrance of a former commander is interesting since Burr and Arnold are not supposed to have been too friendly during those hectic days before the citadel of Quebec in 1775.

Of course, Burr was an abrasive person at times, clashing with George Washington during a brief tour as aide at headquarters in Richmond Hill, as well as others in his career. However, it is true that Washington treated Burr ungraciously later on, for whatever reason. Burr's subsequent appointment to Israel Putnam's staff was a much happier move.

To return to the supposed confession of Peggy, the Shippen family reacted vociferously, denying that Peggy was in any way implicated in her husband's actions. They went further, with a story of their own, that Aaron Burr had been with Mrs. Prevost when Peggy arrived and insisted on attending her for the remainder of her journey home. During this journey he was supposed to have attempted to seduce the poor, distraught Peggy!

For two reasons, this smacks of the ridiculous. One—when orphaned as a very young child, Aaron Burr and his sister, Sally, were placed in the care of Dr. William Shippen, Peggy's uncle. While they did not remain long with the doctor, it is probable the children would have known each other, and shared a family friendship. Strange that Burr would have attempted an attack under these circumstances. Two—it is fact that David Franks, Arnold's former aide, and not a little smitten with Peggy Arnold himself, attended the lady for the entire journey.

In the years ahead, evidence shows that the Arnolds, at least to all outward appearances, maintained a more than adequate marriage. Burdened with frequent pregnancies, Peggy at one point determined not to have any more children—"plagues," she called them. No doubt this decision was a wise one considering the small brood they already had and the difficulties attendant upon providing for their futures. At that time such a decision could only mean a total sexual abstinence, considering the prevailing lack of knowledge concerning birth control. One doesn't need much imagination to know what this would mean to a man of Arnold's nature.

Whatever one wonders about this marriage between two people so ill suited to one another, there can be nothing but admiration for Peggy Arnold as she struggled to salvage what she could from the disaster of Arnold's estate upon his death. She had a family to provide for and she exerted everything, approaching everyone in her power to make secure their futures as well as her own. Her letters to her family in the United States, as well as to Arnold's sons by his first marriage living in Canada, are those of a courageous woman.

It is unfortunate that she destroyed Arnold's personal papers upon his death, retaining only those of a business nature concerning the family. If she had not, we might have gained a deeper insight into the last years of a very complex man. We just might have known more of his thoughts and feelings at the end, and whether or not he ever wondered if his defection had been the right decision.

# Chapter X
## Canada Again

The crossing passed uneventfully. Arnold had timed it right and pressed men and ship for the utmost speed. Winter was nearly upon them when the brig *The Lord Middleton*, after a voyage of five weeks, reached Halifax, Canada, November 19, 1785.[1]

His arrival there met with mixed reactions, as it was subsequently in St. Johns. It is necessary to realize at this point that the Loyalists who had settled in Canada following their dismissal from the American Colonies after the peace with Britain were finding survival, for the most part, quite difficult. They had had their properties confiscated and were allowed to take only the bare necessities with them when they left.

The arrival of Benedict Arnold in their midst surely struck a discordant note. Here was an affluent man, as they had been before the war, who, catlike, seemed to have landed very well on his feet. He had played both sides and won. For all their loyalty to the king, they had lost.

He had been rewarded by the king for changing his mind and was here with a tidy ship, loaded with saleable cargo, all set to reconnoitre the area. He hoped to select a base and once more establish his trade with the West Indies. The Loyalist settlements were in need seemingly of everything.

The mixed feelings are evidenced by the comment of Attorney General Samuel Blowers to his friend Ward Chipman in St. Johns: "Will you believe! General Arnold is here from England in a brig of his own, as he says, reconnoitering the country. He is bound for your city, which he will of course prefer to Halifax, and settle with you. Give you joy of the acquisition."[2]

The snide insinuation of the last line apparently didn't have much effect upon the friendship which was later formed between Arnold and Chipman, a friendship which continued between the two men until Arnold's final return to England in 1792. Even then it was continued in their frequent letters.

In fact, while some looked askance at Arnold, others did not. He quickly formed fast and lasting friendships with Ward Chipman and Jonathan Bliss, who acted as his attorney. Both were reputable men, even then, though they later ascended to even greater heights: Ward Chipman to chief justice of New Brunswick and Jonathan Bliss to chief justice and the presidency of the Council.

Unfortunately for Arnold, misfortune struck as his brig, under the direction of the captain and pilot he had hired in Halifax, was brought into the marsh river and onto mud flats.

Arnold, at the time, suffering a bout with the gout, which plagued him throughout much of his life, was beside himself with fury.

According to a letter of Jonathan Sewell, Jr., to his father, the accident regarding the ship was not directed towards Arnold personally, but due to other causes:

> I have one circumstance more to add before I close my letter which is the arrival of the celebrated General Arnold in this part of the world. He came in a small brig loaded by himself. An accident which happened to this vessel coming into this harbor has been the subject of general conversation for some days past. The General first touched at Halifax and as the navigation of the Bay of Fundy is not much known at present, hired a pilot which was recommended to him as a capable one and who it is notorious has been here before. The brig was conducted in safety till she came off the harbor, where they plainly discerned the ships riding at anchor but the pilot insisted upon it that was not the harbor and as General Arnold was at this time confined to his bed by the

gout and unable to look after her himself crowded all the sail he could set—for the marsh river which is behind the town as you will see by the map which I have sent you if you have received it. The consequence was the brig was run upon the flats bilged and it is supposed will be lost from these circumstances and some others such as the winds being directly fair for entering the harbour. There is no doubt but the while was an infamous preconcerted piece of work done with an intention of injuring the credit of the harbour and to deter vessels from coming sound by malevolent conclusions to be drawn from the loss of this brig; and that the Captain was himself privy to it. This is General Arnold's account of the transaction and he has no doubt remaining of the pilot and captain's villainy, nor has any other that have received any injury in entering this harbor has had a Halifax pilot on board!![3]

Arnold, with his usual sixth sense regarding location, had selected a site in Lower Cove adjacent to the water at the intersection of Charlotte and Broad Streets, and erected a store and warehouse near the small house where he lived. He intended to establish a business in trading as soon as possible. The cargo from *The Lord Middleton* was salvaged and he began to stock the store. As he had surmised, just about everything was needed in St. Johns, and his supply of flour, nails, cooper's supplies, hay, shingles, and Tangier wine was a popular selection.

The settlers made their livelihoods by trading in furs, fish—herring was plentiful, as well as cod—and lumber—white and yellow pine, rock maple, black, yellow, and white birch, spruce, fir, ash, and elm, all abounded. White pine was used for ships masts, the production of which was a lucrative one. Oak staves, spars, and square timber also were produced. The West Indies was also another trading source. Once the peace was signed, the New England Colonies would also become a popular market for the settlers' items. Many of these settlers became quite prosperous through the hard work of hewing out an existence in the virgin territory along the St. John River. Evidence of the quickening pace in Saint John is found in the following:

> Ship building, where every material is or may be got on the spot, cannot fail to be an article of great importance in this country. Many vessels large and small are now building on the River, and as the materials are of the best sort, it may be expected that vessels will be lasting and durable and have a preference at foreign markets.[4]

Conditions were not easy. There were few and poor roads and rough log bridges. Transporting anything was far easier by water up and down the river.

The need to establish communications between the various settlements was high on the agenda, and citizens were asked to pledge funds for the building of roads, with each five-pound subscription entitling the donor to purchase a hundred acres of land on the road to which the contribution was being made. Arnold contributed fifty pounds for construction of the Westmorland road.[5]

His sons, Richard and Henry came to join him. Richard, now seventeen, and Henry, thirteen, were the sons of his first wife, Margaret Mansfield. His elder son, Benedict, had joined the British army. The boys had remained loyal to their father and were now eager to work with him to form a successful business venture. Since his sister Hannah had remained with the boys upon his defection, it is quite probable that she, too, joined them. Christmas that year might just possibly have been somewhat happier than the last several, when the family was scattered and caught up in the midst of the turmoil that existed following the peace.

About this time Arnold took as a partner Munson Hayt (variously and incorrectly spelled Hoyt), a Loyalist who had served as lieutenant, duty of quartermaster in the Prince of Wales American Volunteers. Arnold would be sorry before too long that he had formed this association.

By March of 1786, Arnold had purchased Lot 1329 from Jedediah Fairweather, a farmer, for a nominal price of £50.[6] He didn't stop there. Further frontage was available and he purchased one-half of the adjoining Lot 1328 in May, for £63.[7]

The city of St. Johns owned a number of lots and also all land below high water mark. The city was conservator of the waters and the river harbor and bay of the city, and had the right to allow construction of wharfs and piers. The city charter gave control over the entire harbor to the city and allowed it to authorize such construction. Since Arnold planned that his business was to be a trading venture, he needed to have direct access to the harbor. Therefore, he petitioned the city for permission to obtain and use a water lot. This was April. He certainly didn't waste time — ever.

The Common Council received the petition for a grant of lands on the west side of the harbor and ordered a grant of land at a rent of £10 annually. They also authorized a grant for three water lots on the west side, being Lots 18, 19, and 20, to extend to low water at a rental of seven shillings, six pence, annually.[8] This apparently was not related to the other property, which Arnold had acquired first.

The Common Council, in June, received a further petition from General Arnold regarding the ground in front of Lots 1328 and 1329 and the right to build a wharf. Following the next meeting of the Council, the Committee reported that General Arnold should be given the right to build a wharf 160 feet in length, agreeable to a plan attached to the original petition in front of Lots 1328–1329. It seemed he was ready to go.

The previous December he had purchased, from Tristram Hill, a half-interest in his sloop, *Nancy*, which was formerly the *Munson*. To this small beginning, he added a larger ship, the *Lord Sheffield*, no doubt named for John Baker Holroyd, the first Earl of Sheffield, and a local hero of the Loyalists because of the changes he instituted which so improved their lot.

Acquiring this ship caused some unpleasantness. She was purchased, price agreed upon, while still on the stocks at Maugerville, from Nehemia Beckwith. Subsequently, Arnold had some second thoughts and desired some rather expensive changes in the design and structure of the ship, which caused Beckwith to lose part of the original price. It seemed Arnold had acquired another enemy, along with his new ship.

However, he couldn't have been doing everything wrong, judging from the following quotation of the local *Gazette*, June 6, 1786:

> On Thursday last came through the falls of the City, now moored, a new and noble ship belonging to Brigadier General Benedict Arnold, upwards of 400 tons of white oak, the *Lord Sheffield*, to be commanded by Captain Alex Cameron. The General's laudable efforts to promote the interests of this infant colony have, during his short residence, been very productive to its commercial advantage and as such deserve the praise of every well wisher to its prosperity.

In August, the ship would sail for Campobello, an island off New Brunswick, near Eastport, Maine, en route to Jamaica. Accommodations for passengers would be available.[9] A trip like this — a brand-new ship under his feet — Arnold could not resist. He left Hayt in charge of his business in St. Johns and sailed for the West Indies aboard his vessel.

How long Arnold remained in the West Indies has not been recorded, but October 17 finds him once again in St. Johns, attending to business regarding a shipment which would have to leave by November 20.[10]

Since the Royal Navy was actually in residence in the Caribbean, to ensure protection of Britain's interests in the West Indies, provisioning of these ships was of the utmost importance. Arnold's trading between Canada and the Indies stood an excellent chance of prospering because of this.

In 1786, a child was born whom most historians consider pretty much of a mystery. It would be more correct to say that the mystery concerns the circumstances surrounding his birth, rather than the child himself.

In 1800, when Benedict Arnold drew up his will, he mentions John Sage:

> Item, I give devise and bequeath to John Sage now in Canada living with my sons there (being about 14 years of age) twelve hundred acres of land being part of a grant of thirteen thousand four hundred acres of land made to me as an half pay officer for myself and family by order of the Duke of Portland by his letter directed to Peter Russell Esquire President of the Council in Upper Canada dated the 12th June 1798 which said 1200 acres of land I give to him to be located altogether in one place out of the before-mentioned grant as my Executors may judge equal and fair. I also do hereby give and bequeath to the said John Sage £20 per annum to be paid to my sons Richard and Henry for his use for board, clothing and education until he shall be of age of twenty one years to be paid out of the estate I may die possessed of. I also give and bequeath to the said John Sage the sum of £50 pounds to be paid to him when he shall attain the age of twenty one years.[11]

Nowhere, it will be noted, does Arnold specifically say that John Sage is his son. Furthermore, this is the only place that this child is referred to as "Sage." Early historians assumed he spoke of an illegitimate son, giving him the name of "Sage." Perhaps it might have been a desire to spare his wife and family public embarrassment that prompted the subterfuge. The name "Sage" perhaps came to his mind because of his close friendship with Comfort Sage, of Middletown, Connecticut. A business friend before the war, Comfort became a comrade in arms, receiving the rank of major general before the war ended.

The mystery deepens considerably, though, when reading Arnold's petition for the land grants, which was dated April 13, *1798*, two years *before* he wrote his will:

> — praying for lands for himself and family, consisting of Mrs. Arnold and *eight* children as follows: Richard and Henry Arnold now in New York or Canada, Edward, James, Sophia, George, William and *John* in England for their education.[12]

Neither Margaret Mansfield nor Peggy Shippen had a son "John."

John Arnold subsequently was allotted land in the township of Elmsley: Lots 10 and 11, Concession 1; Lots 10, 11, and 12, Concession 3.[13]

When Benedict Arnold petitioned for the grant lands, in 1798, two years before he filed his will, he speaks of John as his son, whether he was with the other children in England for his education, or not (as he mentioned) is not important. What is important is that John was named "Arnold," not "Sage," out of necessity. Only the "Arnold" children would qualify for the grants, and so John was acknowledged as Benedict's son.

The tombstone on John's grave in Lehigh Cemetery, near Frankville, Ontario, adds to the mystery, with the information that John died on October 22, 1831, aged 45 years, 6 months, 8 days. This would place his birthday as April 14, 1786. Since Benedict did not arrive in St. Johns until early December of 1785, it is doubtful John was born the following April. An infant born that prematurely surely could never have survived at that time. Perhaps the date on the tombstone, which was placed on the grave upon the death of John's wife, Sarah, in 1871, is in error. A mistake on the part of someone could have resulted in the 6 *Months*, when 6 *Weeks* would have been more correct, placing John's birth in September of 1786, not April.

Historians have played with the mystery surmising this theory and that, the most ridiculous being the one asserting that Arnold sired a "half-breed" child in Canada, in 1775. This is obviously confused with the incident concerning Aaron Burr who did sire a child at the time of the march through Maine in 1775 in the attempt to capture Quebec. The mother was the Indian maiden Jacataqua, the sachem of Swan Island.

Others have placed the incident resulting in John's birth in the West Indies, and still others have flatly denied it could ever have happened in St. Johns—or, New Brunswick, for that matter, because Arnold's enemies surely would have used this juicy bit of scandal against him. There was never a whisper. The secret was well kept.

Considering the fact that Benedict's sister and his older sons, Richard and Henry, were in St. Johns, and John does turn up at age fourteen, living with them in Upper Canada, it seems probable that John's mother, whoever she was, died either in childbirth or soon thereafter and Hannah took still another of Benedict's sons under her wing.

While John emerges several times in census records and accounts of County Doings,[14] he remains a mystery. That he farmed his land and fathered four sons and three daughters is factual. It is probable that the details of his parentage were handed down to his children. If so, someone along the line stopped passing them on, other than that he'd been a son of Benedict Arnold. It is interesting to note that a military tunic, one of the few items belonging to Benedict that have survived, was treasured by John and remains with his descendants—still treasured to this day. Apparently, John did not resent his father. What he knew of his mother we shall never know. The only surviving legend in the family is that she was the daughter of a sea captain in St. Johns.

*Silverware, Broach, and Seal belonging to Benedict and Peggy Arnold*

These are the few personal items remaining in the family.

## Chapter XI
## Trouble Mounts

In 1787, with his affairs beginning to prosper, his base established, Benedict Arnold planned to move his family from England. He had changed his living quarters from the small house in Lower Cove to the more prestigious location of King Street — considered Upper Cove — the previous year. Surely now the situation in St. Johns would be more appealing to Peggy.

Whether Arnold had not brought her with him when he first sailed out to Canada in 1785, because of the insecurity of his position, or Peggy herself had chosen to remain in London to see how the venture would prosper before joining him, is not certain. That she was not the pioneer type can be gathered from her remark to Jonathan Bliss, when writing from London in 1795, following the family's final return to England: "...and I shall never again try a new settlement, for the benefit of posterity."[1]

In any case, Arnold returned to St. Johns in July, bringing with him his wife; Edward, now seven; James, six; and Sophia, two. Another son, George, would arrive that September.

It is doubtful that Hannah Arnold, and the two older sons, Richard and Henry, shared the house in King Street with Peggy and her young family. There was not a close bond between the two women, and relations would have been too strained.

Peggy soon made fast friends in St. Johns, Mrs. Ward Chipman and Mrs. Jonathan Bliss, to name two. They were seen riding their horses together often.

The Arnolds' social circle grew. St. Johns was not all "frontier town." There were balls, teas, and various other social doings.

131

Assemblies, numbering twenty to twenty-five ladies were not uncommon, and private dances were held at the fort quite often.
"Felicity Hall," Edward Winslow's house at Portland Point, in
front of Fort Howe Hill, would resound with gaiety and music,
and Ward Chipman would set everyone laughing by sharing a
humorous incident with the company.[2]

Along with the gaiety, Arnold continued his business ventures. He engaged Thomas Hanford as master aboard the schooner *George*, operating in the West Indies. Hanford was to be paid
three pounds a month at first, and upon delivery of cargo at Jamaica, he was to receive six pounds. Included in the arrangements was a percentage for the master on commission for goods
purchased and sold.

Arnold continued to branch out in business. With his usual
sagacity he established, besides his trading station in St. Johns,
another on Treat's Island, midway between Eastport and Lubec,
at the mouth of Cobscook Bay, facing Campobello Island. He also
lived for a short time on Campobello, at Snug Cove. It was at
Campobello that his path crossed once again with Captain John
Shackford. Captain Shackford, a member of Captain Ward's Company on the march to Quebec, was subsequently made a prisoner after the failure of the assault on that city.

At Campobello, Captain Shackford helped Arnold load a
ship, and later remembered the experience: "I did not make myself known to him, but frequently...I sat upon the ship's deck,
[and] watched the movements of my old commander, who had
carried us through everything, and for whose skill and courage I
retained my former admiration, despite his treason. But when I
thought of what he had been and the despised man he then was,
tears would come, and I could not help it."[3]

Arnold, with Jonathan Bliss, also signed an agreement, with
others, for protection against fire, promising to acquire fire en-
gines and dig public wells. They pledged £10 each.

Still his plans grew and in April of 1788 Arnold petitioned
the Common Council for the grant of two vacant lots, Nos. 379

and 381, on the west side of the harbor, in order to secure the course of a stream of water which moved through them. He managed to acquire the right to Lot 379 for a nominal annual rent of two shillings, six pence. The other lot had been granted to someone else.

Along with Arnold's increasing prominence and success, the city of St. Johns continued to develop. The pioneers expanded the businesses which they had created. New and more substantial homes were built. There was even an elegant "hair dresser" straight from London and Paris! Shops appeared which offered tobacco, wines, ladies' finery, and there were bakers, merchants, auctioneers, mantua-makers, retailers of dry goods, lodgings, taverns, etc. The ads in the *Gazette* abound with interesting entries. There was even a school for young ladies, where they could be "carefully instructed in needlework, writing, arithmetic, French, reading and English grammar." St. Johns was no longer the "backwoods."

Benedict Arnold had expanded his operations further afield, and had bought property in Fredericton, land and a house on what is now Waterloo Row. Other lots were acquired from Lieutenant Edward Earl and Lieutenant Charles Matheson. In Fredericton he renewed old friendships with former comrades in the British army, amongst them Adjutant Andrew Phair, postmaster, and Dr. William Stairs.

A warehouse he owned at the corner of Waterloo Row and University Avenue was later made into a home called Rose Hall. He built and launched ships near a creek at the lower end of the city.

Whether he actually ever lived there is doubtful, but he certainly spent time visiting back and forth, overseeing his many business ventures in Fredericton.

Arnold must have felt confident and proud that he had proved himself right regarding this adventure. Surely Peggy would regard this place in a favorable light and agree with him that here they would prosper and raise their family in the midst of gentility and affluence.

In December 1789, Peggy sailed for New York on her way to visit her family in Philadelphia. Her reception, outside of her immediate family, was still cold and she only stayed until April of the following year, returning once again to St. Johns. In July she wrote her sister, from a fog-bound St. Johns, a gloomy letter about her feelings concerning the visit and seeing her old friends. In her absence, her "small boys," whom she had boarded out, had been sorely neglected by the woman in charge. Apparently seeking some solace from the boredom she felt, she asked her sister to purchase various lengths of dress material and "anything else elegant" that she thought she might like.

Just when things seemed to be going right, there were the beginnings of unrest. Some of the terms of loans Arnold had extended began to come due and were not being paid. He expected payment by his debtors. Doesn't everyone? After a suitable wait he sought satisfaction in court. Very unpleasant situations developed. It was also evident that his name had been entered, by business associates, as security for debts contracted without his knowledge or consent. The partnership with Munson Hayt began to sour.

Arnold had met Hayt while in New York, following his defection, and they had become friends. While their business association in St. Johns had at first seemed to run smoothly, by October 27, 1789, because of too many differences, they decided to dissolve their partnership by mutual consent.

While Arnold was in England disposing of a cargo in 1788, it was suggested to him by friends there that he insure the Lower Cove warehouse for £1,000, its stock for another £4,000, and goods in the King Street store for another £1,000.

The Lower Cove structure burned in July of that year while Arnold was still in England. His son, Henry, who was in the store, nearly didn't escape. Rumors ran rampant, no doubt fanned by persons whose feathers had been ruffled in court. It was said Arnold had been a party to arson, and the insurance underwriters attempted to evade payment.

Upon his return, Arnold, along with Stephen Sewell, then a law student associated with Ward Chipman, were able to find a possible explanation for the fire, and it might very well have been something as simple as a candle left burning in an empty loft.

The fact that Arnold finally did receive recompense for the damages as claimed, clearly indicates there was no skullduggery involved. However, Munson Hayt, seething with resentment of his own, joined those who had spread the rumors of arson.

Now the situation really began to get out of hand. Arnold's temper, always quick to flare, exploded at the imputations and he cried "slander."

May 8, 1790, Hayt obtained a writ against Arnold, and on the same day, Arnold procured a writ against Hayt. Accusations grew ugly—charges and countercharges of theft, arson, robbery, and slander flew thick and heavy.

As the case began to be heard, young Stephen Sewell wrote his brother, Jonathan:

> The Circuit Court opens today with Judge (Isaac) Allen on the bench. The defamation (Arnold vs. Hayt) case comes up on Friday and if they should have to go into all of the General's transactions in this country, which is not impossible, it will take some days. The General has 30 witnesses.
>
> About a month ago I went up the River after two black men with the General. We found one of them on the Main [St. John] River and the other on the Kennebecasis, both giving evidence as nearly alike as possibly could be, which was to their purpose. One of them went with Harry [Henry Arnold] to the top of the store the night that it was burnt with a candle after some oak to make a boat. There was such an appearance of veracity and fear withal of what might be the consequences, their story so direct which they told without leading questions, the declaration that they had not seen any of the General's family, that no one ever said a word to them respecting the fire, their strong appearance of truth, candor and simplicity, which is always visible particularly

in black men, altogether is sufficiently presumptive evidence against anything that Hayt can allege that the store was burnt otherwise than by accident.

Mr. Chipman takes a great deal of pain in the business and he had told me that it is one of the most hellish plots that ever was laid for the destruction of a man.[4]

Hayt had borrowed various amounts from Arnold and signed promissory notes. Subsequently, he was unable to pay the money back. The debt came to £2,000, a nice round sum. This was one of the reasons the partnership had been dissolved. Also, the remarks Hayt had made against Arnold at the time of the fire had caused the initial hesitance of the insurers to pay the insurance. This, plus the unpaid notes determined Arnold to take action.

In court Arnold was represented by Ward Chipman and Jonathan Bliss. Ward Chipman had been deputy master general of the King's Provincial Forces in New York. He was one of the most prominent and influential lawyers in the province. Hayt was represented by Elias Hardy (take note of that name), a prominent New Brunswicker whose legal feats were notable.

The suit began September 7, 1791, and was a bitter one. Hayt repeated his slanderous statement: "I will convince the Court that you are the greatest rascal that ever was, that you burnt your own store and I will prove it."[5]

The verdict in the slander trial was in favor of the plaintiff — Arnold — but the amount awarded, 20 shillings, was so trivial as to be insulting. The fact that he later recovered part of the money Hayt owed him might have provided balm for the pain Arnold must have felt at the time.

An interesting bit of evidence concerning the reason for the disposition of the court, and which is not at all well known, is that *at the same circuit,* Arnold was sued for failure to pay an arbitration award and lost to the extent of £275.6.0, and costs. An examination of the record shows that the one action had a decided bearing upon the result of the other. John Harvey brought action against Benedict Arnold for debt on an arbitration bond. *Elias Hardy* acted for Mr. Harvey!

Those eligible for jury duty were limited in number, and once a jury panel was drawn, the jury for each trial was selected from the same jury panel. As a result there could be, and there were, jurymen who served on more than one case at a sitting. In this case we discover *nine of the members* of the jury who decided against Arnold on the Harvey trial were selected to try the issue between Arnold and Hayt!

In slander suits damages are usually unlimited and the special prerogative of the jury. A nominal award in effect means a technical slander but no real injury to the reputation, and this in effect was the result.[6]

Perhaps had Arnold not been so involved in suits, arousing so much bitter feeling, and had he not just lost a case brought against him, the slander case would have ended quite differently. What happened instead was that people began to remember the old resentment against him because of his defection and the rewards he received thereby. Feelings grew really hot and a mob gathered outside his home, burning him in effigy and causing the troops to be called out to disperse the demonstrators.

Arnold grew bitter with resentment at the open hostility of the city he thought had become his home at last. The unpleasantness and openly violent action of the mob would have finished the whole project for Peggy, in any event. London represented a safer refuge, and so the September 22, 1791, issue of the *Gazette* carried the following notice of an auction sale at the Arnold residence:

> A quantity of furniture comprising excellent feather beds, mahogany four-post bedsteads with furniture; a set of elegant cabriole chairs covered with blue damask [still in the collection of the New Brunswick Museum], sofas and curtains to match; card, tea and other tables; looking-glasses, a secretary desk and book-case, firescreens, girandoles, lustres, an easy and sedan chair with a great variety of other furniture. Likewise, an elegant set of Wedgewood gilt ware, two

tea table sets of Nankeen china; a variety of glassware, a terrestrial globe; also a double wheel-Jack and a great quantity of kitchen furniture. Also a lady's elegant saddle and bridle.

One other interesting memento survives from those years in Saint John and is exhibited in the American Museum at Claverton Manor, Bath, England. It is a very attractive lady's sewing box made of bird's-eye maple, with various compartments formed of birch-bark covered with the palest of blue satin and delicate embroidery. The box was presented to the museum by the great-great-great-granddaughters of Peggy and Benedict Arnold, descendants of their daughter, Sophia Matilda Phipps. The box was a farewell present to Peggy from a Mic-Mac Indian girl, Elasaba. A rather poignant verse was discovered in the box:

> When more pleasing scenes engage
> And you in polished circles shine
> Then let this wild, this savage page
> Declare that gratitude is mine
>
> Elasaba

*Diane Thomas and Vivian Harvey, descendants of Benedict Arnold's daughter, Sophia, with work box at the American Museum, Claverton Manor, Bath, England*

In December, the Arnolds were on the high seas bound once more for England. For several years, a frequent correspondence was carried on between Benedict Arnold and Jonathan Bliss, who was delegated to look after the unfinished business in St. Johns, along with Ebenezer Putnam. There was property to be sold, 16½ lots of land in the St. Johns area, 1,000 acres elsewhere, two wharves, a house, and the seasoned frame of a 300-ton ship. All chores that were to cost Bliss much time and effort. Some of the debts would never be collected.

The letters between Arnold and Bliss were not all business but contained warm concern between friends. When Bliss lost his wife, Arnold commiserated with him: "It is vain to offer you consolation, time only, with the hope of meeting in happier regions, can reconcile you to so heavy and distressing a loss."[7]

There were lighter moments, concerning the lengths of material and bonnets sent for Mrs. Bliss, and again tragedy with the shattering news of the loss of Arnold's oldest son, Benedict, who died of a fever which developed from a wound he suffered while serving with the British army on the Island of Jamaica.

With the death of the elder Benedict Arnold, in 1801, the correspondence died off. The contact with St. Johns was at an end.

Only one Arnold would ever return—James Robertson Arnold. He was given command of the Engineers in Nova Scotia and New Brunswick from 1818 to 1823. While on this command, he visited his father's house in St. Johns and it is said he wept like a child when he entered it.[8]

While Peggy and Benedict Arnold lived in Canada there had been many developments. The Canada Constitutional Act had divided the country into two Provinces, Upper and Lower Canada, and in the country of their birth, news of which no doubt they followed with great interest: in 1789, George Washington became the first president; John Adams, vice president; Thomas Jefferson, secretary of state; and Alexander Hamilton, secretary of treasury. The year following, Ben Franklin died, Washington,

D.C., was founded, though Philadelphia remained the federal capital of the United States.

Europe, too, was undergoing many changes. France in particular. The French royal family had been captured trying to leave the country and were returned to Paris. The fires of the French Revolution had been lighted!

# Chapter XII
## England Again

The rough winter crossing proved a miserable one for the Arnold family, but at last they were back in England once again. Benedict, suffering an attack of gout, wrote to Bliss from London, on February 26, 1792:

> We had a very rough and disagreeable voyage home, but our reception has been very pleasant, and our friends more than attentive since our arrival. The little property that we have saved from the hands of a lawless ruffian mob and more unprincipled judges in New Brunswick is perfectly safe here, as well as our persons from insult, and tho we feel and regret the absence of the friends we had there, we find London full as pleasant! And I cannot help viewing your great city as a shipwreck from which I have escaped.[1]

It appears they were not forgotten and were about to be once again involved socially with friends. This time they settled into living quarters on Holles Street, a side street opening off Oxford Street. The area is very commercial now, having suffered extensive damage during the last war, so we have no idea what sort of house existed on Holles Street in 1792. However, Holles Street fed into Cavendish Square where the Fitch family was living.

Samuel Fitch, a Loyalist and former barrister in Boston, was of the Fitch family who after settling in America in 1638 had lived in Norwich and New Haven—neighbors of Arnold before the war. In 1776, Samuel, having different feelings than Benedict concerning his allegiance, left his law practice and went to Halifax. When it became evident that the war was to continue, and he was notified of his formal proscription in 1778, he moved his family to England.

Samuel Fitch's wife was Anne Whiting, sister of Nathaniel Whiting, who had presented Benedict Arnold for membership in the Hiram Masonic Lodge in New Haven, before the war. Old friends, indeed.

Samuel's son, William, fifteen years older than Benedict, was living with his parents at the time as a half-pay captain in the British army. The daughters, Ann and Sarah, were closer to Peggy's age, Ann a year older, Sarah a year younger.

A close-knit group formed between the Arnolds and the Fitches, which also included the William Vassall family, Daniel and Sarah Coxe, and Nathaniel and Anne Middleton, living on Harley Street, Cavendish Square. Coxe had been a member of the governor's council in New Jersey. Of this group, the Vassalls were more comfortably situated as far as finances were concerned. Vassall had owned a sugar plantation in Jamaica and had managed to salvage a good part of his fortune. They lived in a fine house facing Clapham Common, at Battersea Rise.

A bit of cheer would come to the Arnolds when they were informed that Peggy was to receive an annual pension of £500 from the Crown.

The domestic family gatherings of friends, no matter how compatible, were not enough to curb Benedict's restlessness. He yearned for an appointment, not just to keep him occupied, but because such an appointment would mean added income, desperately needed.

In May, Arnold presented an elaborate scheme concerning the "forwarding of intelligence to collect troops in the shortest time," coupled with emergency plans to be used in the event of the threatened invasion of the French.[2] Suggesting putting the old Beacon Fire system to use to warn the inland posts of an enemy force approaching from the coast, he also outlined a program to train civilians how to handle fire arms, destroy supplies of use to the enemy, and remove food and livestock from their path. This latter action he had put to good use against Burgoyne's forces as they moved towards the inevitable confrontation at Saratoga.

The scheme was elaborate, concise, and would be very useful if accepted and followed. Whether it was, or not, we cannot be sure, but it was sent to Lord Edward Hawke, son of the renowned admiral, who was to become a close friend in the near future.

On the 31st of May, there was a heated debate in the House of Lords concerning the king's proclamation against seditious meetings. Following addresses of the Marquis of Abercorn, the Earl of Harrington, Lord Hawke, the Prince of Wales, and others, the Earl of Lauderdale entered the fray, charging the ministers with gross inconsistency, comparing their conduct with that of Mr. Pitt and the Duke of Richmond at the close of the American War.

> How the noble Duke and Mr. Pitt would vindicate such a change of conduct he knew not, but would leave it to them, etc.
>
> The Earl at length took notice of the camp at Bagshot, which he said the noble Duke [of Richmond], who had been so strenuous for reform, was appointed to command, to overawe the people, and destroy their endeavors to obtain a reform. He declared he was glad the Duke was to command the camp. If apostasy could justify promotion, he was the most fit person for that command, <u>General Arnold alone excepted.</u>
>
> To these remarks the Duke of Richmond replied in language which called from the Earl of Lauderdale, through Mr. Grey, a demand for an explanation or a meeting. After discussion, the Earl of Lauderdale declared the expression used by him, applied solely to the Duke of Richmond's public conduct, and that he meant nothing in any respect to his Grace's private character. The Duke of Richmond, on his part, declared he did not persist in the terms he used to Lord Lauderdale, those expressions having been suggested solely by the idea of his private character's having been attacked.[3]

During the ten years of Benedict Arnold's exile he had withstood various insults, ignoring them with as much patience as he could command, but now, this slur of the Earl of Lauderdale, the hereditary standard-bearer of Scotland, in the House of Lords, was more than he could bear. Nor could he afford to let it pass, especially since the Duke of Richmond had raised an angry voice concerning the slur directed at him, and had received an apologetic explanation. Arnold could hardly remain silent.

The earl had used Arnold's name in his debate to make a point, or embellish his argument. It was, perhaps, the beginning of the custom of using Benedict Arnold's name as a synonym for the anathema which persists to this day regarding his name. Arnold could not have known this, but he did realize it would add fuel to the derision expressed towards him by his enemies in America, who would assume that all England agreed with the earl. Aside from the pride of the man, which was deeply wounded, he could not afford the slur to go unanswered, if only for the sake of his family. He sought immediate action and indicated his intentions to his personal friend, Lord Hawke, who offered to deliver his demand for an apology, or the alternative — a meeting upon the field of honor.

The earl refused giving an apology, denying he'd said any such thing, and would not sign a statement of apology which Arnold composed and submitted to him. A meeting was arranged. Lord Hawke would act for General Arnold. Charles James Fox, the renowned parliamentary orator, would act for Lord Lauderdale. The time, 7 A.M., Sunday morning, July 1, 1792. The place, Kilburn Wells, the site of an old priory and medicinal well, then occupied by the Bells Inn, a short distance from Regent's Park — open country in those days.

And so, on the Sunday morning appointed, according to a family tradition, recalled by the Reverend Edward Gladwin Arnold (Benedict's grandson) we find Benedict arising early, kissing his wife farewell, though taking care not to awaken her, and leaving the house for his assignation with the earl. Peggy, however, had feigned sleep, hoping to spare her husband an emotional farewell, and it was she who recounted the story to her family.

For an accurate description of the duel we have a statement, made by Lord Hawke, and presented to Mr. Fox, on Monday, 2nd July:

> The mediation of friends having failed to produce an accommodation between Lord Lauderdale and General Arnold, they met this week in a field behind Kilburn Wells. It was agreed that they should fire together. General Arnold fired and his second not seeing Lord Lauderdale fire, said to him your Lordship's pistol had missed fire, no [replied] Lord Lauderdale, I have not fired. I have no enmity to General Arnold. I will not fire. General Arnold's second then said your Lordship then can have no objection to say you did not intend to asperse his character. Lord Lauderdale replied I formerly said I did not mean to wound his feelings. I can give no explanation. General Arnold's second then desired Lord Lauderdale to take his ground, and return General Arnold's fire, and General Arnold keeping his ground for that purpose, repeatedly called on his Lordship to do it, which Lord Lauderdale declined, saying at the same time that he would take his ground again to receive General Arnold's second fire, but would not fire himself. This General Arnold and his second both said was impossible, for neither in such a case would he, General Arnold, fire, nor ought any second to permit it, even should his principal be inclined to it. Lord Lauderdale then said that he was sorry for what he had said, but he could not retract his words. General Arnold replied that was not an apology, or such as he himself would have been ready to make in the same situation, to Lord Lauderdale.

> Lord Lauderdale then said that he had no enmity to General Arnold, that he had had no intention to asperse his character, or wound his feelings, that he was sorry for what

he had said, that General Arnold or any other man, should feel hurt by it, and trusted General Arnold was satisfied. On which General Arnold replied, that he should be perfectly satisfied if both the seconds as men of honor would say he ought to be, which they both did.

Monday, July 2, 1792

Hawke[4]

Later that same week, Peggy wrote to her father with details concerning the duel. In the course of her letter, she makes interesting remarks, which I hereby extract: "I am happy now to have it in my power to relieve; as the affair is settled most honorable for the General, and his conduct upon the occasion has gained him great applause." And: "It has been highly gratifying to find the General's conduct so much applauded, which it has been universally, and particularly by a number of the first characters in the Kingdom, who have called upon him in consequence of it."[5]

It seems that Lord Lauderdale was rather a firebrand on the side of the opposition in the House of Lords, and not well liked. Perhaps Arnold's act of standing up to him was well received because of this. In any case, it brought Arnold pleasure at a time he could sincerely appreciate friendly gestures.

In Peggy's letter to her father, concerning the duel, she makes a request that he advise her concerning a £2,000 investment she and her husband wished to make for their children. She was of the opinion that such an investment could perhaps earn a higher rate of interest in America, than the 4 percent then available in England.

That autumn, Ward Chipman, back in St. Johns, wrote that he was making every effort possible to obtain payment of various notes left unsettled by Arnold when he left Canada the year before. He was a good friend and most anxious that his letters were being received, since mails were so often lost. Duplicates and triplicates were written to ensure delivery.

Money was tight for the Arnolds, even if they didn't live in a very opulent fashion. The social gatherings with Colonel Beverly

Robinson at his home "Mortlake," in Surrey, Lord Hawke in town, and their other Loyalist friends, were not elaborate, but pleasant.

During a great part of 1792, Arnold was attempting to obtain the rest of the money he felt was his due, and correspondence was frequent between him and General Clinton. Pitt was approached, and wished to consult with Clinton. Arnold felt that Clinton could add weight to his request if he would furnish Pitt with substantiation of his claims. After all, Clinton had been in America, knew the situation thoroughly, and could affirm Arnold's risks and the value of his services.

Clinton had a house on Portland Place, near Regent's Park, but usually spent most of his time at his country residence at Weybridge, until he had a falling out over rent with the owner of the house, the Duke of Newcastle. As a result he moved to Orwell Park, in Suffolk, near the Orwell River, between Ipswich and Harwich.

Clinton, traveling between Orwell Park and London, promised to do all in his power to help Arnold. He mentions that his correspondence with Arnold had been mislaid, and he worried that his memory might be a bit foggy. He was sure of one thing, though. "I am sorry that General Arnold should have the occasion to think it necessary to ask my opinion of his motives which influenced his desire of being reconciled to the British Government and joining the King's Army...." and, "I do not hesitate to declare that you never gave me any reason to suppose you expected anything more than indemnification. That I thought it an act of justice, as well as of duty to offer you £600, not as an indemnification for all your losses, for they had not been ascertained, but I thought it was all I could give in that prudence with which I was obliged to temper with liberality." He closes with: "I sincerely hope that it will not be long before your conduct may be fully elucidated to your satisfaction and the motives which influenced it better known than you seem to think them at present."[6]

Arnold submitted an itemized account of the property he possessed at the time of his defection, and also an outline of what he could have realized in half-pay funds, and lands which might have been bestowed upon him had he not defected.

October came and Arnold wrote Clinton again, following his return from a six-week stay on the Isle of Wight, describing his meeting with Pitt, which seemed favorable because Pitt "appeared very much surprised at the small sum I had received, and seemed inclined to do something for me, and in the course of conversation asked me what would make my situation as good as it <u>formerly was</u>, in consequence of this question I stated to him my former and present situation and prospects and left him to judge."[7]

Though Pitt promised to consider the problem, Arnold felt that he would in all probability wish to consult Clinton again. That consideration was being thought of along these lines, is evident by the statement Arnold provided in November, and which Clinton enclosed in a letter to Pitt:

> Sir Henry Clinton will find on examining their correspondence that when General Arnold stated his losses, (after he came into New York) at £10,000 he alluded only to Personal Effects, his real property not then having been lost, <u>nor at that time had he any real idea that it would be eventually lost,</u> and that the sum of £6,000 given him was <u>considered</u> both by Sir Henry Clinton and himself <u>only</u> as a part of his losses, the whole not being ascertained at that time, which General Arnold begs leave to remind Sir Henry Clinton that he fully expressed in his letter of the 2nd of August last, a copy of which General Arnold gave to Mr. Pitt.[8]

Ward Chipman and Jonathan Bliss were still struggling to collect Arnold's outstanding notes in St. Johns. In November, Chipman wrote that he had concluded a couple of small accounts and would send the money as soon as he could obtain a "bill" on London, needed to transmit the funds.[9]

On February 1, 1793, the French National Convention declared war on Britain. The reign of terror in France; the executions of Louis XVI and Marie Antoinette shocked everyone. The bloody excesses disappointed and alarmed the many romantic radicals in Britain. Though they still spoke of and worshiped the idea of freedom and equality for all, which they hoped could be brought about by revolution, the stark reality of war had the effect of stirring second thoughts. The youth down from the universities, with their vivid ideas of reforms and even the abolishment of the monarchy, and the end to the power of the church, greatly worried the British government. There were arrests, but a token solution was offered when the government suspended the Habeas Corpus Acts.

Henry Clinton finally made good his promises in December and furnished Pitt with the information he required in order to increase Arnold's income, but it wasn't until July of 1793 that the Arnolds were formally notified of the decision, by the King's Warrant. An annuity, or yearly pension of £100 each, was to be provided for Edward Shippen Arnold, James Robertson Arnold, Sophia Matilda Arnold, and George Arnold.[10]

Since Arnold, in all his letters to Pitt and Clinton, had expressed his anxiety concerning his children, their continuing education and their situation, should they be deprived of parental support at an early age, this settlement would have given him some peace of mind, if it didn't quite come up to his expectations, nor cover the present financial situation.

## Chapter XIII
## The Last Adventure

In 1794, when Benedict Arnold was fifty-three, the tensions and disillusions of the past year sparked a return of his old restlessness. He just couldn't sit in London with nothing to do—waiting for favors which might never be granted.

Early in the spring he purchased a ship and began to fit her out for trade with the West Indies. Since the French made travel in the English Channel perilous, Arnold went overland by coach to Falmouth, Cornwall, where he waited several weeks for his ship to arrive from London. Whether some sort of sixth sense warned him, or he thought the journey could be achieved with greater speed via a fast-sailing packet, or perhaps his old impatience just took hold—we'll never know, for he boarded the packet and was on his way. It was fortunate that he did because the French captured his ship soon after she left port, while he arrived safely in St. Kitts.

At Falmouth, while Arnold waited impatiently for the arrival of his ship, he had an unexpected meeting with Charles Maurice de Talleyrand, who happened to be staying at the same inn. Talleyrand was on his way to America and when introduced to Arnold, asked him if he could provide letters of introduction to his friends in America in his behalf. This must have been an embarrassing question for Arnold, since this common request was impossible for him to fulfill. After a slight hesitation, he told Talleyrand: "I am perhaps the only American who cannot give you letters for his own country—all the relations I had there are now broken—I must never return to the States."[1] Years later,

Talleyrand remembered the incident and the pity he had felt for Arnold.

At St. Kitts, Arnold traded for a while, then decided to sail for Pointe-à-Pitre, Guadeloupe, to buy sugar. This would not have been a great problem had it not been for the political unrest of the West Indies at that time. With the Negro revolt on the island of Haiti in 1791, French planters had become alarmed and appealed to the British for protection, and British forces had taken control of the French islands as a result. However, the radical Jacobite French government sent a squadron of troop transports that had slipped through the British blockade and recovered Pointe-à-Pitre shortly before Arnold was to arrive. The commander of this force, a mulatto named Victor Hughes, was firmly ensconced at Pointe-à-Pitre, ruling with a ruthless hand. He gave the slaves their freedom and carried out extensive executions of royalists.

Arnold, unwittingly, sailed straight into this situation, believing that the shipping in the harbor was British. When he discovered it was French, it was too late to escape, so he decided to bluff it out by landing and declaring himself an American there to buy sugar.

The French suspected he was British at first, and he was placed aboard a prison ship with other captives. Shortly after his capture, Arnold heard that the British fleet had arrived to blockade the port. This knowledge, coupled with the information of a sentry that Hughes knew his identity and planned to hang him, made Arnold decide on a hasty escape. Hanging might have been the easiest of deaths available at the hands of Victor Hughes, considering the atrocities he was committing — beheading, staking, burial alive, and various forms of mutilation were common. Fortunately, Arnold had been able to secret among his personal effects the £5,000 he had planned to use for the sugar cargo.

His always-alert, quick mind made plans. Passing a few gold coins amongst his guards, he obtained an empty cask. Hiding his treasure in the cask, along with a letter identifying its owner, he lowered it into the sea.

When night came, he climbed down a rope suspended from the cabin window onto a hastily constructed raft of planks provided by the bribed guards. There were no oars, so he paddled the craft with his hands through shark-infested water to a small boat which he found nearby. Shortly after midnight he was on his way, threading through the French squadron with muffled oars. At one point he was hailed from a guard boat, and when he made no answer, they gave chase. Fortunately, he was able to escape by dodging in and out amongst the shipping, and early morning found him near the English fleet. He was quickly taken aboard the *Boyne*, flagship of Admiral John Jervis. He even managed to recover the cask containing his money, which had drifted ashore below Point-à-Pitre and was found by a British landing force.[2]

Arnold had used another of his cat-like nine lives, and operating from St. Pierre, Martinique, quickly made himself useful to Sir Charles Grey, in command of British forces, in a volunteer capacity, expediting and organizing the operation of supply service. The West India Planters and Merchants Company also appointed him their agent.

During this time, Henry Arnold, Benedict's third son from his marriage to Margaret Mansfield, joined his father in the Indies. Henry, while a personable lad, proved unreliable, and his irresponsibility in business matters angered his father to the point that he wrote Josiah Blakesley:

> If my obstinate and imprudent son would [use?] his own interest and common prudence and economy, I would in a short time put him in a very line to make a fortune. I want an assistant very much, but until I can trust him with money and be assured that he will not squander it away and think himself above giving an account of it, I will treat him as a stranger and not as a son. I wish to God he would have a little sense and prudence and determine to reform....Pray give my love to Harry. I expect a letter from him when he has an apology.[3]

They did eventually reconcile, but not much else is known of Henry afterwards.

While Arnold was busy in Martinique, Peggy gave birth, on June 25, in London, to a son, William Fitch Arnold, who was to be their last child. In letters to her sister, Peggy writes of trying not to have any more children.[4] In a letter to Richard Arnold, Benedict's second son from his first marriage, Peggy announces the birth of this child in a curiously cold manner: "On the 25th of June, I made an addition to my family, of another son; a circumstance by no means desirable to me."[5]

There was anxiety in the family for still another son, Benedict, Margaret Mansfield's eldest son, who had been imprisoned in France for a long time. British prisoners held there were being very ill-treated. Peggy finally was able to transmit some funds to the young man, which would make his incarceration more bearable.

Seventeen ninety-five found Benedict Arnold, the elder, still at work in the West Indies. He wrote Ward Chipman again in February about the notes outstanding in St. Johns, and then, on May 4, he wrote again, hoping that the notes will have been settled and he would receive confirmation when he arrived back in England. He stated that while he had made money in the Indies, he had recently met with a loss of £3,000 at Grenada.[6] Considering that, his anxiety over outstanding debts is understandable. He planned to leave for England within a few days aboard a packet, or perhaps His Majesty's 44-gun ship *Assurance*, commanded by Captain V. C. Berkeley. The ship had seen service in the recent political upheavals in the Indies and would be returning, with others, as the British relinquished their struggle to hold the islands.

Arnold would never return to the West Indies, but he must have been gratified the following August, when he was requested to appear before the Standing Committee of West India Planters and Merchants at Wright's Hotel in London to "afford them what information he might be able to communicate, respecting the actual state and condition of the West India Islands, and having attended, and given them information in the most obliging manner.

RESOLVED

That a letter be written and transmitted to General Arnold, by the Chairman of this Meeting, informing him, that the Standing Committee of West India Planters and Merchants, beg leave to return him their thanks for the communications he was this morning pleased to afford them; that on their part they are fully sensible of his services in the West Indies, and feel themselves particularly obliged by his exertions at the request of the Commander in Chief, which were attended with such beneficial effects in covering the retreat of the troops from Guadaloupe, and under these impressions they cannot refrain from expressing their great concern, at finding his having quitted the Islands at a time when their safety is in the utmost hazard; and from the great mortality among the troops and the misfortunes with which some of the late enterprises have been attended, there appears a great deficiency of officers to command the remaining troops in the several islands which are still in His Majesty's possession, and that they beg leave to assure him that it would give them the most entire satisfaction to find he was again in a situation to render further service to His Majesty in that part of the world.

Wrights Hotel,

Soho Square, August 1st 1795.

Sir,

As Chairman of the Standing Committee of West India Planters and Merchants, met at this place, it is with great pleasure I have the honor of transmitting on the other side a copy of their Resolution of this day, and to assure you of the great regard with which I have the honor to be

Sir,

Your Most Obed.t Humble Ser.t

Gilbert Franklyn.[7]

Arnold replied, certainly with much pleasure, and a sense of being really appreciated — for a change:

Sir

I have had the honor of receiving your very obliging letter of this day enclosing a copy of a Resolution of the Standing Committee of the West Indies Planters and Merchants, expressing of their approbation of my conduct in the West Indies, and a wish of my being further employed. The approbation of so very respectable a body of gentlemen cannot fail of being highly gratifying to me, and I beg you will do me the favor of returning them my sincere thanks for the favor they have done me, and assure them that nothing would afford me greater pleasure than having an opportunity of rendering them special service in the West Indies.

I have the honor to be with great respect and esteem,

Sir
Your Most Obedient Humble Servant
B. Arnold[8]

Arnold, as he states in his letter, would no doubt have loved to return to the Indies in some military capacity, or other, but since none was forthcoming, and further problems, of a personal nature, had developed, his traveling days were at an end.

## Chapter XIV
## England — One Final Time

Upon his return to London in June of 1795, Arnold found Peggy ill. She had not completely recovered from the birth of William, the previous year, and also was experiencing a return of a "nervous complaint," which she seemed to suffer from frequently throughout her life. Arnold attempted to provide respites of a month at a time, in such places as Bath, Warwick, and in the Essex countryside, but since he himself, outside of a lifelong tendency to gout, enjoyed a sturdy robust health, Peggy's delicacy would have tried his patience and added to his financial worries.

There was an infant son to be viewed, a pleasure this — Arnold loved his children and maintained affectionate relationships with them. Edward, fifteen, and James, fourteen, would be away at school, but perhaps George, eight, would still be at home with ten-year-old Sophia. The little girl, his only daughter, delicate, but was now growing proficient in her needlework, art, and music. He would also find a wife determined to have no more children!

London was still London, little changed in the short while he had been away, though styles certainly had. A group of young Whigs, in protest against a powder tax imposed by William Pitt, had washed their hair and refused to powder it. It was a fad, slow to take hold, though by 1810 it would become universal.

Henry Clinton had been appointed governor of Gibraltar and had gone off there the year before, and would die there this year of 1795.

In Benedict's absence, Peggy had continued the correspondence with the Bliss family, who were now happily settled into the house on King Street, in St. Johns, the last residence of the Arnolds before their departure to England. In August, Arnold, once again happily involved with his family, wrote Bliss: "Our three boys and little girl are placed at exceedingly good schools where they improve very much. Edward the eldest will soon be the start [*sic*] of me in heighth and is a remarkable forward and fine boy."[1]

Since 1784, when Benedict Arnold first presented his "Memorial," asking to be recompensed for property, potential status and income he had lost because of his defection, nothing definite had emerged. Depositions of friends, social and financial background from before the war began, attesting to his claims had all been filed. A settlement of wastelands in Upper Canada (now Ontario) was being considered. However, at that time, if the grants were given, there was a stipulation which required residency on the grant. The Duke of Portland, secretary of state, interceded for Arnold, requesting that this stipulation be dispensed with, in consequence of "his [Arnold's] late and meritorious services in Guadaloupe."[2]

The Duke of Portland's support was to prove valuable, and his influence surpassed that of another friend, Lieutenant General John G. Simcoe, whose petition, in behalf of Arnold and his family, received little attention. The months dragged on, causing much frustration, but as is usually the case, the workings of government cannot be hurried, unless it suits government to do so.

In September, Arnold wrote again to Bliss that Peggy was still ill and pretty much an invalid—a nervous disorder. He had been asked to go out to the West Indies again in a military character and would accept the appointment if his terms could be met. He mentions that Peggy is sending a bonnet to Mrs. Bliss which, he is "told is very fashionable, a thing of great importance—I think it pretty. Edward nearly as tall as myself and bids fair to be very tall—they are [Edward and James] both excellent scholars and lately received most of the prizes in the academy where there are now one hundred boys. They all speak French as well as English and the master of the school opins me that George, who is Master of his Grammar will make a figure—he has great ambition—if you was [*sic*] not a fond father yourself I would apologize for troubling you with the history of my little family."[3]

On December 5, Peggy wrote to Bliss congratulating him on Mrs. Bliss's delivery of an addition to the family—"as it appears to be a pleasurable circumstance to you—for my own part, I am determined to have no more little plagues, as it is so difficult to provide for them in this country, and I shall never again try a new settlement, for the benefit of posterity. I am much obliged by your good wishes for the General's return, with a handsome addition to his fortune. I have, thank God, got him safe home, but I believe he has, by his trip to the West, gained more credit than money. The West India Planters and Merchants applied to Ministers to send him out again with a Command; they were extremely anxious for him to go, but could not comply with his terms, which were either to go second in command, or have a separate one. They were fearful of putting over the heads of so many old General Officers, but it is universally acknowledged that had his advice been followed, we should now be in possession of Guadalupe, and the necessity of sending such a force as is now going, been prevented."[4]

January of the new year of 1796 brought some cheer when Benedict's son, James Robertson, was accepted as a gentleman cadet in the Royal Regiment of Artillery, under the command of Charles Marquis Cornwallis. A nice gesture from an old friend and it must have provided a semblance of relief to the Arnolds that one more son had been helped towards his future career. Another friend, Colonel Barry St. Leger would provide support, as would Lieutenant General Lake prove helpful to young Edward Arnold when he ventured to India later.

February brought sad news. Arnold's eldest son, Benedict, wounded in a skirmish with maroons, the half Negro, half Indian savages on the island of Jamaica, had died of a fever, a result of his wound suffered in October of the previous years. Arnold wrote Bliss:

I have recently received the melancholy information of the death of my oldest son in Jamaica, who fell a sacrifice to a fever brought on by the severity of duty in that unhealthy climate, where he had distinguished himself, and had been promoted, and was in a fair way of rising fast in the Army, had he lived. I have the consolation to hear that he was much respected and beloved by the officers of his acquaintance. Major General Walpole in particular the Commanding Officer on the North side of Jamaica, was his particular friend and had appointed him his Brigade Major, and Lord Balcarres had promised him further promotion. His death I find is much regretted by them, and is a heavy stroke on me, as his conduct of late years had been irreproachable and I had flattered myself with seeing him rise to eminence in his profession — [5]

There was to be another blow to the little company of Loyalist friends when it was learned that William Fitch had also died on Jamaica during these uprisings.

Arnold's correspondence with Jonathan Bliss and Ward Chipman continued into the spring. Arnold had signed a covenant to rent a parcel of land for use as a shipyard in Carleton, during his residency in New Brunswick. He had paid rent until his departure for England, at which time he was under the impression he could relinquish any claim on that land and the corporation in St. Johns would be free to accept another lessee. Now the corporation was attempting to hold him liable for unpaid rent, and he appealed to Bliss and Chipman to act in his behalf.

At this time, even though he carried on a courteous exchange of ideas concerning farming and navigational problems existing in St. Johns, he must have wondered when he would see an end to the mortifying problems which still pursued him from the other side of the sea.

The months passed and the war with France continued. In 1793, when the French Republic had declared war on Great Britain, Spain had been a British ally, but on June 22, 1795, through the Treaty of Basel, Spain and France joined forces, and Spain declared war against Great Britain.

Benedict Arnold, always the opportunist, conceived a plan for the capture, by the British, of Spanish possessions in the West Indies, as well as the liberation of Chile, Peru, and Mexico, from the dominion of Spain!

The plan was remarkable, an elaborate one, showing a great deal of detailed study of existing situations in these possessions, as well as actual first-hand knowledge gleaned from his experiences in the West Indies. He identifies each area meticulously as to exact lattitude and longitude; topographical details; types of native inhabitants; religious preferences; taxes and injustices imposed by Spain, which would likely persuade the people of the advantages of becoming a part of the British Empire — including suggestions on establishing local government![6]

The plan was submitted to Pitt on December 9, 1796, and was no doubt discussed, since we find Arnold answering a letter from Lord Cornwallis, in which he thanks him for his attention in speaking to Pitt on his behalf concerning the plan. It seems there was some thought of the hazard of deploying so many ships of the line from the service, which might place Britain in danger from a close neighbor, who was also an enemy. He makes suggestions concerning the number of ships required, and offers his services to lead the expedition.[7] He couldn't resist, even at the age of fifty-five, to charge off into the fray once more!

Despite the plan and his personal offer of availability, the year was drawing to a close once again, leaving the old warhorse in a state of suspense, always the most odious situation for such a restless and impatient personality.

News of pleasant sort had come from across the sea. Henry, Benedict's third eldest son, had married a Hannah Ten Eyck of New York and planned to reside in Canada. Also, in America, George Washington had refused to accept a third term as president.

In Europe, Napoleon had also married — his beloved Josephine.

In December of this year of 1796, we find Arnold's correspondence listing a new address — 18 Gloucester Place, London. A new development of the area between Portman Square and Marylebone Road was taking place and rows of Georgian-type architecture were going up. The Arnolds became the first residents of a very respectable new four-storied house on the east side of Gloucester Place, with stables and carriage mews attached at the rear. In the 1930s, when Gloucester Street and Gloucester Place were combined, to be called Gloucester Place, the houses were renumbered — #18 became #62. The area is now partly residential. Number sixty-two has been divided into flats, several commercial. Some of the old imposing Georgian houses along the street have been turned into small hotels.

In January, Arnold wrote to Bliss on business. There were still debts he hoped to collect. He mentions that Peggy had been an invalid for many months, and their recent move into the new house in Gloucester Place, though pleasurable, had only deteriorated her delicate health. He hoped they would remain in the new house for many years. By July, he wrote greatly encouraged by Peggy's response to a new prescription of a Dr. Warren. Unfortunately, the good Dr. Warren could not continue the treatment — he died shortly after taking on his new patient. The treatment, however brief, must have had a substantial effect upon Peggy's health, since Arnold's letter of November 25 to Bliss presents an entirely different picture: "Mrs. Arnold has been at Cheltenham this fall to try the water....I have the pleasure to say she is in better health than she has been for a long time past and I hope will soon be properly well."[8]

Meanwhile, England was delirious with news of the encounter of the British fleet off Cape St. Vincent, Portugal, on February 14, when Admiral Jervis's fleet defeated the Spanish fleet, thanks in a large part to the insubordinate act of young Horatio Nelson, who took his ship out of the line of battle — an unheard of maneuver — to engage the enemy and precipitate the battle. He was forgiven by his commander, Arnold's old friend. It was an unparalleled act of initiative on the part of a subordinate officer, but Jervis, always a fair man, was also intelligent enough to recognize Nelson's potential. Jervis became Lord St. Vincent, and Nelson soon was made a Knight of the Bath in recognition of their feats on that memorable Valentine's Day.

Benedict Arnold, chafing at the bit like a restive thoroughbred, had approached Lord Spencer and volunteered for naval duty in January of that year, and now with the news of the defeat of the Spanish fleet, he again volunteered in June, but was disappointed that he was not accepted. It was very plain he was not wanted, or needed — an awesome blow to a proud man, secure in the confidence of his abilities. It was a time of anxiety and glory to be won. He could not bear to be left out!

# Chapter XV
## Last Heroic Rallies and Death

In January of 1798, Benedict Arnold wrote a lengthy letter to Lord Spencer, at the Admiralty, making some suggestions regarding the preparations for a French invasion. The letter begins in an apologetic vein, hoping to put forth the impression that his ideas might not have occurred to anyone else, but that he does not wish to be thought presumptuous. His grasp of strategy, an ability he had always exhibited, and in which he had excelled, is uncannily shown when he writes:

> I think it reasonable to suppose that tho' their ostensibile object is England, their real design is against Ireland where if they should effect a landing with twenty or thirty thousand men, in the present temper of the people it might probably be attended with fatal consequence to that country and <u>prove ruinous</u> to England in the event.

He goes further:

> But as there is only the Port of Brest in France from which the French can send an Armament against Ireland with any probability of success, I have no doubt that it will be blocked up with a fleet sufficient to oppose their designs, notwithstanding which I think it may possibly happen as it has done before that a fleet of heavy ships crossing from Brest may by a series of strong easterly, or westerly winds be driven from their ground so far to the westward, or up the British Channel as to afford an opportunity for the French fleet to escape from Brest and reach the coast of Ireland before they could be intercepted by our fleet, whether we can put a fleet in any

western harbor of Ireland sufficient to oppose the French should they evade the fleet of Brest I cannot say....[1]

His idea was prophetic! Such an attempt was made by the French, to land a force in Ireland, though they were not successful in maintaining the advantage.

In this same letter, Arnold makes a suggestion of equipping a small group of frigates and fire ships to back up the British fleet, which might be absent, to take care of any such landing forces. Of course, he volunteered to lead such a force.

Lord Spencer acknowledged Arnold's letter politely, but indicates he feels they are taking care of any such eventuality — thank you.[2]

On April 22, 1798, tenacious to a fault, Arnold again tried to enter the fray. He wrote to His Highness, the Duke of York: "Sir, At this important crisis, I feel it a duty that I owe both to the public and to myself, to offer my services to your Royal Highness in any way that I can be most useful to the Country."[3]

The Duke of York's reply was kinder than that of Lord Spencer. He thanked Arnold for his offer and promised to lay it before His Majesty.[4]

Arnold was now fifty-seven years of age. What made him so persistent to enter the military arena once again? Certainly not financial gain because he could not expect any high-paying appointment. Why then? Was it what we would call today a "death wish"? Had he reached that point in his life when there was little that mattered to him? Did he hope to go down in glory — trumpets blaring — just one more time?

In April, Benedict Arnold presented his application for Crown Grant Lands in Upper Canada to Peter Russell, president of His Majesty's Council in Upper Canada, on the basis of his service as colonel of the American Legion of Cavalry and Infantry in the American War and the fact that as a half pay officer he was entitled to such a grant. He requested these wastelands on behalf of himself, Mrs. Arnold, and their eight children: "Richard and Henry, now in New York or Canada, Edward, James,

Sophia, George, William and John [this would have been the boy referred to as "John Sage" in Benedict's Will]." He requests, originally, 15,800 acres—5,000 for himself, 1,200 for Mrs. Arnold and as much for each child in his family—to be located by his sons, or an agent. He requests that he and his children "in England for their education" not be required to reside in Canada."[5]

He later withdrew the request for lands in the names of Richard and Henry since they had already received grants as half-pay officers.

Lord Edward Hawke showed his affectionate regard for Arnold in his letter to William Henry Cavendish, Duke of Portland, home secretary under the prime minister, William Pitt (the younger):

> My Lord,
>
> I shall think myself obliged to your Grace's attention to General Arnold's Petition to His Majesty for a Grant of Land in Upper Canada, in the following Proportions. For Ten Thousand acres for himself, for five thousand for Mrs. Arnold, and as much for each of his children, as some compensation for the great losses of property, the sacrifices which he has made and the services which he has rendered government.
>
> I have much respect and friendship for General Arnold, and I flatter myself at all times, more especially in the present, he could render very essential services to his country. But as I am well acquainted with Your Grace's inclination to do him justice, I will not lay any stress on the above considerations, but rather on what he has lost and the services he has already performed. As a half pay officer only he would be entitled to sixteen thousand acres: I trust he has a claim on government for some further compensation and particularly on the faith, justice and honor of the nation, and, in the way above stated by him. I trust that it cannot be, in the least burdensome to government.
>
> I have taken the liberty of stating the above to Your Grace, and it will give me very particular pleasure and I shall

consider it as an obligation done to myself, should General
Arnold succeed in obtaining his reward.

    I have the honor to remain, with very great respect,

       My Lord, Your Grace's very faithful servant

                          Hawke[6]

It appears that Lord Hawke felt Arnold was deserving of a somewhat larger settlement.

On June 12, Arnold was notified that he had been granted 13,400 acres of Crown Grant lands in Upper Canada, and through the efforts of the Duke of Portland, the anxiety concerning their residency on the lands was over. The stipulation had been waived.

The war with France continued and news would finally reach England of Nelson's victory of August 1, in the Bay of Aboukir, Egypt, where he destroyed the French fleet at their anchorage, thus cutting Napoleon off from France. In England rumors of French spies were rampant and a radical element was stirring up insurrection, though threats of invasion, which had been on everyone's mind for so long, seemed to have slackened.

Life at 18 Gloucester Place settled down to a quiet pace. There were new neighbors to meet—friends to make: The Gardners, Dawsons, Governor and Mrs. Hornby and a Mrs. Petre. The Fitches remained constant, as did the Vassall family. The Vassals had an early connection with America, as had the Arnolds. William Vassall's great-grandfather, Samuel, had been an original patentee of the Massachusetts Bay Colony in 1628, a member of Parliament, an alderman of London and a staunch parliamentarian. William had graduated from Harvard in 1733 and lived for many years in Boston, acquiring considerable property there. At the time the Revolution began, he was high sheriff of Middlesex, Massachusetts. He was known to be a firm Loyalist and so had to make an early exit from the Colonies in 1778. He moved his family and his wife's sister, Ann, to England. The Vassalls, of all Arnold's friends, were the most affluent, having been able to salvage much of their property in Massachusetts by proxy sale. William also owned an extensive plantation in Jamaica and enjoyed revenues from there.

In April, Arnold decided to approach Charles Jenkinson, 1st Earl of Liverpool, a personal friend of the king, for a favor. Benedict's son, George, then twelve, was old enough to begin training for a place in the military. Unfortunately, Lord Liverpool was no longer secretary of war and did not feel it was within his scope to do anything for George.

That same spring, while the Arnold family were seeking refreshment near the sea, at Margate, they were observed by John C. Warren, a near relative of Joseph Warren, whose children Benedict had so kindly aided before his defection: "I met General Arnold, the 'traitor', so called. He was there with his family; I recollect a son, very handsome, and a daughter. Arnold was rather a stout man, broad shouldered, large black eyes. He walked lame from a wound received at the attack on Quebec, I think."[7] How sad that after only twenty-two years, his valor at Saratoga was forgotten — or, not remembered with surety!

Arnold received encouraging news from Charles, Lord Cornwallis. He would be glad to see that young George was placed in training for a situation in the India service.

In June, Jonathan Bliss suffered the loss of his wife. News of this loss did not reach the Arnolds until December. George Washington died this same December, though the news would not reach England for many weeks.

The year 1800 was to be eventful in many parts of the world. The British were to capture Malta; the Royal College of Surgeons would be founded in London; the city of Ottawa would be founded in Upper Canada; Thomas Jefferson would be elected president of the United States, and the U.S. Federal Offices would move from Philadelphia to Washington, D.C., the nation's new capital city.

For the Arnolds there would be two farewells. In May, their good friend William Vassall died and was laid to rest in the crypt of St. Mary's Church, Battersea. In June, Edward Arnold left for military service in Bengal, under the personal patronage of Lord Cornwallis. Neither Benedict, nor Peggy would see him again.

Also in June, Arnold corresponded with President Russell once again regarding his Canadian grants. The grants had been promised in 1797, but in 1798 new regulations went into effect concerning the fees required for their completion. Arnold had to write that his memorial had been filed and approved *before* these new regulations, and therefore did not feel that he was liable for the increased fees. There seemed no end to the annoyance regarding these grants. Richard and Henry were hard at work clearing their lands, and prepared to locate acceptable lands for the rest of the family.

The deterioration of Arnold's health is evident in a letter written to Lord Cornwallis in August, and even more so, in a letter of September 19, to Jonathan Bliss. The handwriting is nearly illegible. He wrote of Peggy being quite ill with a condition which affects her head with spells of giddiness. Edward's departure had apparently caused a setback in her nervous condition. He wrote with pride of Edward and James and their professional accomplishments. "Sophia is grown very tall, but delicate. We hope when she has done growing that her health will be better established. George and William are fine boys and coming on well. You who know the feelings of a parent will indulge me in saying so much of my young family and I assure you with great truth that it will always afford us great pleasure to hear that yours, by their good conduct, are a comfort and blessing to you."[8]

Early in October the Arnolds left London for a trip to Warwick and Bath. Perhaps a change of scene and the waters at Bath would benefit both Benedict and Peggy.

Benedict, conscious of his declining health, had drawn up his will at the end of August. The order for the land grants had finally been approved; therefore he was able to disperse these lands amongst his children as he chose.

The developing decline of his health began to accelerate. He hadn't been really well since he returned from his last escapade in the West Indies. A persistent and chronic cough developed, creating an asthmatic condition that plagued him daily and

disturbed his rest at night. His right leg began to swell, indicative of a dropsical condition complicated by gout. His left leg,
injured at Quebec and shattered badly at Saratoga, became so
painful that he didn't venture out often, or at any great distance.

Arnold could deal with these annoyances and pains, as he
had on so many occasions in his life, but now he was sixty years
old, and suffering not just a physical deterioration, but a spiri-
tual despair which ate at his vitals. Despair—this was the true
disease he suffered. He slowly resigned himself to a useless existence, and a general withdrawal set in—a sort of "letting go,"
not caring about much of anything.

Nothing seemed to go right. His efforts to provide for his
family, who he seemed to sense would soon be on their own,
were frantic. Any scheme which offered a decent recompense
had failed. His ventures into privateering had been more of an
aggravation than anything else. In February, the *Ferret* sent in a
Spanish prize, valued at £20,000, which disappeared quickly into
the hands of his creditors. Not being able to command his own
ships, he had to rely on others, and they proved unscrupulous or
unreliable, allowing captured prizes to be recaptured, instead of
seeing them into port themselves, and cheating him out of nearly
£50,000. The *Earl Spencer* was in port awaiting a refitting, but
Arnold couldn't seem to summon enough enthusiasm to make a
decision to have it completed. Litigation was in the Admiralty
Courts concerning a Swedish captain who sued Arnold for detention of his ship and cargo. The case would ultimately be thrown
out of the courts, two years after Arnold's death.

Peggy wrote to their son, Edward, in February: "But, he is,
at present, in the most harrassed wretched state that I have ever
seen him. Disappointed in his highly raised expectations, harassed
by the sailors who are loudly demanding their prize-money, when
in fact their advances have greatly exceeded anything that is due
to them, and wishing still to do something, without the health or
power of acting, he knows not which way to turn himself."[9]

As spring began, there was news of Nelson's victory at
Copenhagen, but the excitement of his daring probably did little

to stimulate Arnold, or lift him from his acute lethargy. Peggy had hoped that perhaps he would find pleasure in riding his horse again — even that pleasant prospect could not revive him. News of the temporary peace with France, brought about by the Treaty of Amiens, could not rouse him.

On May 23, they went to stay with their friends the Fitches, who had leased a house in Galleywood, near Chelmsford, in Essex, bucolic countryside at that time. Perhaps the change of scene and the opportunity to enjoy the peace of a quiet country-side would help Benedict. They stayed only eight days, being recalled to London on business. The aggravations attending this settlement of litigation in the Admiralty Courts so distressed Arnold that on June 8 he became very ill, and by the tenth had lapsed into delirium.

There is a legend, which cannot be attributed to any reliable source, that during this disturbing time of delirium, Arnold called for his old Continental army uniform (which it is possible he might have retained, since he was wearing it when he escaped from West Point to the British in New York City), saying that he wished to wear it once again, calling on God to forgive him for ever wear-ing another.

That his mind was greatly disturbed is true. He was leaving his affairs in a horrendous state, and his family sadly lacking in funds. Who knows what thoughts agitated his mind during those last days of consciousness, what doubts or torments he might have suffered — it must remain only conjecture.

His doctor prescribed calomel, a universal panacea at that time, used in the treatment of various ailments, more particu-larly heart trouble and dropsy. Calomel, mercurous chloride; mild mercurous chloride; and mercury subchloride, according to the USA Dispensary, a cathartic and diuretic, was also very popular as a laxative. Unfortunately, Arnold experienced a violent reac-tion to the drug, causing his throat to swell to such an extent that he could not swallow. This situation, coupled with his asthmatic cough would have placed an extreme strain on his heart.

On Sunday morning, at 6:30 A.M., of June 14, 1801, Benedict Arnold passed away peacefully, still unconscious. The long fight was over. On June 21, he was finally laid to rest in the crypt of St. Mary's Church, Battersea, London, where his wife and daughter were to join him eventually. Fairly recently, a quite lovely stained glass window was installed in the church, honoring Arnold, by an American admirer, Vincent Lindner. This was a welcome gift since the church had lost nearly all her colored glass during the bombing of London during World War II. Pictured in the window is a portrait of Arnold, with crossed flags of both England and America. The inscription reads: "Beneath this church lie buried the bodies of Benedict Arnold 1741–1801, sometime General in the Army of George Washington, and of his faithful and devoted wife, Margaret Arnold, of Pennsylvania, and of their loved daughter, Sophia Matilda Phipps. The two nations under which he served in turn in the years of their enmity have united in this memorial as a token of their enduring friendship — 1801–1951."

A plaque has been placed on the outside of the house, 62 Gloucester Place, London, Benedict's last residence, by two Americans and one Englishman. It reads: "Major General Benedict Arnold American patriot resided here from 1796 until his death June 14, 1801." It's time the "patriot" was remembered.

# Chapter XVI
## After the Curtain Fell

The story of Benedict Arnold ended with his death, but perhaps a few details concerning other members of his family would be of interest.

Peggy, with the devoted support of her friends, in particular the Fitch sisters, Ann and Sarah, who were with her when Benedict died, assumed the duty of trying to pay the many remaining debts of her husband. To do this she had to terminate the lease of the house on Gloucester Place, sell much of the furniture and other items, and move to smaller quarters at 32 Bryanston Street, Portman Square, London.

The three years following Benedict's death were filled with trials and tribulations. Fortunately, none of her children caused her a moment's concern, other than their proximity to danger in their chosen careers. They were all outstandingly moral young people, kind and considerate of their mother and their siblings.

Peggy's letters home to her beloved father and other relatives are filled with the pride she felt for her children, and the difficulties she was experiencing concerning the debts. They also hint, despite references to "the best of husbands," that her married life had not been as blissful as it began.

She wrote to her brother-in-law, Edward Burd, not long after Benedict had died: "I sometimes fear that my reason will give way. My sufferings are not of the present moment only. Years of unhappiness have past. I had cast my lot, complaints were unavailing, and you and my other friends are ignorant of the many causes of uneasiness I have had."[1]

Childbearing, dealing with anxiety, the shock of their banishment, the collapse of her high hopes for a gay, social, secure life amongst the wealthy, and dealing with the personality of a man who was perhaps not the type of man she'd hoped he was, had all proved disillusioning. Benedict's forceful nature and ever-present restlessness would have been appealing to a young ignorant, romantic girl, but it soon became perplexing and vexing. Peggy's nature was not that of a pioneer woman who had to learn to cope with what fortune had brought.

She was also of a rather unstable nervous constitution. Early fainting spells and hysterics (tantrums?) developed as she became an adult and was plunged into a difficult marriage, and she constantly refers in her letters home to fears of losing her reason. She even refers to thoughts of taking her life, but restrained from doing that because she felt her children needed her. The year after Benedict's death she refers to a "state of irritation not to be described, at present I am neither one or the other, but have a total loss of memory, as far as relates to present circumstances."[2]

Her father was very supportive during these difficult times. There was money in Philadelphia, a savings account of sorts that he thought Benedict's creditors could not touch. He also suggested that she might come home again, now that the war with Britain was over, and bring her daughter with her. In the same letter, with utter kindness, he wrote that it would be better if the boys remained in England, where it would be possible for them to obtain advancement.

There was another worry facing Peggy, concerning her pension, decreed by the king, George III. His mental condition had steadily deteriorated, but while he lived, her pension was secure. Whether it would continue upon his death was quite another matter. His son could decide to discontinue the kindness of his father.

While Hannah Arnold and Peggy had never been close, Peggy assumed the responsibility of seeing that Hannah received the small pension Benedict had been sending her, and in July of

1803 Peggy became uneasy, not having heard from her sister-in-law for some time. Hannah was not well and died August 31, 1803, aged sixty-one, at the home of her favorite nephew, Henry Arnold, in Canada.

The year 1803 boded further misfortune for Peggy when it became apparent she was suffering from cancer of the womb. Surgery for this condition not being known at that time, rest and herbal diet were prescribed. She spent much of the time prone on her back, the only position which brought any comfort at all. The end had begun, and she died August 24, 1804.

Richard Arnold married Margaret, daughter of Samuel Weatherhead, of Augusta, Upper Canada, in 1804, and remained in Canada. They had a number of children, descendants of whom live in Ontario. Richard died in 1847.

Henry Arnold married Hannah, daughter of Richard Ten Eyck, of New York, in 1796, subsequently moving to New York City, following his aunt's death, where he conducted a mercantile business for years. Of his eleven children, only one daughter, Sophia, survived infancy. She married a William Sill. Henry died in 1826.

Edward Shippen Arnold remained in India where he became an officer in the 6th Bengal Cavalry and later paymaster at Muttra, India. He died of a fever at Dinapore in 1813, leaving no issue.

George Arnold also went to India and became an officer with the rank of lieutenant colonel in the 2nd Bengal Cavalry. He married Anne Martinez Brown. Descendants of their several children live in England. George died in 1828.

James Robertson Arnold had the most distinguished career, becoming an officer in the Royal Engineers. He saw action in Malta, Egypt, and the West Indies. He also was involved in the construction of the Citadel in Halifax, Canada. He saw action in Surinam, where he displayed outstanding bravery. For his gallantry in action he was honorably mentioned in the dispatches and was presented by the committee of the Patriotic Fund with a sword of the value of £100. This sword is now in the possession of Benedict's great-great-great-grandson, V. H. C. Arnold. It is believed that such a sword has only been presented to one other subaltern. James, according to his letters to the Shippen family in Philadelphia, would have liked to visit them, but restrained from doing so because he was apprehensive of the insults he might receive because of his father. He eventually became aide to William IV when he became king, and was created a Knight of the Hanoverian Guelphic Order, a Knight of the Crescent, and promoted to lieutenant general. He married Virginia, daughter of Bartlett Goodrich of Saling Grove, Isle of Wight. He died without issue in 1854 at his home in Ormonde Square, London.

William Fitch Arnold became a captain in the 19th Royal Lancers. He eventually retired from the military and settled at Little Missenden Abbey, Buckinghamshire, where he served as justice of the peace until his death in 1846. He married Elizabeth, daughter of Captain Alexander Ruddock, R.N., of Tobago. They had two sons and four daughters. Of these children, one son, William Trail Arnold, was a captain in the 4th Foot, taking part in the Crimean War against Russia, where he died in the assault upon Sebastopol. The other son, Edward Gladwin Arnold, became a clergyman, marrying Lady Charlotte Georgina, eldest daughter of the Marquis of Cholmondely. Georgina Phipps Arnold, one of William's daughters, married the Reverend John Stephenson. Their son, Theodore, became a major general, C. B., and served in the British army in World War I. Descendants of William Fitch Arnold and his brother George are living in England today.

Sophia Matilda Arnold, following the death of her mother, joined her brother Edward in India, where she met Edward's friend and fellow officer, Pownoll Phipps, a recent widower. They fell in love and married, having a family of five children. She died of tuberculosis in 1828. Survivors of descendants of this marriage are living in England.

*Sophia Matilda Arnold Phipps,*
*daughter of Benedict Arnold and Peggy Shippen*

Courtesy of Clive Hammond

John (Sage) Arnold married a Sarah Brunson and had seven children. He lived a quiet and unpretentious life on his farm in Ontario, dying in 1831. The secret identity of his mother died with him. Descendants of John live in Ontario and also Saskatchewan, Canada.

# Appendix I
## And Now to the Tales

> Scholars always have an intellectual edifice and the edifice reposes on a cornerstone of fundamental dogma that you're not allowed to touch because if you take away the cornerstone, the whole beautiful edifice tumbles down.
>
> — Sten Forshufvud
> *The Murder of Napoleon*

Any study of Benedict Arnold, no matter how casual, brings to light information so contradictory that one feels as though some sort of a balance sheet must be compiled.

In one breath he is portrayed as a vile, selfish, brutal cowardly scoundrel about whom one could believe anything or everything of the lowest nature. In another he emerges as a heroic, courageous, brilliant, kind, tasteful, well-read...gentleman.

Excerpts exist from the letters and diaries of his contemporaries; some bitter because of their disappointment in a former hero; others, openly libelous; still others are warm, kind — according honor to a former comrade despite his change of politics.

The purpose of this section of the book is to examine some of this material, some well known, some perhaps surprising. I hope it will not add to the existing confusion, but temper opinion and therefore provide a more realistic balance. To achieve this balance, certain arguments are grouped together, others treated separately.

## The Damage of Jared Sparks

Every heroic story — and the story of how the American Colonies broke away from Great Britain to become the United States of America was indeed a most heroic story — must have a list of characters, much like the list drawn up by a novelist building a story. There are the heroes and heroines and, of course, the villain. There must always be a villain. Good must triumph over evil.

Heroes abound in the story of the Revolutionary War. They did not have to be created; they came forward as event after event unfolded. Washington, Morgan, Montgomery, Greene, Knox, Marion, are some of the names which come instantly to mind. Along with these were many whose names will never be known, but who shared in the glory every bit as much.

The villain of the piece, Benedict Arnold, was not always a villain. For a considerable length of time during the war he was, to many, more than a hero. His name was sung throughout the Colonies, his deeds recounted at every fireside. His fame had even spread to Europe. The common people in England admired him and wished he were on their side, secretly hoping he could be captured.

Admired by his enemy, who had found him a formidable adversary in battle, feared by the Indians, and loved by his own men because he never asked of them what he would not do himself, he had become a veritable "folk hero."

After his defection, which was completely incomprehensible to his admirers, the bitterness grew, feelings flamed out of control. His change of sides could not be accepted. The hysteria generated by this bitterness resulted in the people of Norwich, Connecticut, storming the cemetery where his family were buried, and destroying the tombstones of his father and infant brother simply because their names also happened to have been "Benedict Arnold." While the flames died down somewhat eventually, they smolder to some degree to this day. The first American "folk hero" became the first, and therefore unique, "traitor." During the years which followed the Revolution, great pride existed in accomplishment. The land that had freed itself of oppression and established a precedent which would affect the thoughts of the world and the lives of many for generations to come. The heroes could do no wrong; the villain could never be forgiven.

To ensure unforgiveness, stories grew and spread which were not always true. A major contributor to this trend was the biography of Benedict Arnold, by Jared Sparks, published in 1830.

Jared Sparks, born into a farming family in Willington, Connecticut, in 1789, became fiercely interested in the events of the Revolution so recently ended. As he slowly acquired schooling, which eventually brought him to Harvard University, where he showed evidence of a brilliant mind and a great facility for writing, he made it a practice to accumulate many oral tales, many of which were colored and expanded by time. This collection, along with letters and inaccurate written accounts, became the nucleus for his historical biographies of various personages active during the Revolution.

He had access to George Washington's writings, as well as those of Horatio Gates. That he made use of his editorial talents is well known. Deletions and additions were frequent. Modern historians are agreed though that much of which survives of a scarcity of printed period material can be attributed to the efforts of Jared Sparks.

His discretion, or sense of "delicacy," was practiced to a great degree in his treatment of Washington's papers. What he chose to eliminate to make them readable is not known. Also, Washington, in his old age, completely rewrote his early letters, and Sparks generously "touched up" the later letters when it was evidently required to do so. His flair, as the editor of the *North American Review*, was exercised to a great degree, when it should have been repressed when dealing with historical material.

Sparks's treatment of the material available to him concerning Benedict Arnold came under the same regrettable tendency. What did he add to enhance the already blackened reputation of the man?

Benedict Arnold, if not the only, certainly the most notorious defector during the Revolutionary War to earn the title of "traitor," had achieved a certain distinction, which grew in volume until the subsequent conflicts of the War of 1812 and the War Between the States provided other distractions and a new set of heroes and villains. He has been virtually "enshrined" as America's first and worst "traitor." During the establishment of this infamous title, his great contributions to his country have been not only forgotten, but distorted and denied in most cases. Jared Sparks, as his first biographer, contributed to this in a large sense, not only because of the bias of much of the book, but because of colored hearsay evidence which he assumed to be the truth. He states that "Several gentlemen now living, who were personally acquainted with circumstances attending the treason of Arnold, have made valuable communications, either written or verbal, for the present work," and goes further to say: "The author will only add, that he has everywhere aimed at strict accuracy in his statements, and certified them whenever it was possible, by reference to manuscript authorities."[1] It would have been extremely helpful if Sparks had listed these gentlemen and manuscript references. A search of his papers at the Houghton Library, at Harvard, does not provide adequate clues. Yet, because the Jared Sparks biography was, in 1830, the very first, he has since been quoted by every subsequent biographer of Arnold.

Sparks begins to vilify Arnold when writing of his childhood: "To an innate love of mischief, young Arnold added an obduracy of conscience, and a cruelty of disposition, an irritability of temper, and a reckless indifference to the good or ill opinion of others, that left but a slender foundation upon which to erect a system of correct principles or habits. Anecdotes have been preserved (where?) illustrative of these traits. One of his earliest amusements was the robbing of birds nests, and it was his custom to maim and mangle young birds in sight of the old ones that he might be diverted by their cries...."[2]

That Arnold was a mischievous boy in his early youth is no secret, as a perusal of the *History of Norwich, Connecticut*, by Frances Manwaring Caulkins will prove, but surely the darker accusations are quoted from the interviews Sparks might have had with aged contemporaries of Arnold whose bitterness was allowed to color their memories.

Sparks also presents a defamatory picture of Benedict's father, portraying him as "a man of suspicious integrity, little respected, and less esteemed."[3] Again, Caulkins states otherwise: "Benedict Arnold, Sen., and his brother Oliver, were natives of Rhode Island, and coopers by trade, but became seamen, and as each had the title of Captain, it is inferred that they rose to the rank of ship-masters. They appear to have been honest, reputable citizens. Benedict took an interest in public affairs, serving occasionally in town offices as collector, lister, surveyor, constable, and selectman.[4] That Benedict, Senior, did suffer business reverses and turned to drink is a known fact. The father's fall from respectability, and the resulting humiliation young Benedict suffered because of it, made a deep impression on him, and influenced his subsequent intolerance of drunkenness. For his day and age he became fairly abstemious, and while he indulged, in a social sense, with wine at dinner, and rum aboard ship—he would never drink to excess or tolerate drunkenness amongst his men. This characteristic makes the later accusation of General Anthony Wayne (who rather liked the bottle himself) ridiculous: "I had long known the man [Arnold], as early as 1776 he produced a conviction to me that honor and true virtue were strangers to his soul—and, however contradictory it may appear, he did not possess either fortitude or personal courage. He was naturally a coward, and never went into danger but when stimulated by liquor, even to intoxication; consequently not capable of conducting any command committed to his charge."[5] Charles Neilson, when writing of his father's experiences at the battles of Saratoga, recounts that General James Wilkinson also accused Arnold of "intoxication," but goes on to say..."but Major

Armstrong, who assisted in removing him [Arnold] from the field, was satisfied that this was not true. Others said he took opium. This is conjecture, unsustained by proofs of any kind, and consequently improbable. His vagaries may perhaps be sufficiently explained by the extraordinary circumstances of wounded pride, anger and desperation, in which he was placed."[6]

The latter is quite possibly the true explanation. A man of Arnold's temperament, still seething from the galling behavior of Gates, his disappointment at how the whole Northern campaign was being handled, his belief that all would be lost if an aggressive action was not taken against Burgoyne, would have become so infuriated that perhaps he did seem "mad," or even "drunk," to place himself in continuous danger—the act of a man not only desperate, but disillusioned by the actions of a blundering, inept Congress, which allowed their distrust and fear of the military to addle their brains to such an extent that they could not formulate an intelligent course of action.

Now we come to the "tale of the horse," used by Arnold in his mad charge at Saratoga, another of Sparks' dramatic fabrications.

"It has been seen in the preceding narrative, that the horse on which Arnold rode in the second battle of Bemus's Heights was shot under him, just as he was entering the Hessian redoubt. The animal was a beautiful Spanish horse, which had formerly belonged to Governor Skene, but was now the property of Colonel (Morgan) Lewis, and borrowed by Arnold for the occasion. A short time after the action, Colonel Lewis called on him, and requested a certificate of the horse having been killed, that he might obtain the value of him, according to usage, from the public treasury. Arnold declined giving the certificate, saying it would have an ill appearance for a major-general to sign a certificate for a horse, that had been shot under him in battle. Lewis said no more, till Arnold was about to leave the camp, when he again went to him, and insisted on being allowed a proper compensation for the loss of his horse. Arnold assigned motives of delicacy for refusing a certificate, but told Lewis that he had a fine Narraganset mare in the public stables, which he would give him in the place of his horse, and immediately wrote an order to the keeper of the stables, directing him to deliver the mare into the hands of Colonel Lewis. Meantime Arnold went off, and two or three days afterwards the order was presented. The keeper said there was no mare belonging to General Arnold in the stables; that there had been one of that description some time before, but she was sold to another officer, who had taken her away. It was subsequently ascertained, that Arnold sent in a certificate, and received pay from the government for the horse that had been shot.

"Nor was this the end of the affair. When he was on the point of sailing for England, he borrowed two hundred dollars from a Captain Campbell in the British service, for which he gave an order on Colonel Lewis, telling Campbell that Lewis owed him for a mare purchased three years before, and that, as he was about to leave the country, and should not have an opportunity to collect the debt, it would be a convenience to him if Campbell would undertake that small service. Captain Campbell, having been acquainted with Colonel Lewis before the war and expecting to see him again, took the order as an equivalent for his two hundred dollars. When the news of peace arrived in New York, a passport was obtained from General Washington by the British Commander, for a person to proceed through the country with the intelligence to the Governor of Canada. Captain Campbell was the bearer of the message, and on the way he visited his friend Lewis in Albany, and presented Arnold's order. Their mutual surprise may be imagined, both having been equal sufferers by this refinement of knavery."[7]

This story proves interesting in its many complexities, and when examined closely provides numerous questions.

First of all, it seems highly unlikely that Arnold would have shown any hesitation whatsoever in providing a certificate for Colonel Lewis so that he could be reimbursed for the loss of his horse. Such a certificate would have cost him absolutely nothing, and to say that his excuse was that "it would have an ill appearance for a major-general to sign for a horse that had been shot under him in battle," is ridiculous. Such occurrences certainly were not uncommon at the time, so why would he demur? Such "delicacy" would have been foreign to Arnold's nature—he was a blunt, outspoken man.

This tale had intrigued me for years until, quite by accident, I located Benedict Arnold's Day Book of October 6, 1777, to August 31, 1779. Always the shopkeeper, all accounts are neatly entered in Arnold's hand in detail, in both dollars and pounds. The very first entry drew my immediate attention:

> Morgan Lewis, Esq. Dep.$^y$ Q$^r$ M. Gen$^l$
> To a Sorrel Mare 200 Dollars — £60.[8]

The date of the entry interested me even more since it was: "1777 October 6"—the day *before* the second battle of Saratoga! The mare Benedict Arnold rode onto the field at Saratoga, October 7, 1777, and which was killed by the same musket ball that shattered his left thigh when he stormed the sallyport of Breymann's Redoubt, was not a *borrowed* mount belonging to Colonel Morgan Lewis, but the *sorrel mare* he had *purchased from Lewis the day before the battle!* And, of course, he would have sent in a certificate so that he could be reimbursed for the loss of *his own horse!*

The second part of Sparks's "tale of the horse," concerning the $200 Arnold borrowed from Captain Campbell, and which he informed the captain he could collect from Colonel Morgan Lewis in lieu of a debt Lewis owed Arnold for a mare Lewis had purchased some three years before, is not as scurrilous a deal as Sparks would have us believe.

In a private collection of manuscripts I have found a letter dated July 27, 1780, written by Colonel Lewis to a Colonel Udny Hay: "The Mare purchased from General Arnold was on Account of the Public. I know not that they allow of Depreciation. When they do, I shall with Pleasure pay it to the General or his order."[9]

Unfortunately, Colonel Lewis does not give the purchase price of the mare, or directly say that it was $200.00, but it appears that there was a sum *owing* General Arnold for a horse purchased *by* Colonel Lewis.

On the whole, a remarkably cordial understanding appears to have existed between Arnold and Lewis. The situation concerning the horse killed at Saratoga could not have occurred as Sparks states. Also, we see that Morgan Lewis *purchased* a mare from Arnold in *1780,* for which he had not paid. This places an entirely different light on Arnold suggesting that Captain Campbell collect the $200 Arnold had borrowed from him, from Morgan Lewis in lieu of the money Lewis owed Arnold for the mare. A transaction of this sort was very common. "Orders" were frequently exchanged. Lewis had stated he would pay the money to Arnold or "his order."

Another tale recounted by Sparks concerns the departure of the Arnolds from New York City in December of 1781. I quote directly from Sparks:

> At the time he [Arnold] was to sail from New York, two Scotch officers, wishing to return to England, requested a passage in the same vessel. The captain told them, that General Arnold had taken the whole cabin for himself and family, and that there was no more room for passengers; but, if they could make an arrangement with him, there would be no other obstacle. They accordingly consulted with Arnold, who agreed to receive them into the cabin. Nothing further was said on the subject, till the vessel arrived in London. The Scotch gentlemen then went to the captain, and offered to pay for their passage, but he declined taking the money, and referred them to Arnold. He did not see them again, till they departed for Scotland. When Arnold came to pay his bill, he insisted that the proportion for their passage should be deducted. To this the captain would not consent, alleging that he had no claim upon the officers, and requiring a fulfillment of his contract. As this could not be evaded, Arnold was obliged to pay the demand, but he persuaded the captain to draw on the two officers, in favor of Arnold, and in

his own name as captain of the ship, for their passage money, and recovered the amount. It had also been paid to him by the officers before they left London.[10]

The first inaccuracy occurs when Sparks writes: "General Arnold had taken the whole cabin for *himself* and family." Benedict Arnold did not travel in the same ship with his family, but aboard the *Robust*, a 74-gun British navy ship of the line. This decision was determined by General Clinton. The reason—assured safety for Arnold, should the convoy suffer an attack by either American or French ships. Lord Cornwallis was also a passenger on the *Robust*, as well as the notorious Colonel Banastre Tarleton, whom besides Arnold, the Americans would have dearly loved to capture. Tarleton's reputation of extreme brutality during the late campaign in the Carolinas earned him the justifiable hatred of the Americans. It is also well known that during Arnold's active part in the campaign in the Chesapeake and Virginia regions, there was a concerted effort and a great deal of hope, on the part of the Americans, to capture him. Two such trophies, Arnold and Tarleton, would be tempting in the extreme.

If there were any Scottish officers, it would have been natural for the captain of the ship to direct them to Arnold for permission to share the cabin with the ladies and children, even if the situation would have appeared to be a bit unseemly.

It is unfortunate that Sparks's references to these officers are so vague—no names, or regiments. However, suppose we acknowledge that they did, in fact, exist. We have them approaching Arnold, receiving permission to share the cabin with Peggy, her children, and their maid. What we do not know is what arrangements they made with Arnold concerning their fares. Did they pay him then, or, merely make an agreement to pay, as Sparks indicates Arnold did, at the end of the voyage?

Next we have the Scottish officers going to the captain, at their destination, and attempting to pay for their passage. Would they have done that if they had already paid Arnold? Hardly likely. And, if Arnold had not yet paid the captain, as Sparks says, wouldn't he have accepted the money from the Scottish officers, as he expected payment from Arnold, rather than refer them back to Arnold, who had not paid his portion as yet? We must remember that Arnold was in all probability not on the scene when the merchant vessel arrived in England. The *Robust* had had a difficult journey and Arnold was forced to transfer to another ship, which would have delayed his arrival.

The plot becomes even more complicated when we find Arnold coming to the captain to settle his account and insisting that the fares of the Scottish officers be deducted from his account — a fair request. After all, they had only required permission from Arnold to travel with his family — none of them paid in advance. Knowing this it seems most strange that the captain would have refused payment offered to him by the Scottish gentlemen, particularly since Arnold, due to his delay, was not on the scene. Isn't it more than likely that the captain accepted payment when offered, rather than wait to take the matter up with Arnold? The fact that the officers were offering to pay the captain, upon arrival, indicated that they had made no payment to Arnold, nor any arrangement to pay him. They could very well have been told that they could travel on the ship, but should settle with the captain for their fare upon arrival in England. That they did indeed pay the captain would account for their subsequent refusal to honor the draft issued against them. Sparks tells us that Arnold was forced to pay the entire amount, and after prosecuting the captain, he recovered the overpayment. Apparently, the situation was settled to the satisfaction of the court, yet Sparks insists: "It [the fare] had also been paid to him [Arnold] by the officers before they left London."[11] This they could not have done since Arnold was not there!

This tale, as is the case with others, is not substantiated in any way. However, Sparks achieves his goal: the further maligning of Arnold.

Jared Sparks, not content with writing disparagingly about Benedict Arnold in every way possible, enlarged his scope to include Arnold's children. Perhaps he believed in the adage that the sins of a man were visited upon his children, which anyone who believes that the whole concept of Jesus Christ is "love" would find unacceptable.

Early in the biography, Sparks, when writing of Arnold's first marriage to Margaret Mansfield, states: "They had three sons, Benedict, Richard and Henry. The first died young in the West Indies. He was a violent, headstrong youth, and *it is supposed* [italics added] he came to an untimely end. He had a commission in the British service after the Revolution. There is a letter written by Hannah Arnold, in which, after mentioning that this nephew had gone to the West Indies, she says, 'He went entirely contrary to the wishes of his father, what has been his fate, God only knows, but my prophetic heart forebodes the worst.'"[12]

This report coincides with one passed on to us by Lorenzo Sabine: "Benedict was an officer of artillery in the British Army, who *it is believed* [italics added] was compelled to quit the service."[13]

It is interesting to note the increase in severity of the offense, and still more interesting to note that Sabine, writing in 1864, very probably lifted his comment on young Benedict from Sparks' biography of the father, printed in 1830, rather than confirming the young man's military career, which he could easily have done.

Isaac Arnold, writing his biography of Benedict,

*Bruce Arnold, great-great-grandson of Benedict Arnold via Richard Benedict's son of Margaret Mansfield*

Senior, in 1880, gives a rather different story. "Benedict, Jr., saw active service as an officer in the artillery. He died October 24, 1795 at Iron Shore; on the north side of the Island of Jamaica, in the West Indies, aged 27 years. He had been wounded in the leg, in a recent action, and refusing to have the leg amputated, the wound resulted in his death."[14]

Benedict Arnold, Senior, writing to Jonathan Bliss, after he'd heard of the death of young Benedict, said: "I have recently received the melancholy information of the death of my oldest son in Jamaica. I have the consolation to hear he was much respected and beloved by the officers of his acquaintance. Major General Walpole was his particular friend...and Lord Balcarres had promised him further promotion. His death...is much regretted by them, and is a heavy stroke on me...."[15]

Upon his return to England, Sir Grenville Temple brought young Benedict's sword with him and presented it to his father.

Aside from these last two reports, which present an entirely different light upon the career of young Benedict, the brief reference to Lord Balcarres, in Benedict Arnold, Senior's letter, indicates a friendship between the two men which must cancel the wild story recorded by Malcolm Decker in his biography of Arnold: "...and scornfully frozen one day in the King's very presence by Earl Balcarres..."[16]

Mr. Decker does offer an explanation in his notes to this chapter: "There were always fresh rumors circulating in America concerning Arnold's last years in London. One of these related to a duel Arnold is *supposed to have had* [italics added] with the Earl Balcarres following an insult directed at him by the Earl in the very presence of the King. 'Why don't you fire, my Lord?' Arnold is reported to have shouted after he had fired his weapon. 'Sir' replied the Earl, turning upon his heel, 'I leave you to the hangman.'"[17]

These "rumors" evidently persisted, hounding Benedict Arnold from the moment of his defection until his death. Who compiled them, and why? Was it the unrelenting opinion of those early patriots who could never forgive one of their own that had separated from them because of a difference of belief? Was this so unforgivable?

The impact of Jared Sparks, and his early biography, upon the recorded story of Benedict Arnold cannot be minimized. Reference to it can be found in every subsequent biography of Benedict Arnold.

# Appendix II
## The West Point Caper:
## A Few Loose Ends

The factual information contained in the collection of the Secret Service Papers of the British Headquarters in North America, so brilliantly presented and analyzed in Carl Van Doren's *Secret History of the American Revolution*, is so detailed and conclusive that I do not see any reason to re-examine the material to any great extent. I do, however, wish to draw attention to several inconsistencies which have come to my notice concerning certain incidents that occurred during the same period of time.

A definite target date for the capture of West Point had evidently not been decided upon. Negotiations were still being discussed, and correspondence was passing between Arnold and the British. If an attack were imminent, it would appear that Arnold would be placing his wife and son in danger, since they were expected to arrive from Philadelphia any day. Did he, despite the danger, wish to have them with him so that they would be together when the attack came and not separated, if it were unsuccessful? Or, did he have such confidence in the success of the plan that he felt they would instead be safer with him than at a distance in Philadelphia?

These arguments become still more confusing when one reads the letter Arnold wrote to Catherine Van Rensslaer Schuyler, wife of General Philip Schuyler, on September 2, 1780 (just twenty-three days before he was forced to flee), a letter which rings of a future social gathering:

191

Dear Madam,

On Friday week General Schuyler arrived here in perfect health, and left this Sunday for camp. He informed me that you intend us the honor of a visit soon. I expect Mrs. Arnold and her sister here in ten days or a fortnight, who as well as myself will be extremely happy in seeing you and the young ladies here. I hope Miss Schuyler, and Miss Peggy (if returned) will give us the pleasure of their company, not for a few days but as long as you can make it convenient and agreeable to be from home. You will here have an opportunity of seeing the General very often, which — I am sure will be a sufficient inducement to you to come and to induce Miss Schuyler to come I promise she then shall have the happiness of seeing a certain person of her acquaintance, very much devoted to her, and who will be more than happy to see her.

I do not know what promise to make Miss Peggy unless it is to promise her some agreeable gentleman to flirt with her, but as we have very few at present, if I do not succeed, I will enjoy to flirt with her myself as much as I possibly can.

I beg you will present my best respects to the ladies, and believe me very sincerely and affectionately,

Dr. Madam
Your Obed.^t & very Humble Serv.^t
B. Arnold.[1]

The "Miss Schuyler" mentioned is Betsy, and the "person" she would enjoy seeing was Alexander Hamilton, whom she eventually married.

Certainly a house filled with family and guests would be cumbersome and inconvenient should there be an attack upon the works at the fort across the river.

The lack of a definite target date also concerns the theory that Arnold planned the capture of Washington to coincide with that of West Point. Arnold could not have known of Washington's plans to be in the vicinity until he received, on the 13th of September, the following note from his superior: "I shall be at Peekskill on Sunday evening (September 17th), on my way to Hartford to meet the French Admiral and General. You will be pleased to send down a guard of a Captain and 50 at that time, and direct the Qr. Master to endeavor to have a nights forage for about forty horses. You will keep this to yourself, as I want to make my journey a secret."[2]

Arnold, of course, hastened to provide this information to the British, realizing that though it had been unforeseen, it would be a coup to capture Washington, if it could be carried off. He wrote, on September 15: "General Washington will be at King's Ferry Sunday evening next on his way to Hartford, where he is to meet the French Admiral and General and will lodge at Peak's Kill."[3]

It is apparent that this information did not reach André in time, if ever. He bid goodbye to Clinton in New York City on the 20th. Arnold joined Washington at Smith's house in Haverstraw, where the general had dined, and accompanied him across the river to Peekskill. There was no attempt at interference by the British.

Although Trevelyan cites that it was widely believed Washington was to be captured at this time, Washington himself was not so sure that it had been intended.

"How far he meant to involve me in the catastrophe of this place does not appear by any indubitable evidence — I am rather inclined to think that he did not wish to hazard the more important object of his treachery by attempting to combine two events, the less of which might have marred the greater."[4]

---

When Benedict Arnold escaped from West Point and made his way to the *Vulture*, the sloop which had delivered John André to his assignation with Arnold, he was conveyed to the ship by a six-oared barge, manned by a crew who were constantly at his disposal in order that he could be taken across the river whenever necessary, from his headquarters at the Robinson house to the fort at West Point. They would have been in particular readiness since Washington was expected and they would be required for his transport across the river.

Arnold knew that he had very little time to reach safety and urged the men to make all possible haste, directing them to row for Teller's Point, telling them that he had an errand there from which he wished to return in time to greet General Washington upon his arrival. When the boat passed the installation at Verplank's Point, Arnold produced a white handkerchief and raised it so that it would appear to be a flag of truce. He then directed the men to row directly to the *Vulture*, which was riding at anchor in Haverstraw Bay. The men were no doubt surprised, but probably thought he had business under the flag. They soon were no longer surprised, but alarmed, when Arnold, after speaking with the commander of the *Vulture*, told them: "My lads, I have quitted the rebel army and joined the standard of his Brittanic Majesty. If you will join me I will make sergeants and corporals of you all, and for you Larvey [the coxswain], I will do something more. Larvey replied: 'No, sir, one coat is enough for me to wear at a time.'"[5]

General William Heath, in his memoirs, recalls the details of the incident: "When Arnold had got under the guns of the *Vulture*, he told Corporal Larvey, who was coxswain of the barge, that he was going on board the ship, not to return, and that if he, Larvey, would stay with him, he should have a commission in the British service. To this Larvey, who was a smart fellow, replied, that he would be d — — d if he fought on both sides. The General replied that he would send him on shore. Arnold then told the barge crew that if any of them would stay with him they should be treated well, but if they declined staying, they should be sent on shore. One or two stayed, the rest with the coxswain, were sent on shore in the ship's boat; the barge was kept. Larvey, for his fidelity, was made a sergeant. He thought he merited more, and that he ought to have had as much as Arnold promised him.

He continued uneasy until, at his repeated request, he was allowed to leave the army."[6]

Here we have two separate sources, with much the same
information, yet Arnold is accused of having had his bargemen
detained as prisoners aboard the *Vulture*. James Flexner (providing no documentation) has Arnold demanding that the men be
"thrown in the hold of the *Vulture* as prisoners of war."[7] Willard
Wallace goes along with this, though he cites, among other references, Heath's memoirs.[8]

Even Major Henry Lee contributes: "The poor bargemen
whom he made use of on this occasion were, at his instance, retained as prisoners of war."[9] However, an interesting footnote to
the above is provided: "When they reached New York, Clinton
at once gave them their parole, an unusual favor to private men.
Two of them, English deserters, had wept bitterly on the ship at
the prospect of going to New York to be identified and hanged;
once there, they shipped on board a letter of Marque just ready
to sail, and got away undiscovered. The remainder were released
with a parting word and some money from Arnold, and were
soon again with their friends."[10]

When Arnold reached New York City, another tale was con-
cocted. A flurry of activity, which resulted in numerous arrests
of American spies in the city, is laid at Arnold's doorstep. A malicious action on his part, against his former compatriots, he is
supposed to have informed on them. However, an interesting
account was preserved by a Right Reverend A. A. Reinke of a
Moravian congregation of New York, written by a diarist, Ewald
Gustav Schaukirk:

> September 30th, Saturday — This week the rebel General
> Arnold came in. Upon hearing of this (André's capture) Gen-
> eral Arnold made off, got on board the *Vulture*, and thus to
> the City at the same time a commotion was occasioned, and
> several persons in the City and on Long Island, were arrested
> and put in jail. The report was that Arnold had informed
> against them, as keeping a prejudicial correspondence with

the rebels, but the truth is, that one Pool arrested as a spy some weeks ago and condemned, has impeached these persons. This he did to save his life."[11]

All of this makes very interesting reading, and it is a shame that the details are so scattered that they would not readily be discovered by the average reader of history. Nevertheless, they do exist and paint a very different picture.

---

Major John André, talented, handsome, fervently anxious to further his career, is always seen as the martyr of the piece. That he was a vain, foolish exhibitionist is also true. During the time when Charleston was in the hands of the Americans and under siege by the British, André delighted in exchanging his regimentals for the garb of a back countryman, thus enabling him to pass through the American lines. He would pose as a Virginian, connected in a civil capacity with the Virginian Continentals and stroll about the streets. His disguise was so deftly carried off by this consummate actor, that even his host, Edward Shrewsbury, never guessed he was a spy.[12] Did he enjoy some sort of a thrill from such reckless behavior?

Although Benedict Arnold admitted that it was upon his suggestion that André set aside his regimentals at Joshua Smith's house in exchange for civilian clothes, when it became apparent that he would have to get back to his own lines via an overland route, did it take much persuasion from Arnold, even though Clinton had emphatically warned André against any such action? Was this streak of thrill-seeking in evidence once again when he *dismissed* Joshua Smith from accompanying him any further on his journey, which ultimately exposed him to taking the wrong turn in unfamiliar territory, placing him in the hands of his captors?

When Arnold first approached the British with plans to defect, André, as aide to Clinton, recognized a chance to further his career if he could carry off such an important assignment, and appointed himself as case officer. From there on he exhibits a lack of intelligence, or just plain common sense.

None of the arrangements for his meeting with Arnold were well designed. The whole mission should have been handled by someone experienced in this type of liaison, but André's impulsive ambition clouded both his and Clinton's vision. André wanted to have the glory of bringing off the coup, and Clinton wanted him to have it. They would both have cause to regret the decision.

Clinton's orders concerning any change of clothing, or accepting any documents (couldn't he have memorized the content of the papers given him by Arnold?) were not followed, nor was there adequate provision made for such a risk, or any change of plans.

Further information comes to light in the letter of Lieutenant Will Pagett (quoted before in chapter 6). Joshua Smith has been thought to have abandoned André, which resulted in his taking a wrong turn. While Lieutenant Pagett laments the fate of the popular young major, he writes:

> ...there not being a man more beloved in the Army, and who in a few years without connections, has raised himself to be Adjutant General of this Army...it is strange that with uncommon cleverness, he should have been guilty of such a fatal oversight, and indeed breach of orders, for the General [Clinton] had desired him to trust all to memory without putting anything on paper.[13]

Surely André, in his position of a headquarters aide, was ill prepared for such an important undertaking. Here Clinton was at fault, allowing his friendship to interfere with his judgment, but it is more than likely that André's vanity cost him the mission.

It seems that André's aplomb completely deserted him when he was halted by John Paulding, Isaac Van Wort and David Williams. Being confident that all dangers were passed, he was shaken and fluffed his lines miserably. Assuming from the captured Hessian coat, worn by one of the men, that he was within the British line, he blurted out the information that he was a

British officer. Paulding, the leader of the group, stated: "Had he pulled out General Arnold's pass first, I should have let him go."[14]

With the mission lost, Arnold escaped to the British in New York City, André hanged, we come to the proceedings of a court of inquiry into the behavior of Richard Varick, Arnold's recent secretary.

Richard Varick had previously been secretary to General Schuyler, who recommended him to Arnold shortly after he arrived at West Point and assumed the command there. Arnold wrote him a polite invitation:

> Headquarters, Robinson's House
> August 5, 1780
>
> Dear Sr.
>
> I am in want of a secretary, having within a few days been appointed to this command. General Schuyler informed me yesterday that he believed it would be agreeable to you, as the duty would engross only a part of your time and leave a considerable part of yours to persecute your studies, if you chose.
>
> I shall be happy to find the General is not mistaken, being with great regard, dr, Sir,
>
> Yr. Obed. Humble servant,
> B. Arnold
>
> P.S. As this has the appearance of a quiet post, I expect Mrs. Arnold will soon be with me. The bearer waits your answer. If my proposal should not be agreeable to you, perhaps you can recommend a gentleman of industry and abilities of your acquaintance.[15]

David Franks, who had served as aide to Arnold during his command at Philadelphia, also joined him at West Point, only being absent for the brief period of his going back to Philadelphia to escort Peggy to the Point.

The Robinson house, a plain frame farmhouse, was not at all pretentious. It had served as headquarters for Generals Putnam and Robert Howe, since the fortifications at West Point were crude, a mere stockade affair, and unsuitable to house officers. The space within the house was meager, and conditions would be crowded when Arnold and his military family were all in residence.

The situation of the house was rather remote and indeed "quiet," as Arnold had mentioned. Any communications would be carried by messengers on horseback — couriers. With the intimacy of such crowded conditions, which must have curtailed privacy, the comings and goings of such couriers, it has always amazed me that it was possible for Arnold to carry on such an extensive correspondence with the enemy. After all, while he was a prolific writer, his secretary would have done most of his letters and memorandums, and Arnold couldn't very well run down to the corner postbox to mail anything of his own. So, I find it rather perplexing that David Franks and Richard Varick knew absolutely nothing of Arnold's conspiracy. At the court of inquiry they both denied any knowledge, and Arnold himself, in his letter to Washington, written from the *Vulture* soon after his escape, states: "In justice to the gentlemen of my family, Colonel Varick and Major Franks, I think myself in honor bound to declare that they, as well as Joshua Smith, (who I know is suspected) are totally ignorant of any transaction of mine, that they had reason to believe were injurious to the public."[16]

How was this possible? We read of petty squabbles, Varick arguing with Smith, when at a dinner party he voiced the opinion that America might have made an honorable peace with Great Britain when the Commissioners came out in 1778; the general suspicion that Joshua Hett Smith was in fact, an undeclared Loyalist; Varick's disappointment that Arnold kept him so busy he had little time left for his studies, and so on.

It is no small wonder that all this bickering did not erupt much sooner than it did. But finally Arnold, who never did have much patience, exploded when Varick threatened to leave if Arnold didn't discontinue his intimacy with Smith. Rather a strong stand for a new member of the staff to take with a superior, and Arnold told him in short order that he "was always ready to receive advice from the gentlemen of his family, but, by God, would not be dictated to by them!"[17]

At this same court of inquiry, mention is made of a certain memorandum book, in the handwriting of Benedict Arnold, which contained an account of sales of public salt, wine, and pork. This book could not be found amongst the papers concerning the case, yet testimony is given by David Franks concerning the sale of such supplies, and it is further stated that the presence of the book is "unimportant."[18]

Surely Arnold, in his hurried escape, did not have time to search out this book and take it away with him, since he left behind far more incriminating papers. One wonders if it ever existed, though Arnold did have the shopkeeper's penchant for keeping these records. Several still exist. Would he, though, have kept a record of illicit transactions involving public stores — not likely. Arnold was no fool.

Joshua Hett Smith wrote an interesting narrative, following his escape to England, concerning the death of Major André. Whether true or not, the following extract makes very interesting reading:

> There is now a person in this Kingdom [England], who was informed by Samuel Colquhoun [one of the boatmen involved in bringing André ashore for his meeting with Arnold], that while I was on my trial, he was taken into a field by some of General Washington's officers, who read to him a paper purporting to be a declaration of the means which I had adopted, and which if he would attest against me on the trial, he should have a purse of gold, which was then offered him, and a promise of support for life; Colquhoun answered, that although he was a poor man, he could not sweat falsely for money, which he should do if he

attested the paper; and, if made rich by such means, he added, that he should be miserable for life.[19]

Very intriguing are these obscure tales regarding the aftermath of the West Point chronicle.

# Appendix III
## The Wolf Pack

Jared Sparks certainly began, in print, the "blackballing" of Benedict Arnold, but the questionable honor of being the first to engender the hornet's nest, which seemed to follow Arnold throughout his military career, must be accorded to the combined efforts of three gentlemen: James Easton, John Brown, and Moses Hazen. The damage they created undoubtedly generated a prejudice in the minds of certain members of Congress, which contributed towards the acts of injustice towards Arnold.

Easton, a Massachusetts recruit, was a tavern keeper, churlish and rather forceful; Brown, a smart-talking young lawyer, Yale graduate, and the husband of a cousin of Arnold's; Hazen, a former Tory, and a one-time ranger in the Montreal region. Of the three, John Brown was to be the outstanding protagonist. Brown's persistent harrying of Arnold seems strange upon examination. He is the only one of the three having a personal connection with Arnold, through his marriage. One can only assume that his antipathy towards Arnold was based upon some personal, private issue between the two men. Since no evidence has survived, any theory is pure supposition.

Moses Hazen, a former Tory turned Rebel, was perhaps overzealous in his actions in order to present a chaste impression to anyone who might be tempted to doubt his newly adopted loyalties.

To quote Kenneth Roberts, in speaking of the plot for his novel *Rabble in Arms*: "The continued attacks on Arnold cannot be explained by impartial historians. Schuyler, Carroll of

Carrollton and other bigwigs knew that Arnold was going to, and did, seize goods in Montreal for his destitute army. Yet attacks on him for it never ceased. Twice he was courtmartialled for it, and both courts were dreadful miscarriages of justice. The attacks can, and reasonably, be explained by counter-espionage working on men who had been bawled out by Arnold for their blunders or luke-warm efforts."[1]

Has Roberts, once again, in his inimitable expertise, found the explanation for many of Arnold's problems? Did Brown, Easton, and Hazen try to get back at him, like cowardly hyenas snapping at the heels of a quarry larger than themselves, by accusing him of mismanagement or stealing supplies in Canada?

We really meet these gentlemen amidst the confusion surrounding the capture of the lake forts, Ticonderoga and Crown Point. The squabbling which existed at many of the events of the American Revolution is never more evident than before, during, and after these attacks. It ranges from the competition between the states of Connecticut and Massachusetts — each wanted to beat the other out and so each sent a delegation to organize the assault on Ticonderoga. Then, there were the gentlemen who claimed they were first to come up with the idea: Colonel Samuel H. Parsons, James Easton, Captain Edward Mott, Ethan Allen, and Benedict Arnold. Despite the many arguments concerning one or the other, we shall never really know who first had the thought. That they all responded, and it was successful, is a miracle.

In the midst of all this, an explosive incident occurred between Benedict Arnold and James Easton, which became rather physical. Arnold had had quite enough of Easton's arrogance and attempts to assume full credit for capture of the lake forts, and admitted in a letter to General Schuyler: "I took the liberty of breaking his head, and on his refusing to draw like a gentleman, he having a hanger [cutlass] by his side, and case of pistols in his pocket, I kicked him very heartily, and ordered him from the Point [Crown] immediately."[2]

After all these goings-on it is ludicrous to find that, after the victory and securing of the much-sought-after cannon, Congress had second thoughts about the action and its propriety. They feared it would appear offensive to Great Britain and perhaps they should be returned!

Brown, Easton, and Hazen appear next in the situation following the unsuccessful attempt to capture Quebec.

That Arnold had been authorized to seize certain goods in Montreal is evident from his letter to Schuyler:

> I wrote you a few days since, from Montreal, that I had seized a parcel of goods for the use of the army, by particular orders from the Commissioners of Congress. Our hurry and confusion was so great when the goods were received, it was impossible to take a particular account of them. Every man's name was marked on his particular packages, with intention of taking a particular account of them at Chamblee, or St. John's where the goods were ordered to be stored. Major Scott was sent with them with orders to have them stored under the care of Colonel Hazen, who commanded at Chamblee.[3]

Arnold has often been accused of "taking" these supplies for himself with nefarious intent. It is obvious from the above that he was "ordered" to take them and made all preparations for their safe delivery and keeping until he received further orders concerning them.

Hazen always asserted he had not received orders concerning the supplies and therefore had refused to store them, even if he'd had space to do so.

Colonel James Easton and Major John Brown had assisted General Montgomery in his march on Canada, capturing Chambly, St. Johns, and Montreal.

The charges and countercharges, snapping at Arnold's heels with threats of investigations and court-martials must have resulted, in part, from Arnold's frank assessment of Brown's worth and his hopes for promotion, when he wrote a very frank and damaging letter to the president of Congress, concerning Brown's and Easton's part in the plundering of officer's baggage, taken at Sorel:

> Major John Brown, who came down with General Montgomery, with about 160 men, collected from different regiments, now assumes and insists on the title of Colonel, which he says the General promised him at Montreal. That the General promised him promotion, he told me some time before his death. When Major Brown wrote to him reminding him of his promise, the General handed me the letter, and told me, at the same time, as Colonel Easton and Major Brown were publicly impeached with plundering the officers' baggage, taken at Sorel, contrary to articles of capitulation, and to the great scandal of the American Army, he could not, in conscience or honor, promote him [Major Brown], until these matters were cleared up. He then sent for Major Brown, and told him his sentiments on the matter very freely; after which I heard of no further application for promotion. This transaction, Col. Campbell, Maj. Dubois, and several gentlemen were knowing to. As Col. Easton and Major Brown have, doubtless, a sufficient share of modest merit to apply to the Honorable Continental Congress for promotion, I think it my duty to say, the charge before mentioned is the public topic of conversation at Montreal, and among the officers of the Army in general; and, as such conduct is unbecoming the character of gentlemen or soldiers, I believe it would give great disgust to the Army in general, if those gentlemen were promoted before those matters were cleared up.
>
> P.S. The contents of the enclosed letter I don't wish to be kept from the gentlemen mentioned therein. The public interest is my chief motive for writing. I should despise myself were I capable to asserting a thing in prejudice of any gentleman, without a sufficient reason to make it public.[4]

Arnold's postscript could not be more forward or blunt. Easton and Brown were no doubt subsequently informed.

Arnold had advanced credit for supplies needed at Crown Point and Fort Ticonderoga, and due to the litigations and doubts instilled in the minds of members of Congress, he had to cover these expenditures out of his own pocket.

Brown even went so far as to have a handbill published, defamatory to Arnold, because he had been unsuccessful in every other way to have him arraigned before a court-martial. His lack of success was only due to the efforts of Washington, Schuyler, and, yes, Horatio Gates, who acknowledged Arnold's worth and credited his courage and valor, which had been tested to the extreme during the Canadian campaign.

Gates, friendly towards Arnold at this time, set Brown down, when he submitted detailed accusations against Arnold and insisted that they be submitted to Congress, telling him it would be up to Congress to deal with the situation when they thought it proper.

General Schuyler wrote to Gates: "If courts-martial would severely punish officers for illiberal abuse of their superior officers, such violent and ill-founded complaints as you mention to be made by Lieutenant Colonel Brown against General Arnold, would soon cease. The latter gentleman will always be the subject of complaint, because his impartiality and candor will not suffer him to see impropriety of behavior with impunity."[5]

When Benedict Arnold was serving as military governor of Philadelphia, in 1778, we meet another member of the "wolf pack," in the person of Joseph Reed, member of both the Congress and the Executive Council of Pennsylvania.

The necessity of establishing martial law, until such time as proper distribution and identity of property in the only recently evacuated city could be determined, was an unpopular act. Arnold's occupation of the John Penn house on Market Street, formerly headquarters of Sir William Howe, was considered ostentatious, and his attempts at various personal speculations, a necessity since his officer's pay was in arrears and his trading business in Connecticut was suffering from lack of his personal attention, began to draw fire from Joseph Reed. The "espionage action" would begin again, this time with Reed writing Nathaniel Greene: "Will you think it extraordinary that General Arnold made a publick entertainment the night before last of which not only Tory ladies, but the wives and daughters of persons proscribed by the State, and now with the enemy in New York, formed a very considerable number."[6]

This must have disturbed Greene since he wrote to General John Cadwallader, on November 10, 1778: "I am told General Arnold is become very unpopular among you owing to his associating too much with the Tories. Pray how is the fact? At this distance it is difficult to get at the truth. I should be sorry to hear that he had done anything to forfeit the good opinion of the truly deserving. But all men have their friends and enemies."[7]

It is interesting to find an entirely different interpretation of Arnold's social activities given by Cadwallader to Greene: "General Arnold is become very unpopular [among the] men in power in Congress, and among those of this State [Pennsylvania] in general. Every gentleman who has a liberal way of thinking, highly approve his conduct. He has been civil to every gentleman who has taken the oath, intimate with none. The ladies, as well as those who have taken an active part (as our low-lived fellows will call it), as those who are good approved Whigs, have been visited and treated with the greatest civilities."[8]

On the same day Nathaniel Greene wrote John Cadwallader, Arnold wrote to Greene, apparently making an effort to maintain his sense of humor: "A few days since I was favored with yours of the 16th Inst. and was happy to hear you were well — The history you allude to is short: some Gentlemen, or rather Officers of the Army, and Members of Congress, were offended with my paying polite attention to the Ladies of this City, without first discovering if they were Whigs at Bottom. Those Gentlemen who avow such illiberal sentiments, I shall treat with the Contempt which I think they deserve by taking no notice of them."[9]

Short-tempered as Arnold always was, it is debatable as to how much longer he would treat the situation humorously.

---

Following the first part of the Battle of Valcour Island, on October 11, 1776, when Benedict Arnold and his small fleet made a heroic stand on Lake Champlain against the far superior force of Sir Guy Carleton, a desperate attempt was made by Arnold to escape the net of British ships and flee up the lake to Crown Point. Unfortunately, the situation became acute when the winds, which had served the Americans well up to this point, became erratic, fierce headwinds for the most part, but generally more favorable to the British.

Arnold, on October 13, faced with a second encounter in three days, after a hasty repair of damage off Schuyler Island, made an enormous effort to save the remnants of his fleet, which had survived the initial battle. In the midst of trying to gain every possible inch of passage that could possibly be gained from the fickle winds and the exhausted, continuous rowing of the men, he had to aim every cannon on board his ship, the *Congress*, and encourage his men to superhuman efforts. The winds separating the fleet, and the constant bombardment of the enemy made contact between the ships virtually impossible.

The galley *Washington*, under the command of General David Waterbury, was so badly damaged, with so many men killed or wounded, that she could not keep up with the rest of the retreating fleet, and surrendered to the enemy. General Waterbury maintained that he wished to scuttle his galley, rather than surrender, but Arnold had given express orders that he was not to do so. It would seem doubtful that Arnold, in the perilous situation in which he found himself, could have made any such order. If he had so instructed Waterbury before the fleet made a run for it, he could not have expected him to follow such an order as his situation rapidly deteriorated. However, Waterbury always maintained his story, and when he heard that malicious stories were perpetrated behind his back at Fort Ticonderoga, following the engagement, he accused Arnold of being the instigator. His lengthy letter to General Gates is one long complaint against his commanding officer, with whom he had disagreed on every plan concerning the battle.[10]

Arnold managed to maneuver the *Congress* galley and four gondolas into the shelter of what was then known as Ferris Bay, now Arnold's Bay, on the Vermont shore. And now we encounter a very interesting story, another of the tales. It's a mystery that upon each occasion Benedict Arnold accomplished a major heroic and valuable feat, there would evolve, from some source or other, a defamatory tale. Although he was criticized for losing the mini-fleet, it is historically agreed that the engagement at Valcour Island delayed the British invasion from Canada, which was intended to split the Colonies, allowing American forces to muster a greater defense and defeat Gentleman Johnny Burgoyne on the field at Saratoga the following year.

The tale which arose from this accomplishment is that, when Arnold abandoned his ships in Ferris Bay, and set them ablaze to keep the enemy from salvaging from them anything of value, he abandoned the sick and wounded men who were unable to disembark.

The first thought of anyone who has studied Arnold is that this act would have been impossible for the man who had always captured the hearts of his men as a field commander—the man who was always concerned for their welfare, and who on many occasions provided for them out of his own pocket.

The tale evolves from two separate sources. Major General Friederich Riedesel, who was not there, repeats a rumor which was circulating through the British military "That General Arnold, while burning his five ships had also burned about thirty sick and wounded men who were on board."[11]

It is probable that this rumor stemmed from the eyewitness account of Dr. Robert Knox, chief medical officer to the British army in Canada, and who was on board the British flagship *Maria* during the entire battle. His story is that "Mr. Arnold run [*sic*] five ships ashore, and remained on the beach till he set fire to them, burning the wounded and sick in them.[12]

Arnold, himself, factually records this part of the engagement: "The sails rigging and hull of the *Congress* was shattered and torn to pieces, the first Lieutenant and three men killed, when to prevent her falling into the enemy's hands, who had seven sail around me, I ran her ashore in a small creek ten miles from Crown Point on the east side when after saving our small arms, I set her on fire with four Gondolas...."[13]

Arnold not only does not refer to any disposition of his sick and wounded, but the fact that the story has never surfaced amongst American sources, always so eager to condemn his actions, seems strange. If they had known, surely it would have been used against him at some time or other.

Somewhere between these two stories is the thought that it would have been extremely difficult for Arnold and his surviving men to have transported ill and possibly seriously injured men through the difficult forest route they followed on their ten-mile trek to Crown Point. A forced march of desperate men, unfed for days, knowing full well that hostile Indians would have been landed on the shore by the British to harry them, and couldn't be far behind, would explain a decision which would be distasteful to anyone.

We could easily assume that the British story was true, and the existing conditions of their escape would require such a decision, if it were not for the survival of another eyewitness story — that of Squire Ferris, a young lad at the time, and an old man of eighty-three when he recounted it.

Peter Ferris, father of Squire, originated in Nine Partners, New York, removing his family to the Vermont side of Lake Champlain, near Panton, in 1765. He soon settled his wife and young son into a log cabin and began to farm his land, which he had selected on a bluff overlooking the small bay, which was to bear his name and that of Arnold. Art Cohn, in his excellent article in *Vermont History*, details the history of the Ferris family, who due to their proximity to the popular water route between Canada and the American Colonies, which the British determined to control, were to suffer frequently throughout the war.[14]

When Arnold beached the shattered remnants of his small fleet in Ferris Bay, Peter and Squire Ferris were witnesses to the event. Many years later Squire recalled: "Lieutenant Goldsmith of Arnold's galley had been severely wounded in the thigh by a grape shot in the battle near Valcour Island, and lay wholly helpless on the deck, when orders were given to blow up the vessels. Arnold had ordered him to be removed on shore, but by some oversight he was neglected, and was on the deck of the galley when the gunner set fire to the match. He then begged to be thrown overboard, and the gunner, on returning from the galley, told him he would be dead before she blew up. He remained on deck at the time of the explosion, and his body was seen hurtling into the air. His remains were taken up and buried on the shore of the lake. To his credit Arnold showed the greatest feeling upon the subject, and threatened to run the gunner through on the spot. The British fleet arrived at the mouth of the bay before the explosion of Arnold's vessels and fired upon his men on the shore, and upon the house of Mr. Ferris, which stood near the shore."[15]

The reaction of Arnold would have been typical of the man, and no doubt he had to be restrained from carrying out his threat. When the unfortunate Lieutenant Goldsmith was blown into the sky, could he have been seen by Dr. Knox from the deck of the *Maria*? Would Dr. Knox have assumed that this had been the fate of Arnold's "abandoned" men? How easily opinion can create a narrative.

## Appendix IV
## The Visible, or Invisible Man — September 19, 1777

The arguments concerning Benedict Arnold's presence on the battlefield at Stillwater, on September 19, 1777, are numerous and extremely argumentative — much like a dog worrying an old bone. At the risk of picking up this much worn and chewed bone, I am going to re-examine the evidence, which exists, both that of contemporary sources, and the latter day historians, who have based their opinions and summations on the original material, but have allowed their bias or adulation to color their conclusions. There will also be several new additions I have discovered, which will lend their individual credence.

In examining this material we must, once again, allow for the execration which surrounded Arnold immediately following his defection to the British, and which has had the tendency to increase in volume since then. It has a definite effect and must be taken into account if a fair decision is to be reached.

The sources are divided into three categories: that he *was* definitely on the field; that he was *not* on the field; and, he *might* have been, but it is more likely, only his men were there.

The first two are emphatic — yes, or no. The third, while it must be considered with the other two, in all fairness, is rather intricate, or to be more explicit, inconsistent with Arnold's nature, which he had faithfully exhibited on a regular basis — that was his tendency to *lead* his men, not *direct* them onto the field. The theory has been raised that in this instance he acted quite differently, due to being in charge of the largest volume of men, some four thousand, he had ever commanded. This position, it is argued, would have had a sobering effect on his usual reckless behavior. He would have realized he could not dash about with his men — could not cover all positions at once. He would have to be levelheaded and remain in camp and direct his various divisions from there. Just how he could have done this, considering the conditions of the terrain, is not known. And, realize each situation as it developed, he apparently did, hence his demands for re-enforcements of Gates who, incidentally *was* in camp, supposedly brilliantly deploying his army according to a master battle plan. Arnold's patience would have lasted just so long. A battle that commenced at 1:30 P.M. and continued through 6:30 P.M. would have had him climbing the wall!

A lot of the comments regarding Arnold's presence on the field the 19th of September came years after the battle, either from historians who were not there, or from contemporaries who were. In this last group are several who add conflicting reports.

Ezra Buel (a guide to the American army during the battle) told William Wirt in 1821, during a tour of the battlefield, that Arnold *was* on the field, pointing out his position, as well as Morgan's saying: "Here Morgan was posted. Here was Arnold, then a patriot and excellent soldier", etc. He goes on to describe the battle under Arnold's leadership.[1]

This same gentleman told Jared Sparks in 1830, that Arnold *was not* on the field! He admits he saw General Enoch Poor, with two or three other officers, quite in the rear of the American army, and taking no part in the action. Fighting, he maintained, was handled chiefly by Daniel Morgan, Alexander Scammell, and Joseph Cilly.[2] Apparently, the passing of some nine years had an effect on the memory of Mr. Buel.

Another source which vacillated between two opinions, is that of Colonel and Judge John Marshall, the biographer of George Washington. In the first edition of his "Life of George Washington," he writes that "reinforcements were continually brought up, and about 4 o'clock, Arnold, with nine continental regiments and Morgan's Corps, was completely engaged with the whole right wing of the British Army. The conflict was extremely severe and only terminated with the day."[3]

However, in the second edition of this book, Marshall, in a footnote, explains a change in the text: "<u>The accounts of the day</u> [written before Arnold's treason] stated that the Americans were commanded by General Arnold, but General Wilkinson says that no general officer was on the field."[4]

Marshall knew Wilkinson and believed him, yet his footnote is confusing, since he does allow that "accounts of the day" differed from that of James Wilkinson. This gentleman will be dealt with in the segment of this appendix which concerns the positive denials of Arnold's presence during this first battle. In conclusion we are left to determine which opinion we wish to believe.

Major Henry Brockholst Livingston, an aide to both Schuyler and Arnold, wrote Schuyler, September 23, 1777, "[Arnold] is the life and soul of the troops — Believe me, Sir, to him and to him alone is due the honor of our late victory. Whatever share his superiors may claim they are entitled to none."[5] Rather strong plaudits for a man he doesn't actually say was "on the field" personally.

Richard Varick, aide to Arnold, in his letter to Schuyler, September 22, 1777, only mentions that Arnold "was ordering out troops." Yet, in another letter to Schuyler, written after the surrender of the British, he elaborates a bit further: "During Burgoyne's stay here he gave Arnold great credit for his bravery and his military abilities, especially in the action of the 19th."[6]

Samuel Patterson, biographer and friend of Gates, leaves it an open question.

Brigadier General Poor doesn't actually say that Arnold was on the field, but that he *was told* he was by another (probably Scammel).[7]

While Poor was not actually a fan of Arnold (Poor chaired the court-martial board in Hazen's trial and had sought Arnold's arrest because of his behavior toward the board), it was he who got together the address which commended Arnold for his actions on the 19th of September, and asked him to remain in camp following his row with Gates, and his subsequent resignation. The only officers who did not sign this were Learned's, because they were afraid to give umbrage to Gates, but they did acquiesce the measure. It was signed by every other man *but* Lincoln. It seems most strange that the officers who had participated in the battle of September 19 would sign, or even be a party to an address thanking Arnold "particularly for his conduct during the late action," if he had not been there![8]

We also have the opinion of a contemporary historian, William Gordon, another friend of Gates. Gordon writes that Arnold was not on the field September 19. However, his recounting of American history has been critically examined, and found wanting, in the annual report of the American History Association for 1899.[9]

The letter of Robert R. Livingston to Washington, January 14, 1778, which seems to construe that Arnold was not present on the field September 19, is admirably explained in Isaac N. Arnold's article, "Benedict Arnold at Saratoga," in reply to J. A. Stevens' attack, "Benedict Arnold and His Apologist." Mr. Arnold (Isaac N.), being a reputable attorney, examines the letter word for word and concludes that Bancroft and others made rather hasty opinions of what the letter actually said, and that this letter must stand along with the other affirmations of Benedict Arnold's *personal* presence on the field on September 19, 1777.[10]

The most prominent source on the negative side of this argument is Colonel James Wilkinson, the twenty-year-old adjutant to Gates. As a young captain, he had served with Arnold in Canada. Whether he had formed a personal dislike of Arnold, or just wished to advance his own career by whatever means came to hand, he aligned himself firmly on the side of Gates.

On September 21, 1777, in a letter to St. Clair, Wilkinson says: "General Arnold was not out of camp during the whole action." In his *Memoirs of My Times*, published in 1816, he goes even further: "It is worthy of remark, that not a single general officer was on the field of battle on the nineteenth of September, until the evening when General Learned was ordered out."[11] He also contended that all orders on the 19th came from Headquarters, not from Arnold, but he spoiled the effect of his words, by adding: "though it is not known what conversation passed between the generals."[12]

Wilkinson, whose opinions colored the writings of George Bancroft, Edward Channing, James Austin Stevens, and Lynn Montross, went on to become one of the disgraces of the military fraternity. A Gates man, hostile to Arnold and violently anti-Schuyler, he became, in the course of his life, a liar, coward, corrupt politician, and very nearly a traitor to his country. He was always in hot water with the authorities, and after facing ruin because of involvement in Aaron Burr's conspiracy, he went to Mexico to end his days.[13]

Now we come to a review of evidence that will confirm Benedict Arnold's *personal* participation in the battle of September 19. Since it is so profuse we shall begin with the historians, both contemporary and latter day.

Isaac N. Arnold, a Benedict Arnold biographer, covers the battle thoroughly in his book, and then, using his legal expertise, in a rebuttal to an unfavorable review of the book, he substantiates the opinion that Benedict Arnold was indeed on the field, September 19, 1777.

Charles Botta, an Italian and contemporary to many of the foreign officers serving in the war, states, in his *History of the War of Independence*, "[Arnold] encouraged his men by voice and example."[14]

Henry Carrington was an expert in the field of military battles. He would have attended West Point had he enjoyed better health. When the Civil War began, he became active in recruiting and training troops in Ohio; saw combat duty on two fronts; and, following the end of the war was assigned duty as professor of military history at Wabash College. At about that time he began his *Battles of the American Revolution*, which includes detailed maps of both American and British positions. It is considered a classic and most accurate. He wrote that in his estimation: "Arnold must stand credited with personal valor and a gallant defense of the left wing of the American Army on the 19th day of September, 1777."[15]

Henry B. Dawson, a military historian, also credited as having accurate and meticulous judgment, wrote: "in falsifying history for the purpose of robbing General Arnold of his hard-earned fame, he [Wilkinson] at the same time impeached the military character of General Gates, in maintaining that an action of this importance, where the destiny of the country and of the great principles on which the parties had taken issue was involved, was intrusted to the individual caprices of colonels of regiments, without the controlling superintendence of a general officer; and 'was fought by the general concert and zealous cooperation of the corps engaged, and sustained more by individual courage than discipline.'"[16]

Major General J. Watts de Peyster, after examination of the various testimonies, confided to Isaac N. Arnold, "it is impossible that Arnold, with his temper and temperament, being in command this day, was not actively engaged. For him to have participated was simply the conclusion of a syllogism."[17]

John Fiske, also an eminent historian, places Arnold on the field. John W. Fortescue, historian of the British army, also concurs, as does General Francis V. Greene and Benson J. Lossing.[18]

Hoffman Nickerson, in his *Turning Point of the Revolution*, while often criticized for his lack of documentation, explains his reasons in his appendix I, "On Method," for deciding not to use footnotes. His further appendices furnish sources and his choice of information which led to his expressed opinions. Appendix II details his decision that Arnold was on the field on September 19, 1777.

The list of positive opinions regarding Arnold's presence on the field grows with Charles Stedman, a contemporary English historian and Loyalist officer, most highly regarded: "The enemy were led to battle by General Arnold, who distinguished himself in an extraordinary manner." Willard Wallace, biographer of Arnold, believes he was on the field, as does Christopher Ward, who writes "deserters from the American Army stated they were commanded on this occasion by General Arnold." Mrs. Ellen Hardin Walworth, a local historian, who collected reports from visitors, whose ancestors had been soldiers who fought in the battle, wrote: "Now following Arnold with Learned's Brigade.... Arnold led with his usual spirit." Woodrow Wilson also agrees Arnold was personally present on the field.

However, of the various quotes, George G. Trevelyan's comment seems to be the most emphatic. He writes that "[Wilkinson's] impudent falsehood has been judged worthy of refutation by several excellent historians.... One might as well demand evidence to prove that Nelson was in the sea fight off Cape St. Vincent."[19]

Finally we come to the statements of actual participants, or witnesses, of that struggle of September 19, 1777.

Major Cochran, who rode express from Gates's headquarters to report to the Vermont Council of Safety, and also escort Major General Lincoln back to Stillwater, states: "General Arnold, with his division, attacked a division of Burgoyne, in which General Arnold gained the ground."[20]

General William Hull, a major of the Eighth Massachusetts Regiment (Colonel John Brooks's), on September 19, 1777, left manuscripts of his Revolutionary War services, which were gathered together by his daughter, and published in book form. He states: "On the 19th of September, about 12 o'clock, General Burgoine advanced towards the left wing of the American lines....General Burgoine then brought his effective force into action, when Morgan was in his turn compelled to retreat. But he was soon reinforced by a number of regiments from the left wing of the army, *commanded by General Arnold* [italics added], and about one o'clock the action was renewed with great obstinacy." "As soon as the action recommenced, *General Arnold rode to the ground* [italics added] which was occupied by the guard of Major

Hull. He called the officers around him, and inquired what number of men was at that post. He was informed that it consisted of the guard of two hundred and fifty men and two regiments. General Arnold then said that three hundred volunteers, to be commanded by a field officer, must immediately reinforce the troops which were engaged. He repeated that he wished them all to be volunteers. As none of the field officers offered their services, Major Hull observed to him that he commanded the guard on that day by an order from the adjutant general, but if he could be excused from that duty *he* would be happy to command the detachment. General Arnold replied that *he* would excuse him and directed the colonels of the two regiments to call for three hundred volunteers and a suitable number of captains and subalterns to command them. In a few moments the number required was paraded and formed into four companies, with the officers assigned to them."[21]

Charles Neilson, in his *Burgoyne's Campaign*, states: "About the time General Phillips arrived on the field with the artillery, General Arnold, on a gray horse, and under full speed from the scene of action, rode up to General Gates, who was on the Heights at the time, sitting upon his horse, and listening to the tremendous firing, and addressed him in the following laconic manner: 'General, the British are reinforced; we must have more men.' General Gates immediately replied, 'You shall have them, sir,' and immediately ordered out General Learned's brigade; when Arnold again hurried back at a full gallop, and the men after him in double quick time."

Charles evidently wrote what he believed was a true account. It was based upon family tradition. His father, John, owned the farm at Bemus Heights and was a witness to many events of both battles. Charles was raised on his stories. Yet, it is interesting to note that in his latter years, John, when interviewed by Jared Sparks, stated that Arnold was not on the field for the first battle.[22] It seems strange that he would have recounted a story many times to his son and then changed it in his latter years. It is a fact that the past memories of the elderly are amazingly accurate, while those of more recent events are often wrong, or nonexistent. Is it more likely that his change of mind could be attributed to a belated attempt to deprive Arnold of any credit because he had become a traitor?

Joshua Pell, Jr., an officer in Burgoyne's army, wrote in his diary of Arnold's advance in force on the British right at half past five in the afternoon.[23]

Samuel Poppleton, who was a participant in the battle, provided information, which was recounted to Isaac N. Arnold by his grandson, O. Poppleton, of Birmingham, Michigan: "My grandfather was in the battle of September 19, in the skirmish line under Arnold, and said, 'Arnold, Poor, and Morgan, with less than three thousand men, sustained the unequal contest during that whole day....Arnold was conspicuous in the fight. I saw him frequently on that eventful day, seeming to be ubiquitous. He appeared to be present at all points of the battlefield. If our lines weakened anywhere, he discovered it and strengthened them, *directing in person* [italics added] the movements of the troops, and infusing into them his own energy and confidence of success."[24]

Reverend Hezekiah Smith, D. D., chaplain to Nixon's regiment, left a diary of the events of the battle, which was used as a base for a paper read to the Rhode Island Historical Society by R. A. Guild, a librarian of Brown University. An extract from the paper states: "His diary and letters contain a very full account of the battle of Stillwater, utterly refuting the representations of some distinguished historians. He makes Arnold the hero of this great battle, thereby sustaining the ground taken by Isaac N. Arnold in his *Life of Benedict Arnold*.[25]

Colonel Philip Van Courtlandt, a participant, states: "My regiment was ordered to march, keeping to the left, and in order to oppose their [the enemy's] right. This order was given me first by General Poor on my parade, and as I was marching by General Arnold."[26]

Max von Elking, in his compilation of journals and letters of the German troops, states: "They [the Americans] were led by

General Arnold." It is a fact that von Elking drew heavily upon General Riedesel's memoirs, and often misquoted, or embroidered. But if we are to treat with suspicion his reference to Arnold, it is interesting to note that Riedesel himself makes the same statement.[27]

Captain Ebenezer Wakefield—who was in the trenches at Bunker Hill, accompanied Arnold to Quebec, helping him to safety when he was wounded in the assault, and fought in both battles of Saratoga—leaving a detailed report of the events of both days, writes concerning the battle of September 19, 1777: "I shall never forget the opening scene of the first day's conflict. The riflemen and light infantry were ordered forward to clear the woods of the Indians. Arnold rode up, and with his sword pointing to the enemy emerging from the woods into an opening partially cleared, covered with stumps and fallen timber, addressing Morgan, he said, 'Colonel Morgan, you and I have seen too many red-skins to be deceived by that garb of paint and feathers; they are asses in lions' skins—Canadians and Tories; let your riflemen cure them of their borrowed plumes.'.... Nothing could exceed the bravery of Arnold on this day; he seemed the very genius of war, infuriated by the conflict and maddened by Gates' refusal to send reinforcements, which he repeatedly called for, and knowing he was meeting the brunt of the battle, he seemed inspired with the fury of a demon. Riding in the front of the line, his eyes flashing, pointing with his sword to the advancing foe, with a voice that rang clear as a trumpet and electrified the line he called upon the men to follow him to the charge, and then dashing forward, closely followed by his troops he hurled them like a tornado on the British line and swept it away. There seemed to shoot out from him a magnetic flame that electrified his men and made heroes of all within his influence. Arnold was not only the hero of the field, but he had won the admiration of the whole army. There was not a man, officer or private who participated in the battle, or who witnessed the conflict who did not believe that if Gates had sent reinforcements, as Arnold again and again begged him to do, he would have utterly routed the whole British army. So general was this belief, and so damaging to Gates, that as an excuse to save him from reproaches coming from every side he gave out as the reason that the store of powder and ball in the camp was exhausted, and that the supplies of ammunition from Albany had not arrived. No one could dispute this, yet no one believed it."[28]

Now, at last, we come to what Benedict Arnold had to say: "On the nineteenth, when advice was received that the enemy was approaching, I took the liberty to give it as my opinion that we ought to march out and attack them. You desired me to send Colonel Morgan and the Light Infantry, and support them; I obeyed your orders, and before the action was over, I found it necessary to send out the whole of my division to support the attack. No other troops were engaged that day except Colonel Marshall's regiment."[29]

We observe that Arnold did not specifically mention himself as being on the field in person when he wrote to Gates. This, according to some historians who have a low opinion of Arnold, constitutes conclusive proof that he was not on the field, since he is supposed to have never neglected the opportunity to paint a rosy picture of his personal heroic endeavors.

However one wishes to interpret these reports, which could have been dictated expressly because of his disappointment over lack of credit being given to *his men*, there is one final source which should end the argument once and for all. This source is the entry of September 20, 1777, in the Orderly Book of Colonel Thadeus Cook, of Wallingford, Connecticut: "General Arnold returns his thanks to the officers and soldiers of his Division for their brave spirited conduct yesterday in withstanding the force of the whole British Army whose loss a deserter from their army says is upwards of one thousand men killed and wounded... which ours is very trifling, not one fourth part of the enemies... a convincing proof of the mercifull interposition of Heaven in covering our heads in the day of battle, and loudly calls for our grateful acknowledgement. The General *observed* [italics added] yesterday that too many officers that zeal and spirit pushed on in the front of their companies, whose business it was to have brought up those in the rear, and hopes they will in future observe their proper stations and suffer no man to retreat until an order is given by the commanding officer of the regiment or detachment....those who are found to have deserted their posts in time of action may expect instant death."[30]

If Benedict Arnold was not present, how could he have *observed* anything? How could he have noticed that the zeal and bravery of the men went beyond the control of their officers, resulting in these officers winding up at the head of their companies, rather than at the rear, where it was their duty to be in order to curtail deserters as much as possible? A commander, holding forth in camp, and supposedly issuing orders from that position certainly would have seen nothing of this situation. This leaves us with an *invisible* man becoming very visible!

In a final summation, I wish to quote from John R. Elting's *Battles of Saratoga*: "Gates had done nothing to aid the battle, unless finally allowing Arnold to commit Learned is to be counted. He could have over-whelmed Specht, leaving Burgoyne without supplies or ammunition. He could have risked another brigade, or at least a few guns, to reinforce Arnold. He might have patrolled his front aggressively enough to detect and possibly check Riedesel's difficult uphill advance. Instead, he simply squatted in place. This may have been sagacity; more likely, it was complete indecision. Had Arnold not carried the fight to the British, forcing them onto the defensive, 19 September's early afternoon would have seen Fraser and Breymann out in the open high ground at Neilson's farm."[31]

# Notes

## Chapter I

Nautical details concerning the sailing of the *Robust* can be found in the Master's Log. ADM52/ 1962, PRO, Kew, England.

## Chapter II

Basic biographical facts concerning Benedict Arnold's early years may be found in any of his biographies and in the *History of Norwich, Connecticut*, by Frances Manwaring Caulkins., pp. 409–14. Original edition published in 1866, by Case, Lockwood & Co., Hartford, Conn., reprint in 1976 for The Society of the Founders of Norwich, Connecticut, Inc., by The Pequot Press, Chester, Conn.

1. Records of Hiram Masonic Lodge, New Haven.
2. Original letter in Collection of Glenn Z. Stevens, State College, Pa.; (a copy is in the Library of Morristown National Historical Park, Morristown, N.J.)
3. Lecture of W. G. George Hall, Masonic Historian, June 3, 1937.
4. Christine Baker. *The Arnold House*, in New Haven Colonial Historical Society.

## Chapter III

1. Benedict Arnold to Massachusetts's Committee, April 30, 1775, in American Archives, 4th Series, Vol. 2, p. 450.
2. "Origin of Expedition against Ticonderoga in 1775," a paper read before the Connecticut Historical Society, by J. H. Trumbull. January 1868, "The Proposition Came from Benedict Arnold, etc."
3. Collection of Connecticut Historical Society, Vol. 1, p. 182.
4. Hall, "History of Vermont," p. 199.
5. Letter of Dr. Joseph Warren, April 30, 1775, quoted in Frothingham, *Life and Times of Joseph Warren*, p. 474.
6. Ibid., p. 490.
7. Arnold to Washington. September 25, 1775, in American Archives, 4th Series, Vol. 3, p. 960.
8. John Joseph Henry's Journal. p. 77; also in Kenneth Roberts, *March to Quebec*, p. 347.
9. Ibid., appendix, p. 185.
10. Montgomery to Schuyler. December 5, 1775, in American Archives, 4th Series, Vol. 4, p. 189.
11. Dr. Isaac Senter's Diary in Kenneth Roberts, *March to Quebec*, pp. 233–34.
12. Ibid., p. 234.
13. Arnold to Wooster, January 2, 1776; Dr. Isaac Senter's Diary, p. 105.
14. "The Journal of Charles Carroll of Carrolton." pp. 49–50.

15. American Archives. 5th Series, Vol. 1, pp. 1272–73.

16. Ibid., 4th Series, Vol. 6, p. 596.

17. *The Revolution Remembered.* John C. Dann, Editor. Eyewitness Accounts of the War for Independence, p. 21.

## Chapter IV

1. Arnold to Gates. September 7, 1776, in American Archives, 5th Series, Vol. 2, p. 354.

2. Details of the battle of Valcour Island can be found in these excellent sources: Bird, *Navies in the Mountains: The Battles on the Waters of Lake Champlain and Lake George. 1609–1814*; Fowler, *Rebels under Sail: The American Navy during the Revolution*; and Hagglund, *A Page from the Past*. It was through the efforts of Mr. Hagglund that the gondola *Philadelphia*, which sank early in the battle, was raised from the bottom of Valcour Bay. She is now a permanent exhibit at the Smithsonian Institute in Washington, D.C.

3. Arnold to Mrs. Knox. March 4, 1777, in New England Historical and Genealogical Register, Vol. 2, p. 75.

4. Thomas Glyn, Ens.. "Journal on the American Service," in Princeton Library.

5. Descriptions of the battle of Ridgefield can be found in: McDevitt, *Connecticut Attacked: A British Viewpoint, Tryon's Raid on Danbury*; Sandra Foster, "The Battle of Ridgefield," in *Connecticut* Magazine, October 1972, pp. 29–31, 56; Bedini, *Ridgefield in Review*.

6. Adams, "Familiar Letters," p. 276.

## Chapter V

1. Nickerson, *The Turning Point of the Revolution*, Vol. 2, pp. 273–75.

2. Ibid., p. 315.

3. I. N. Arnold, *Benedict Arnold at Saratoga*, reprinted from The United Service, September 1880, p. 12.

4. Manuscript letter of L. F. S. Foster, October 27, 1877, to I. N. Arnold. Quoted in Arnold "Arnold". p. 204.

5. Stone's *"Burgoyne's Campaign,"* p. 66.

6. *Connecticut* Journal, May 6, 1778.

7. A State of the Expedition from Canada as Laid before the House of Commons. by Lieutenant General Burgoyne. p. 60.

8. Ibid., p. 26.

9. Decker, *Arnold*, pp. 285–86.

10. Ibid., pp. 287–88.

11. Sellers, *Arnold*, p. 19.

12. Elizabeth Tilghman to Betsy Burd. March 13, 1779, in L. B. Walker "Margaret Shippen," PMH&B 25, p. 39.

13. Arnold to Peggy. February 8, 1779, pp. 38–39.

14. Arnold to Deane. March 22, 1780, in Deane Papers (New York Historical Society Collections 22), 4, p. 116.

15. Council of Pennsylvania to Congress. February 3, 1780, in Proceedings of Arnold's Court Martial, p. 168.

16. Ipswitch Antiquarian Papers. 2 (May 1881), No. 19. The author of the story was Professor Daniel Treadwell of Harvard College, who grew up in the home of Nathaniel Wade, his guardian.

17. Arnold to Washington. September 25, 1780, in Sparks, "Writings of Washington," 7, p. 533.

## *Chapter VI*

1. Peckham, *The War for Independence*, p. 144.
2. Original draft among the Force Papers, Library of Congress, Washington, D.C.
3. Benjamin Gilbert Letterbook, 1780–1783, W. L. Clements Library, Ann Arbor, Mich.
4. Letter of Lieutenant Will Pagett, October 12, 1780, in Collection of Herman Herst, Jr.
5. Hatch, *Major John André*, p. 175.
6. Letter of Benedict Arnold to Nathaniel Greene, November 10, 1778, Houghton Library, Harvard University.
7. George Washington to Henry Laurens, October 13, 1780, in Fitzpatrick, "Writings of Washington," 20, p. 173.
8. William Smith's Diary, entry for October 5, 1780.
9. Letter filed at end of 1781, Clinton Papers, WLCL.
10. Letter of Admiral Arbuthnot to Benedict Arnold, November 2, 1780, in Collection of Vere A. Arnold, great-great-grandson of Benedict Arnold.
11. Letter of Admiral Rodney to Sir George Jackson, judge advocate of the admiralty, October 30, 1780, in Collection of Richard Maas.
12. Ibid.
13. Flexner, *The Traitor and the Spy*, p. 381.
14. Letter of Benedict Arnold to Lord Cornwallis, December 10, 1799, in *Historical Magazine*, August 1870, 8, No. 2., p. 110.
15. Original document of appointment in Collection of Vere A. Arnold.
16. Tallmadge folder, Litchfield Historical Society, Litchfield, Conn.
17. Clinton to Colonel Dundas and Colonel Simcoe, Dec. 14, 1780, in Clinton Papers, WLCL.
18. Henry Clinton to Benedict Arnold, March 13, 1781, in Clinton Papers, WLCL
19. Letter of Benedict Arnold to Earl Cornwallis, May 12, 1781, PRO (Kew, England) 30/11/6 in the Cornwallis Papers, p. 63.
20. William Smith Diary, entry of February 1, 1781.
21. Ibid., entry of March 26, 1781.
22. Knox Papers, 6, p. 7; also Mackenzie Diary, 2, p. 466.
23. Phillips to Cornwallis, April 8, 1781, PRO SO 11/5/193 195v; also, to Clinton, March 20, 1781.
24. Cornwallis to Tarleton, May 15, 1781, PRO 30/11/86, pp. 33 and 34.
25. Cornwallis to Arnold, May 17, 1781, PRO 30/11/86, pp. 35 and 36.
26. Isaac N. Arnold, *Life of Benedict Arnold*, p. 20.
27. Caulkins, *History of Norwich, Connecticut*, p. 414.

## *Chapter VII*

1. I. N. Arnold's biography, *Benedict Arnold*, p. 363.
2. Sally Smith Booth, *The Women of '76*, Fern Park, Fla. 1974, p. 287.
3. Drake, *Historic Fields and Mansions of Middlesex*, p. 258; Bigelow, *Life of Franklin*, letter to R. R. Livingston, Vol. 3, p. 48.
4. Hatch, *Letters of Jervis*, American Neptune, 7, pp. 106–7.
5. John Bull to Clinton, March 5, 1782.
6. Ibid.
7. B. F. Stevens' Facsimiles, 10, No. 1050.

8. Burgoyne to Clinton, October 25, 1777, in Clinton Papers, W. L. Clements Library; Burgoyne, statement to House of Commons in 1779; see Burgoyne, *State of the Expedition*, pp. 26, 50.

9. Elizabeth Carter's Diary, February 12, 1782.

10. Sargent, *Life of André*, p. 456.

11. Malcolm Decker's biography, *Benedict Arnold: Son of the Havens*, pp. 435, 436, 495.

### Chapter VIII

1. Marvin Kitman, *George Washington's Expense Account*, p. 32.

2. Isaac N. Arnold, *Life of Benedict Arnold*, p. 24.

3. Sparks, *Life of Benedict Arnold*, p. 5.

4. Ibid., p. 12.

5. Ibid., p. 13.

6. Wallace, *Traitorous Hero*, p. 80.

7. Letter of Benedict Arnold to George Washington, February 27, 1776, in "Letters Of Eminent Men to George Washington." From the time of his taking command of the Army, to the end of his Presidency, Jared Sparks, Vol. 1, p. 154.

8. Ibid., p. 534.

9. Letter of Benedict Arnold to Mercy Scollay, July 15, 1778, in bMs Jared Sparks 49 (16), Houghton Library, Harvard University.

10. Letter of Benedict Arnold to Mercy Scollay, February 19, 1779, bMS Jared Sparks, 49.1 (18), Houghton Library, Harvard University.

11. Malcolm Decker, *Son of the Havens*, p. 283.

12. Letter of Benedict Arnold to Nathaniel Greene, November 10, 1778, in Arnold Collection; Houghton Library, Harvard University.

13. Stone, *Visits to the Saratoga Battle-Grounds*, 1780–1880, pp. 36, 37.

14. Hillard, *The Last Men of the Revolution*, p. 35.

15. Ibid., p. 71.

### Chapter IX

1. Shelburne Papers, 152 6 & 7, W. L. Clements Library.

2. Memorial, *Pro Ao* 13/96.

3. PMHB, 25, p. 38.

4. Ibid., pp. 35, 36.

5. Ibid., p. 39.

6. Ibid., pp. 160, 161.

7. Letter of Benedict Arnold to Robert Howe, September 12, 1780, Washington Papers, Library of Congress.

8. Hannah Arnold to Benedict Arnold, September 4, 1780.

9. PMHB, 35, p. 399.

10. Matthew L. Davis, *Memoirs of Aaron Burr*, Vol. l, p. 219.

### Chapter X

1. Wallace, *Traitorous Hero*, p. 290.

2. Lawrence, *Footprints, Or, Incidents in the Early History of New Brunswick*, p. 71.

3. Letter in the Public Archives of Ottawa, Canada (MG23G11,10, Vol. 2 - Jonathan Sewell, Jr., to his father, dated 5 Dec. 1785.

4. William Donaldson, a merchant of Saint John, W. L. Clements Library.

5. Jean E. Sereisky, *Benedict Arnold in New Brunswick, The Atlantic Advocate*, March 1963, p. 37.

6. Saint John Registry of Deeds, Book A2, p. 10.

7. Ibid., p. 124.

8. E. L. Teed, *Q.C., M.L.A. Canada's First City*.

9. Sereisky, p. 37.

10. Letter, October 17, 1786, Benedict Arnold, Litchfield Historical Society.

11. I. N. Arnold, Appendix, *Life of Benedict Arnold*.

12. Public Archives of Canada: R.G. 1, L-3 Vol. 3; a bundle 5, No. 24; also Microfilm C–1609.

13. O.A.: Surveyor General's Locations, 1803–7; p. 26 (Crown Land Papers), Shelf 18, #4.

14. Thad. W. H. Leavitt, *History of Leeds and Grenville*.

## Chapter XI

1. Letter of Margaret Arnold to Jonathan Bliss, December 5, 1795, Odell Collection, New Brunswick Museum.

2. Bell, *Early Loyalist Saint John*, pp. 56–57.

3. Wells, *Campobello*, p. 446; "Arnold at Campobello," Folder 23, New Brunswick Museum.

4. Jean E. Sereisky, *Benedict Arnold in New Brunswick, The Atlantic Advocate*, March 1963.

5. Teed, *E. L., Q. C., M.L.A., Footprints of Benedict Arnold*, Late Major General Congressional Army of the American Colonies, Late Brigadier General British Army, in Collections of the New Brunswick Historical Society, No. 20, 1971, p. 76.

6. bid., pp. 77–79.

7. Letter of Benedict Arnold to Jonathan Bliss, December 20, 1799, Odell Collection, New Brunswick Museum.

8. Wallace, *Traitorous Hero*, p. 311.

## Chapter XII

1. Arnold to Bliss, February 26, 1792, in Odell Collection, New Brunswick Museum.

2. Collection of Vere A. Arnold.

3. Cobbett, *Parliamentary Debates*, Vol. 29, pp. 1518–19.

4. Lord Hawke's statement regarding the duel between Lord Lauderdale and Benedict Arnold, in Collection of Vere A. Arnold.

5. Arnold, Isaac N., *The Life of Benedict Arnold*, p. 383.

6. Letter of Henry Clinton to Benedict Arnold, August 2, 1792, W. L. Clements Library.

7. Letter of Benedict Arnold to Henry Clinton, October 17, 1792, W. L. Clements Library.

8. Letter of Benedict Arnold to Henry Clinton, November 14, 1792, W. L. Clements Library.

9. Letter of Ward Chipman to Benedict Arnold, November 17, 1792, in Lawrence Collection, New Brunswick Museum.

10. Original Warrant, July 20, 1793, in Collection of Vere A. Arnold.

## Chapter XIII

1.  Broglie, *Talleyrand's Memoirs*, Vol. 1, pp. 174–75.
2.  *Gentleman's Magazine* 64, p. 685.
3.  Letter of Arnold to Josiah Blakesley, September 20, 1794, in New Haven Colony Historical Society.
4.  Balch Papers, Shippen, Vol. 2, p. 20, Pennsylvania Historial Society, Philadelphia.
5.  Letter of Margaret Arnold to Richard Arnold, August 18, 1794, Collection: Arnold, Mrs. Margaret Shippen, Chicago Historical Society.
6.  Letter of Benedict Arnold to Ward Chipman, May 4, 1795, New Brunswick Museum.
7.  Resolution in Collection of Vere A. Arnold.
8.  Letter of Benedict Arnold to Gilbert Franklyn, August 1, 1796, in Houghton Library, Harvard University.

## Chapter XIV

1.  Letter of Benedict Arnold to Jonathan Bliss, August 15, 1795, in Bliss Papers, New Brunswick Museum.
2.  Letter of the Duke of Portland to Peter Russell, President of His Majesty's Council in Upper Canada, June 12, 1795, in Collection of Vere A. Arnold.
3.  Letter of Benedict Arnold to Jonathan Bliss, September 5, 1795, in Bliss Papers, New Brunswick Museum.
4.  Ibid., December 5, 1795.
5.  Ibid., February 20, 1796.
6.  Plan in Collection of Vere A. Arnold.
7.  Letter of Benedict Arnold to Charles, Lord Cornwallis, December 29, 1796, in Collection of Vere A. Arnold.
8.  Letter of Benedict Arnold to Jonathan Bliss, November 25, 1797, in Bliss Papers, New Brunswick Museum.

## Chapter XV

1.  Letter of Benedict Arnold to Lord Spencer, January 14, 1798, in Collection of Vere A. Arnold.
2.  Ibid., Lord Spencer to Arnold, January 21, 1798.
3.  Ibid., Arnold to the Duke of York, April 22, 1798.
4.  Ibid., Duke of York to Arnold, April 24, 1798.
5.  Benedict Arnold's application for Crown Grant Lands, Public Record Office (Kew) 42/88, pp. 875–76.
6.  Letter of Edward, Lord Hawke, to the Duke of Portland, May 2, 1798, in Collection of Vere A. Arnold.
7.  Diary of John C. Warren, in Isaac N. Arnold's biography of Benedict Arnold, p. 221.
8.  Letter of Benedict Arnold to Jonathan Bliss, September 19, 1800, in Bliss Papers, New Brunswick Museum.
9.  For Privateering information, see *Pennsylvania Magazine of History and Biography* 23, 188–92, and Peggy Arnold's letters in Ibid. 25, 473, 482, 486, 488–89.

## Chapter XVI

1.  Letter of Margaret Arnold to Edward Burd, August 15, 1801, *Pennsylvania Magazine of History and Biography* 25, p. 177.
2.  Ibid., Margaret Arnold, June 2, 1802, p. 174.

## Appendix I

1. Jared Sparks's biography, *Benedict Arnold*, vii, Preface.
2. Ibid., p. 5.
3. Caulkins, *History of Norwich, Connecticut*, pp. 411, 412.
4. Ibid., p. 409.
5. Letter of General Anthony Wayne to a party unknown, October 1, 1780, found pasted inside the cover of a copy of Sparks's biography, *Benedict Arnold*, W. L. Clements Library.
6. Neilson, *Burgoyne's Campaign and the Memorable Battles of Bemis's Heights, September 19 and October 7, 1777*, p. 184.
7. Sparks, *Benedict Arnold*, pp. 329, 330.
8. General Benedict Arnold's Day Book, October 6, 1777–August 31, 1779, in Collection of Pennsylvania Historical and Museum Commission, Division of Archives and Manuscripts, Harrisburg, Pa.
9. Letter of Colonel Morgan Lewis to Colonel Udny Hay, July 22, 1780, in Collection of Richard Maas.
10. Sparks, *Benedict Arnold*, p. 328.
11. Ibid.
12. Ibid., p. 10.
13. Lorenzo Sabine, *Biographical Sketches of Loyalists of the American Revolution*, Vol. 1, p. 182.
14. Isaac N. Arnold, *Benedict Arnold*, p. 404.
15. Letter of Benedict Arnold to Jonathan Bliss, February 20, 1796, in Odell Collection, New Brunswick Museum, Saint John, N.B.
16. Malcolm Decker, *Benedict Arnold: Son of the Havens*, p. 431.
17. Ibid., p. 495, note #3 to Chapter 31.

## Appendix II

1. Letter of Benedict Arnold to Catherine Schuyler, September 2, 1780. In Charles H. Collins Papers, Colorado College Library.
2. Letter of George Washington to Benedict Arnold, September 13, 1780. In Sparks's "Writings of Washington," 7, 524, 525.
3. Benedict Arnold to John André, September 15, 1780. Van Doren, *Secret History*, p. 473.
4. Letter of George Washington to Lt. John Laurens, October 13, 1780, in Fitzpatrick's "Writings of Washington," 20, 173.
5. Thatcher, *American Revolution*, p. 472.
6. Heath's Memoirs, 1798, p. 255. This account is confirmed by Larvey himself, as given by Dr. Eustis, in Mass. Hist. Soc. Col., Vol. 14, p. 52.
7. Flexner, *The Traitor and the Spy*, p. 369.
8. Wallace, *Traitorous Hero*, p. 251. His references: B.F. Stevens Facsimiles, 739; Mass. Hist. Soc. Col., 2nd series, 4, 51–52; Mass. Hist. Soc. Proc., 2nd series, 12, 346–48; Mass. Hist. Soc. Col. (Heath Papers, 3), 7th series., 5, 171–72.
9. PMH&B, Vol. 4, p. 63–64.
10. Sargent's, *André*, p. 330.
11. PMH&B, Vol. 5, pp. 433–34.
12. Bass, *The Green Dragoon*, p. 93.
13. Letter of Lieutenant Will Pagett, October 12, 1780. In Collection of Herman Herst, Jr.
14. Sargent, *André*, p. 314.

15. Letter of Benedict Arnold to Richard Varick, August 5, 1780, in Proceedings of Varick Court of Inquiry, pp. 82–83.

16. Letter of Benedict Arnold to George Washington, September 25, 1780, in Sparks, "Writings of Washington," 7, p. 533.

17. Proceedings of Varick Court of Inquiry, p. 128.

18. Ibid., p. 156.

19. Narrative of Joshua Hett Smith, printed in *The Historical Magazine* for July, August, September, October, and November 1866, pp. 10–11, fn.

## *Appendix III*

1. Kenneth Roberts Collection, Dartmouth College, concerning the plot for *Rabble in Arms*, (1932).

2. PMHB, 8, p. 373; American Archives, 4th Series, 2, 1–87.

3. Letter of Benedict Arnold to General Philip Schuyler, from St. John's; June 13, 1776. In Correspondence of the American Revolution, being letters of eminent men to George Washington from the time of his taking command of the army to the end of his Presidency, Edited by Jared Sparks.

4. Ibid., Benedict Arnold to the President of Congress, from his camp before Quebec, February 2, 1776.

5. American Archives, 5th Series, Vol. 2, p. 250.

6. PMHB, Vol. 3, p. 365.

7. Letter of Nathaniel Greene to General Cadwallader, November 11, 1778. Historical Society of Pennsylvania.

8. Lee papers in Publications of the New York Historical Society, 1873, Vol. 3, pp. 250–52.

9. Letter of Benedict Arnold to Major General Nathaniel Greene, in Houghton Library, Harvard University bMs Am 1446.

10. Original letter of General David Waterbury to General Horatio Gates, February 26, 1777, in Gates Papers, New York Historical Society; copied in NDAR 7:1294–97.

11. Stone, "Memoirs, Letters, and Journals of Major General Riedesel," p. 80.

12. Dr. Knox's letter, written to an unidentified party in England, is in J. Robert Maguire's personal collection.

13. Brig. Gen. Benedict Arnold to Maj. Gen. Philip Schuyler, October 15, 1776, NDAR 6:1276.

14. Samuel Swift, "History of the Town of Middlebury," includes the original article by P. C. Tucker, published in the Vergennes *Vermonter*, February 26, 1845.

15. Art Cohn, "An Incident Not Known to History: Squire Ferris and Benedict Arnold at Ferris Bay, October 13, 1776," Vermont History, The Proceedings of the Vermont Historical Society, Vol. 55, No. 2, Spring 1987.

## *Appendix IV*

1. Letter of William Wirt to William Pope, August 20, 1821, in Kennedy's "Life of William Wirt," Vol. 2 (Buffalo, N.Y., 1973), p. 115.

2. Jared Sparks Collection, Houghton Library, Harvard University.

3. Marshall, *Life of George Washington*, Vol. 3, p. 277.

4. Ibid., (second edition), Vol. 1, p. 201.

5. Henry Brockholst Livingston to General Schuyler, September 23, 1777, in Schuyler Papers (NYPL).

6. Letters of Varick in Schuyler Papers (NYPL), and are published in full or in part in Isaac N. Arnold's biography of Benedict Arnold, pp. 178–81, 189.

7. Poor's letters in Moore, "Diary of the American Revolution," Vol. 1, pp. 497–98.

8. Schuyler Papers (NYP.)

9. William Gordon, *History of the Rise, Progress and Establishment of the United States*, Vol. 2, p. 250; Libby, "A Critical Examination of Gordon's History of the American Revolution," in Annual report of the American Historical Association for 1899, I, pp. 367–88.

10. James Austin Stevens, "Benedict Arnold and His Apologist," in *Magazine of American History 4*, pp. 181–91; Isaac N. Arnold, *Benedict Arnold at Saratoga*, reprinted from The United Service, September 1880, pp. 1–16.

11. Ward, *The War of the Revolution*, Vol. 2, p. 941.

12. Wilkinson, *Memoirs of My Own Times*, Vol. 1, p. 255.

13. Bancroft, *History of the United States*, Vol. 9, p. 410; Edward Channing, *History of the United States*, Vol. 3, pp. 276–78; Montross, *Rag, Tag and Bobtail*, pp. 235–37; James Austin Stevens, "Benedict Arnold and His Apologist," in *Magazine of American History 4*, pp. 181–91.

14. Isaac N. Arnold, *Benedict Arnold*, pp. 163–90; 1. N. Arnold, *Benedict Arnold at Saratoga*, p. 10; Botta, *History of the War of Independence*, 2, p. 11.

15. Carrington, *Battle Maps of the American Revolution*, pp. 342–44.

16. Dawson, *Battles of the American Revolution*, I, p. 290.

17. Isaac N. Arnold, *Benedict Arnold at Saratoga*, p. 15.

18. Fiske, *The American Revolution*, Vol. 1, p. 327; Fortescue, *A History of the British Army*, Vol. 3, pp. 234–36; Greene, *Revolutionary War*, pp. 116–18; Lossing, *Life and Times of Philip Schuyler*, Vol. 2, 344.

19. Stedman, *History of the Origin, Progress and Termination of the American War*, 2; Wallace, *Traitorous Hero: The Life and Fortunes of Benedict Arnold*, Appendix 2, pp. 326–32; Ward, *The War of the Revolution*, Vol. 2, p. 942; Mrs. Ellen Hardin Walworth, *Saratoga, the Battle and the Battle-Ground*, p. 23; Trevelyan, *The American Revolution*, Vol. 3, p. 186n.

20. Records of the Council of Safety and Governor and Council of the State of Vermont, 1, p. 176.

21. Maria Campbell, Editor, *Revolutionary Services and Civil Life of General William Hull*, pp. 92, 93, 97.

22. Jared Sparks Collection, in Houghton Library, Harvard University.

23. "Diary of Joshua Pell, Junior," in *Magazine of American History 2*, p. 109.

24. Isaac N. Arnold, *Benedict Arnold at Saratoga*, p. 15.

25. "Diary of the Reverend Hezekiah Smith, D. C. ," in Library of Congress Manuscript Collection; I.N.A., *Benedict Arnold at Saratoga*, p. 16.

26. "Autobiography of Philip Van Courtlandt," in Magazine of American History 2, p. 286.

27. Max von Elking, *Journals and Letters of the German Troops*, published in Hanover, 1863, Part 1, p. 298; Riedesel, "Memoirs," 1, p. 150.

28. Stone, *Visits to the Saratoga Battle-Grounds, 1780–1880*, pp. 151–53; also, I. N. Arnold, *Benedict Arnold at Saratoga*, pp. 10, 11.

29. Letters of Benedict Arnold to Horatio Gates, September 22 and 23, 1777, in Gates Papers (NYHS).

30. "Orderly Book of Colonel Thaddeus Cook," p. 18, in Collection of Orderly Books, Octavo Vol. 12, American Antiquarian Society of Worcester, Mass.

31. John R. Elting, *Battles of Saratoga*, p. 54.

# Bibliography

## Notes

Material concerning Benedict Arnold is vast and clearly exhibits the long-held love/hate theories regarding the man. Therefore, while examining this material, a student of Arnold is pulled first one way and then another, at times experiencing total confusion. Arnold is either represented as the "arch Devil of all time," or "the most heroic figure of the entire American Revolution." He was neither.

Somewhere in between these two labels is a man whom we shall never really know—never really understand. To even attempt an analysis of such a controversial figure, anyone searching for his true identity can only study thoroughly *all* the material concerning him directly, as well as that which is included in works that reconstruct the times in which he lived. A balance sheet can be compiled, based on the evidence and theories, and then it is necessary to sit back and do a lot of serious thinking. How Benedict Arnold will finally emerge from such a study is thought-provoking, but emerge he will. The reader will form an opinion. Either he will stand with those who hate Arnold, or those who would deify him. Both positions are extreme and wrong in many ways. One must remember that the opinions of his contemporaries are often couched in the bitterness which surrounded his defection and therefore must be treated with caution.

No historical personage can ever be understood completely. The study of human nature is far too intricate. The scholar cannot personally interview the person concerned in his study. He cannot observe his response to probing questions, measure his facial expressions, nor be aware of emotion contained in the spoken word—a decided disadvantage. He is faced with the monumental chore of sifting through the printed records which have survived, attempting to read between the lines. He must measure prejudice and bias and make allowance for it while not actually discounting information that does not agree with his own preconceived opinions. A hostile biographer will represent his subject as he believed him to have been. It is quite possible that he will, therefore, either exclude, or even alter, certain evidence. Of course, the overzealous biographer could be found guilty of the same tactics. In the case of Benedict Arnold one finds more of the hostile variety, especially amongst the earlier biographers.

All of the biographers of Arnold are included in my listing, as well as more than one of several of his contemporaries, in the hopes of presenting the most complete picture possible.

I have also included fiction in my listing, at the risk of being criticized, to ensure a complete bibliographic record of Benedict Arnold.

The colossus, certainly one of the greatest writers of historical fiction, known for his copious research, was Kenneth Roberts. His treatment of Benedict Arnold in three novels, *Arundel, Rabble In Arms,* and *Oliver Wiswell,* was tempered by an insatiable mind and a great desire for justice. Of course, he was censured in certain quarters and accused of trying a "whitewash" job of a man so long maligned that scarcely anyone could think of him in any other way.

Roberts did not make a hero of Arnold. He merely presented the man as he believed him to have been, and the new approach was resented. An examination of Roberts's papers, bequeathed to the library at Dartmouth College, shows his indefatigable research and his determination to uncover facts. He not only corresponded with descendants of Arnold here, in Canada, and England, but he submitted samples of Arnold's handwriting (unidentified) to two separate graphologists of note in the hopes of discovering clues to the character of this often abstruse man. It is unfortunate that Roberts did not live to write a book that would have covered the period of Arnold's conspiracy with the British and his subsequent defection.

The respect with which Kenneth Roberts was treated by publishers will be confirmed by Harper Bros. submitting Willard Wallace's manuscript for his 1954 biography of Benedict Arnold, *Treasonous Hero,* to Roberts for his opinion! A rare accolade indeed.

Finally, it is interesting to conjecture how different the treatment of Benedict Arnold would be today, if he'd received his wish at Breymann's Redoubt, on October 7, 1777. When Henry Dearborn reached him and asked:

"Where are you hit?" he'd replied: "In the same leg. I wish it had been my heart." At that moment he wished just that.

If it is interesting enough to give even the slightest consideration to that supposition, it is surely even more so to give a *great deal of thought* to his reasons for changing sides. For this reason it is imperative that every facet of the man, which exists in the copious material of his times, along with the later meritorious studies, be examined and weighed before a judgment of any kind is made. Even then — can it be conclusive?

## *Books*

Abbatt, William. *The Crisis of the Revolution*. New York: 1899.

Alden, John Richard. *The American Revolution: 1775–1783*. New York: 1954.

Alderman, Clifford Lindsey. *The Dark Eagle: The Story of Benedict Arnold*. New York: 1976.

Allen, Ethan. *A Narrative of Col. Ethan Allen's Captivity from the Time of His Being Taken by the British near Montreal, to the Time of His Exchange*. Walpole, N.H.: 1807.

Allen, Gardner W. *A Naval History of the American Revolution*. Boston: 1913.

American Archives: *Minutes of the Committee of Fifty-One*. Washington: 1833–53, 9 vols.

Anburey, Lt. Thomas. *Travels through the Interior Parts of America, 1776–1781*. Boston: 1923.

Anderson, William James. *Canadian History: The Siege and Blockade of Quebec by Generals Montgomery and Arnold in 1775*. Quebec: 1872.

André, John. *The Case of Major John André*. New York: 1780.

———. *Minutes of a Court of Inquiry upon the Case of Major John André with Accompanying Documents*. Albany, N.Y.: 1865.

———. *Proceedings of a Board of General Officers, Held by Order of His Excellency General George Washington, Commander-in-Chief of the Army of the United States of America, Respecting Major John André, Adjutant-General of the British Army, September 29, 1780*. Philadelphia: 1865.

*Appleton's Cyclopedia of American Biography*. New York: 1887.

Armes, Ethel, Editor. *Nancy Shippen, Her Journal Book*. New York: 1935.

Arnold, Benedict. *Proceedings of a General Court Martial for the Trial of Major-General Arnold.* Philadelphia: 1780.

———. *Proceedings of a General Court Martial of the Line, June 1, 1779–1780.* Philadelphia: 1779.

———. *The Present State of the American Rebel Army, Navy and Finances.* Brooklyn., N.Y.: 1891.

Arnold, Isaac Newton. *The Life of Benedict Arnold: His Patriotism and His Treason.* Chicago: 1880.

Arnold, John R. *The Descendants of Benedict Arnold in Canada.* Peterborough, Ont., Canada: 1983.

*The Arnold Family.* Arlington, Va.: 1972.

Augur, H. *The Secret War of Independence.* New York: 1955.

Bakeless, John. *Turncoats, Traitors and Heroes.* Philadelphia: 1959.

Baldwin, Alice M. *The New England Clergy and the American Revolution.* New York: 1928.

Bancroft, George. *History of the United States of America from the Discovery of the Continent.* Boston: 1876.

Barbé-Marbois, F. *Complot D'Arnold et de Sir Henry Clinton.* Paris: 1816.

Bass, Robert Duncan. *The Green Dragoon: The Lives of Banastre Tarleton and Mary Robinson.* New York: 1957.

Becker, Carl Lotus. *The History of Political Parties in the Province of New York: 1760–1776.* Madison, Wis.: 1960.

———. *The Spirit of '76.* Albany, N.Y.: 1971.

Bedini, Silvio A. *Ridgefield in Review.* Ridgefield, Conn.: 1958.

Beebe, Lewis. *Journal of Dr. Lewis Beebe.* New York: 1971. Reprint, Pennsylvania Magazine of History and Biography, Vol. 59, Oct. 1935.

Beirne, Francis F. *The Trial of Aaron Burr.* New York: 1959.

Bell, D. G. *Early Loyalist Saint John: The Origin of New Brunswick Politics 1783–1786.* Fredericton, N.B. Canada: 1983.

Bemis, Samuel Flagg. *The Diplomacy of the American Revolution.* Bloomington, Ind.: 1967.

Bennett, C. E. *Advance and Retreat to Saratoga in the American Revolution: American Offensive: Advance to Quebec: Retreat to Ticonderoga*. Schenectady, N.Y.: 1927.

———. *Vacant Niche or Land of Gold*. Schenectady, N.Y.: 1928.

Bernier, Olivier. *Lafayette: Hero of Two Worlds*. New York: 1983.

Bird, Harrison. *Attack on Quebec: The American Invasion of Canada, 1775*. New York: 1968.

———. *Navies in the Mountains: The Battles on the Waters of Lake Champlain and Lake George, 1609–1814*. New York: 1962.

———. *March to Saratoga: General Burgoyne and the American Campaign 1777*. New York: 1963.

Blades, Marie E. *The March to Quebec: A Mystery Solved: Journal of Matthias Ogden, 1775*. Morristown, N.J.: 1980.

Botta, C. *History of the War of Independence*. New Haven, Conn.: 1840. 2 Vols.

Boylan, Brian Richard. *Benedict Arnold: The Dark Eagle*. New York: 1973.

Boynton, Edward Carlisle. *History of West Point and Its Military Importance during the American Revolution*. New York: 1863.

Bradford, Gamaliel. *Damaged Souls*. Boston: 1923.

Brandow, John Henry. *The Story of Old Saratoga and History of Schuylerville*. New York: 1901.

Burgoyne, John. *State of the Expedition from Canada*. London: 1780.

Bush, Martin H. *Revolutionary Enigma: A Re-Appraisal of General Philip Schuyler of New York*. Port Washington, N.Y.: 1969.

Callahan, North. *Daniel Morgan: Ranger of the Revolution*. New York: 1961.

———. *Royal Raiders: The Tories of the American Revolution*. Indianapolis, Ind.: 1963.

Calvert, George Henry. *Arnold and André*. Boston: 1876.

Carrington, Henry B. *Battle Maps and Charts of the American Revolution*. New York: 1974.

Carroll, Charles. *The Journal of Charles Carroll of Carrollton As One of the Congressional Rommissioners to Canada in 1776*. New York: 1976.

Caulkins, Frances Manwaring. *History of Norwich, Connecticut.* Chester, Conn.: 1976.

Chapman, John Jay. *The Treason and Death of Benedict Arnold: A Play for a Greek Theatre.* New York: 1910.

Clark, Ronald W. *Benjamin Franklin.* New York: 1983.

Codman, John. *Arnold's Expedition to Quebec.* New York: 1901.

Coffin, Robert P. Tristram. *Kennebec: Cradle of Americans.* New York: 1937.

Coggins, Jack. *Ships and Seamen of the American Revolution.* Harrisburg, Pa.: 1969.

Cohen, Sheldon. *Canada Preserved: The Journal of Captain Thomas Ainslee.* New York: 1968.

Connecticut: *A Guide to Its Roads, Lore and People.* Boston: 1938.

Crary, Catherine S., Editor. *The Price of Loyalty: Tory Writings from the Revolutionary Era.* New York: 1973.

Cuneo, John R. *The Battles of Saratoga: The Turning of the Tide.* New York: 1967.

Cunliffe, Marcus, Editor. *The Life of Washington.* Cambridge, Mass.: 1962.

Dann, John C., Editor. *The Revolution Remembered: Eyewitness Accounts of the War For Independence.* Chicago, Ill.: 1980.

Dawson, Henry B. *Battles of the United States.* New York: 1858, 2 Vols.

———. *Record of the Trial of Joshua Hett Smith, Esq. for Alleged Complicity in the Treason of Benedict Arnold.* Morrisania, N.Y.: 1866.

Decker, Malcolm. *Benedict Arnold: Son of the Havens.* Tarrytown, N.Y.: 1961.

———. *Ten Days of Infamy: An Illustrated Memoir of the Arnold-André Conspiracy.* New York: 1969.

Decker, Peter. *Trekking Arnold's Trail to Quebec.* Lakeville, Conn.: 1976.

Desmond, Alice Curtis. *Sword and Pen for George Washington.* New York: 1964.

*Dictionary of American Biography.* 20 Vols. 1928–37.

*Dictionary of National Biography.* 1885.

DiMona, Joseph. *The Benedict Arnold Connection.* New York: 1977.

Dupuy, R. Ernest, and Trevor N. Dupuy. *The Compact History of the Revolutionary War.* New York: 1963.

Einstein, Lewis. *Divided Loyalties: Americans in England during the War for Independence.* London: 1933.

*Eleven Exiles: Accounts of Loyalists of the American Revolution.* Toronto, Canada: 1982.

Emerson, Edwin. *Benedict Arnold, a Drama of the American Revolution, in Three Acts and a Prelude.* New York: 1924.

Emery, Noemie. *Alexander Hamilton: An Intimate Portrait.* New York: 1982.

Ferguson, Eugene S. *Truxtun of the "Constellation": The Life of Commodore Thomas Truxtun, USN.* Annapolis, Md.: 1956.

Fiske, John. *The Critical Period of American History.* Boston: 1888.

———. *The American Revolution.* Boston: 1891, 2 Vols.

Flexner, James Thomas. *George Washington in the American Revolution.* Boston: 1967.

———. *The Traitor and the Spy: Benedict Arnold and John André.* New York: 1953.

Ford, Cory. *A Peculiar Service.* Boston: 1965.

Fortescue, J. W. *A History of the British Army.* New York: 1899–1930, 14 Vols.

*Fort Stanwix: Construction and Military History.* Washington: 1976.

Fowler, William M. *Rebels under Sail: The American Navy during the Revolution.* New York: 1976.

Fritz, Jean. *The Case of Benedict Arnold.* New York: 1981.

Frothingham, R. *Life and Times of Joseph Warren.* Boston: 1865.

Fryer, Mary Beacock. *Buckskin Pimpernel: The Exploits of Justus Sherwood, Loyalist Spy.* Toronto, Canada: 1981.

Furneaux, Rupert. *Saratoga: The Decisive Battle.* London: 1971.

Gipson, Lawrence H. *American Loyalist: Jared Ingersoll.* New Haven, Conn.: 1971.

Graham, James. *The Life of General Daniel Morgan of the Virginia Line of the Army of the United States with Portions of his Correspondence.* New York, 1856.

Greene, Francis V. *General Greene.* New York: 1893.

Groh, Lynn. *The Culpeper Spy Ring.* Philadelphia, Pa.: 1969.

Guild, R. A. *Chaplain Smith and the Baptists.* Philadelphia: 1885.

Hadden, Lt. James M. *Hadden's Journal and Orderly Books: A Journal Kept in Canada and Upon Burgoyne's Campaign in 1776 and 1777.* Boston: 1884.

Hagglund, Lorenzo F. *A Page from the Past: The Story of the Continental Gundelo Philadelphia on Lake Champlain, 1776–1949.* Lake George, N.Y.: 1949.

Haight, Charles S. *Benedict Arnold: The Man, a Character Study.* Library of Congress: 1903.

Hamilton, Edward P. *Fort Ticonderoga: Key to a Continent.* Boston: 1964.

Hart, G. B. *The Varick Court of Inquiry to Investigate the Implication of Col. Richard Varick (Arnold's Private Secretary) in the Arnold Treason.* Boston: 1907.

Hatch, Robert McConnell. *Thrust for Canada: The American Attempt on Quebec, 1775–1776.* Boston: 1979.

———. *Major John André: A Gallant in Spy's Clothing.* Boston: 1986.

Higginbotham, Don. *Daniel Morgan: Revolutionary Rifleman.* Chapel Hill, N.C.: 1961.

Hill, George Canning. *Benedict Arnold.* New York, 1887.

Hilliard, Rev. E. B. *The Last Men of the Revolution.* Barre, Mass.: 1968.

Hough, Frank O. *The Neutral Ground.* Philadelphia: 1941.

———. *Renown.* New York: 1938.

Hughes, Rupert. *George Washington: The Savior of the States, 1777–1781.* New York: 1930.

Jellison, Charles A. *Ethan Allen, Frontier Rebel.* Taftsville, Vt.: 1969.

Jones, Charles H. *History of the Campaign for the Conquest of Canada in 1776.* Philadelphia: 1882.

Jones, Thomas. *History of New York during the Revolutionary War.* New York: 1878.

Koke, Richard J. *Accomplice in Treason: Joshua Hett Smith and the Arnold Conspiracy.* New York: 1973.

Kraske, Robert. *The Treason of Benedict Arnold, 1780: An American General Becomes His Country's First Traitor.* New York: 1972.

Labaree, Benjamin W. *Patriots and Partisans: The Merchants of Newburyport, 1764–1815*. New York: 1962.

Laing, Alexander. *The American Heritage History of Seafaring America*. New York: 1974.

Lamb, Martha J., and Mrs. Burton Harrison. *History of the City of New York: Its Origin, Rise and Progress*. New York: 1877.

Lawrence, J. W. *Footprints, Or, Incidents in The Early History of New Brunswick, 1783–1883*. St. John, N.B.: 1883.

Leake, Isaac Q. *Memoir of Life and Times of General John Lamb*. Albany, N.Y.: 1857.

Lee, Henry. *Champe's Adventure: An Account of the Attempt of John Champe to Seize Benedict Arnold in 1780, Taken from the Author's Memoirs of the War in the Southern Department of the United States*. New York: 1864.

Lengyel, Cornell I. *Benedict Arnold: The Anatomy of Treason*. Garden City, N.Y.: 1960.

Little, Shelby. *George Washington*. New York, 1929.

Livingston, William Farrand. *Israel Putnam: Pioneer, Ranger and Major-General 1718–1790*. New York/London: 1901.

Lomask, Milton. *Aaron Burr*. New York: 1979–82, 2 Vols.

Lonergan, Carroll Vincent. *Ticonderoga, Historic Portage*. New York: 1959.

Lossing, Benson J. *The Life and Times of Philip Schuyler*. New York: 1872.

———. *The Pictorial Field-Book of the Revolution*. Rutland, Vt.: 1859, 2 Vols.

———. *Hours with the Living Men and Women of the Revolution: A Pilgrimage*. New York: 1889.

Lowell, Edward Jackson. *The Hessians and the Other German Auxiliaries of Great Britain in the Revolutionary War*. New York: 1884.

Lowenthal, Larry, Editor. *Days of Siege: A Journal of the Siege of Fort Stanwix in 1777*. New York: 1983.

Luzader, John. *Decision on the Hudson: The Saratoga Campaign of 1777*. Washington: 1975.

MacNutt, W. Stewart. *New Brunswick and Its People: The Biography of a Canadian Province*. New Brunswick, Canada: n.d.

————. *New Brunswick: A History: 1784–1867.* Toronto, Canada: 1963.

Mahan, A. T. *The Major Operations of the Navies in the War of American Independence.* Boston: 1913.

Marshall, John. *The Life of George Washington.* Philadelphia: 1836, 2 Vols.

McDevitt, Robert. *Connecticut Attacked: A British Viewpoint: Tryon's Raid on Danbury.* Chest, Conn.: 1974.

McDowell, Bart. *The Revolutionary War.* Washington: 1967.

McGee, Dorothy H. *Sally Townsend, Patriot.* New York: 1952.

Middlekauff, Robert. *The Glorious Cause: The American Revolution 1763–1789.* New York: 1982.

Millar, John F. *American Ships of the Colonial and Revolutionary Period.* New York: 1978.

*Minutes of a Court of Inquiry Upon the Case of Major John André.* Albany: 1865.

Mitchell, Lynn. Col. Joseph Brady. *Decisive Battles of the American Revolution.* New York: 1962.

————. *Discipline and Bayonets: The Armies and Leaders in the War of the American Revolution.* New York: 1967.

Montross, Lynn. *Rag, Tag and Bobtail: The Story of the Continental Army.* New York: 1952.

————. *The Reluctant Rebels: The Story of the Continental Congress.* New York: 1950.

Moody, Sid. *'76 The World Turned Upside Down.* New York: 1975.

Morpurgo, J. E. *Treason at West Point: The Arnold-André Conspiracy.* New York: 1975.

Morris, Richard B. John Jay: The Making of a Revolutionary (Unpublished Papers, 1745–1780). New York: 1975.

Morris, Robert. *Morris, Arnold and Battersby: Account of the Attack I Made on the Character of General Arnold.* London: 1782.

Muzzey, A. B. *Reminiscences and Memorials of Men of the Revolution and Their Families.* Boston: 1883.

Neilson, Charles. *Burgoyne's Campaign and the Memorable Battles of Bemis's Heights, September 19, and October 7, 1777.* Albany: 1844.

New Brunswick Historical Society. *Collections.* Saint John, N.B., Canada: 1890–1930.

New York State Historic Trust. *The Hudson Valley and the American Revolution.* Albany: 1969.

Nickerson, Hoffman. *The Turning Point of the Revolution, Or Burgoyne in America.* Port Washington, N.Y.: 1967.

Nolan, Jeannette Covert. *Benedict Arnold: Traitor to His Country.* New York: 1956.

———. *Treason at the Point.* New York: 1944.

Norris, George. *What Made Benedict Arnold a Traitor?* Philadelphia: 1934.

Norwich, Vital Records of. Hartford, Conn: 1913, 2 Vols.

Nowlan, Alden. *Campobello: The Outer Island.* Toronto, Canada: 1975.

Orton, Jason Rockwood. *Arnold and Other Poems.* New York: 1854.

Ostrander, William S. *Old Saratoga and the Burgoyne Campaign.* Schuylerville, N.Y.: 1897.

Paine, Lauran Bosworth. *Benedict Arnold: Hero and Traitor.* London: 1965.

Palmer, Dave Richard. *The River and the Rock: The History of Fortress West Point, 1775–1783.* New York: 1969.

Palmer, Peter S. *History of Lake Champlain from Its First Exploration by the French in 1609 to the Close of the Year 1814.* Albany, N.Y.: 1866.

Patterson, Samuel White. *Horatio Gates: Defender of American Liberties.* New York: 1941.

Pausch, Georg. *Journal of Captain Georg Pausch.* Albany: 1886.

Peckham, Howard H. *The War for Independence: A Military History.* Chicago: 1958.

Pell, John. *Ethan Allen.* Boston: 1929.

Pennypacker, Morton. *General Washington's Spies on Long Island and in New York.* Brooklyn: 1939.

Perkens, Col. J. J. *Historical Views: Saratoga Battleground and Vicinity.* Schuylerville, N.Y.: 1906.

Post, Lydia Minturn. *Personal Recollections of the American Revolution: A Private Journal Prepared from Authentic Domestic Records.* New York: 1859.

Ragan, Roger Kemper. *Benedict Arnold: Our First Marine, His Contemporaries and the Story of His Life*. Cincinnati, Ohio: 1931.

Randel, William Pierce. *Mirror of a People*. Maplewood, N.J.: 1973.

Reed, William B. *Life and Correspondence of Joseph Reed*. Pennsylvania: 1847.

*Revolutionary Characters of New Haven: The Subject of Addresses and Papers Delivered before the General David Humphreys Branch #1 Connecticut Society Sons of the American Revolution, 1775–1783*. New Haven, Conn.: 1911.

Reynolds, Paul R. *Guy Carleton*. Toronto, Canada: 1980.

Roberts, Kenneth. *I Wanted to Write*. New York: 1949.

———. *Arundel*. Garden City, N.Y.: 1930.

———. *March to Quebec: Journals of the Members of Arnold's Expedition*. New York: 1946.

———. *Oliver Wiswell*. Garden City, N.Y.: 1940.

———. *Rabble in Arms*. Garden City, N.Y.: 1933.

Roberts, Robert B. *New York's Forts in the Revolution*. Cranbury, N.J.: 1980.

Rossie, Jonathan G. *The Politics of Command in the American Revolution*. New York: 1975.

Royster, Charles. *A Revolutionary People at War: The Continental Army and American Character, 1775–1783*. Chapel Hill, N.C.: 1979.

———. *Light-Horse Harry Lee and the Legacy of the American Revolution*. New York, 1981.

Ryerson, Egerton. *The Loyalists of America and Their Times from 1620 to 1816*. Toronto, Canada: 1880.

Sabine, Lorenzo. *Biographical Sketches of Loyalists of the American Revolution*. Port Washington, N.Y.: 1966, 2 Vols.

Sabine, William. H. W. *Murder, 1776 and Washington's Policy of Silence*. New York: 1973.

Salsig, Doyen, Editor. *Parole: Quebec; Countersign: Ticonderoga. Second New Jersey Regimental Orderly Book 1776*. Toronto, Canada: 1980.

Sargent, Winthrop. *The Life and Career of Major John André, Adjutant-General of the British Army in America*. New York: 1902.

Schachner, Nathan. *Alexander Hamilton*. New York: 1946.

Schroeder, Rev. John Frederick. *Life and Times of Washington*. New York: 1987–61, 2 Vols.

Sellers, Charles Coleman. *Benedict Arnold: The Proud Warrior*. New York: 1930.

Sherwin, Oscar. *Benedict Arnold: Patriot and Traitor*. New York: 1931.

Smith, J. H. *Arnold's March from Cambridge to Quebec*. New York: 1903.

Smith, Joshua Hett. *An Authentic Narrative of the Causes Which Led to the Death of Major André*. London: 1909.

———. *Record of the Trial of Joshua Hett Smith, Esq. for Alleged Complicity in the Treason of Benedict Arnold, 1780*. Morrisania, N.Y.: 1866.

Smith, Paul H. *Loyalists and Redcoats: A Study in British Revolutionary Policy*. North Carolina: 1964.

Smith, William. *Historical Memoirs from 16 March 1763 to 9 July 1776 and from 12 July 1776 to 25 July 1778, of William Smith, Historian of the Province of New York*. New York: 1956–1958, 2 Vols.

Sosin, Jack M. *Agents and Merchants: British Colonial Policy and the Origins of the American Revolution, 1763–1775*. Nebraska: 1965.

Sparks, Jared. *Correspondence of the American Revolution*. Boston: 1853.

———. *Life and Treason of Benedict Arnold*. Boston: 1835.

———. *The Life of George Washington*. Boston: 1825–1835, 7 Vols.

Spicer, Bart. *Brother to the Enemy*. New York: 1958.

*The Spirit of 'Seventy-Six: The Story of the American Revolution as Told by Participants*. New York: 1983.

Sprague, Rev. Delos E. *Descriptive Guide of the Battlefield of Saratoga* Ballston Spa, N.Y.: 1930.

Squire, Marjorie. *British Views of the American Revolution*. Boston: 1965.

Stedman, Charles. *History of the Origin, Progress and Termination of the American War*. London: 1794, 2 Vols.

Stimson, F. J. *My Story: Being the Memoirs of Benedict Arnold*. New York: 1917.

Stinchcombe, William C. *The American Revolution and the French Alliance*. Syracuse, N.Y.: 1969.

Stone, William L. *Visits to the Saratoga Battle-Grounds, 1780–1880*. Albany, N.Y.: 1895.

———. *Burgoyne's Campaign and St. Leger's Expedition*. Albany: 1877.

*Stories about Arnold, the Traitor: André, the Spy: and Champe, the Patriot: For the Children of the United States*. New Haven, Conn.: 1895.

Strach, Stephen G. *Some Sources for the Study of the Loyalist and Canadian Participation in the Military Campaign of Lieutenant-General John Burgoyne, 1777*. New York: 1983.

Styles, Showell. *Gentleman Johnny*. New York: 1962.

Sullivan, Edward Dean. *Benedict Arnold, Military Racketeer*. New York: 1932.

Tallmadge, Benjamin. Memoir of Col. Benjamin Tallmadge Prepared by Himself at the Request of His Children. New York: 1858.

Taylor, John G. *Some New Light on the Later Life and Last Resting Place of Benedict Arnold and His Wife Margaret Shippen*. London: 1931.

Thatcher, James. *Military Journal during the American Revolutionary War from 1775 to 1783*. Boston: 1823.

Thompson, Ray. *Benedict Arnold in Philadelphia*. Pennsylvania: 1975.

Thompson, Richard. *The Robinson House: Or Reminiscences of West Point and Arnold the Traitor, by a Member of the Board of Visitors*. New York: 1840.

Tillotson, Harry Stanton. *The Beloved Spy: Life and Loves of Major John André*. Caldwell, Idaho: 1948.

———. *The Exquisite Exile: Life and Fortune of Mrs. Benedict Arnold*. Boston: 1932.

Todd, Alden L. *Richard Montgomery, Rebel of 1775*. New York: 1966.

Todd, Charles Burr. *The Real Benedict Arnold*. New York: 1903.

Tracy, Frank Basil. *The Tercentenary History of Canada, from Champlain to Lauier, 1608–1908*. New York: 1908.

Trevelyan, George Otto. *The American Revolution*. Condensation of six volumes into one. New York: 1964.

Trueman, Stuart. *An Intimate History of New Brunswick*. Toronto, Canada: 1970.

Tuckerman, Bayard. *Life of General Philip Schuyler: 1733–1804*. New York: 1905.

Vail, Philip. *The Twisted Saber: A Biographical Novel of Benedict Arnold*. New York: 1963.

Van Doren, Carl Clinton. *Secret History of the American Revolution: An Account of the Conspiracies of Benedict Arnold and Numerous Others Drawn from the Secret Service Papers of the British Headquarters in North America Now for the First Time Examined and Made Public*. New York: 1941.

Van Tyne, Claude Halstead. *The Loyalists in the American Revolution*. Gloucester, Mass.: 1959.

Von Elking, Max. *Memoirs and Letters and Journals of Major General Riedesel*. Albany: 1868, 2 Vols.

————. *Journals and Letters of the German Troops*. Hanover, Germany: 1863.

Wallace, Willard M. *Appeal to Arms: A Military History of the American Revolution*. New York: 1951.

————. *Traitorous Hero: The Life and Fortunes of Benedict Arnold*. New York: 1954.

————. *Connecticut's Dark Star of the Revolution: General Benedict Arnold*. Connecticut: 1978.

Ward, Christopher. *The War of the Revolution*. New York: 1952.

Washington, George. *The Writings of George Washington from the Original Manuscript Sources 1745–1799*. Washington USGPO: 1931–44, 39 Vols.

*The Waterman Family*. New Haven, Conn.: 1939, 2 Vols.

Weems, Mason L. *The Life of George Washington: With Curious Anecdotes Equally Honorable to Himself and Exemplary to His Young Countrymen*. Philadelphia: 1837.

Westrate, E. V. *Those Fatal Generals*. Port Washington, N.Y.: 1968.

Weyl, Nathaniel. *Reason: The Story of Disloyalty and Betrayal in American History*. Washington: 1950.

Wilkinson, James. *Memoirs of My Own Times*. Philadelphia: 1816, 3 Vols.

Willcox, William G. *Portrait of a General: Sir Henry Clinton in the War of Independence – An Analysis of the Strategy That Cost Britain the War*. New York: 1962.

Willyams, C. *The Account of the Campaign in the West Indies*. London: 1796.

Wilson, Woodrow. *A History of the American People.* New York/London: 1902, 5 Vols.

Winsor, Justin. *Narrative and Critical History of America.* Boston: 1889, 8 Vols.

Wistach, Paul. *Hudson River Landings.* Indianapolis, Ind.: 1933.

## *Manuscript Sources*

Albany Institute of History and Art, Albany, N.Y.

    Philip Schuyler Papers

American Antiquarian Society of Worcester, Mass.

    Orderly book of Colonel Thaddeus Cook

Arnold, Vere Arbuthnot (great-great-grandson of Benedict Arnold) "Ardmore," Great Barrow, Chester, England. Originals of correspondence with Lord Germain, Hawke, Cornwallis, Henry Clinton, Admiral Arbuthnot, the Duke of York, Pitt, and Memorial for the Canadian Grants.

British Museum, Manuscript Department, London, England

    Lord Liverpool Collection

    Miscellaneous Papers

Chicago Historical Society, Chicago, Ill.

    Collection of Benedict Arnold

    Collection of Hannah Arnold

    Collection of Isaac Newton Arnold

    Collection of Joseph Ward

William L. Clements Library, University of Michigan, Ann Arbor, Mich.

    Henry Clinton Papers

    Thomas Gage Papers

    George Germain Papers

    Benjamin Gilbert Letterbook

    Nathaniel Greene Papers

    MacKenzie Papers

    Miscellaneous Collection, Cornelius Russell Schoff Collection

Shelburne Papers

Simcoe Papers

Columbia University, New York City

John Jay Collection

Gouverneur Morris Papers

Connecticut Historical Society, Hartford, Conn.

Jonathan Trumbull, Sr., Papers

Jonathan Trumbull, Jr., Papers

Joseph Trumbull Collection

Jeremiah Wadsworth Papers

Oliver Wolcott, Sr., Papers

Journal of Capt. Edward Mott

Connecticut State Library, Hartford, Conn.

Map of various passes into Canada from our lower provinces.

Benedict Arnold correspondence with Josiah Blakeley

Joseph Trumbull Collection

Cornell University, Ithaca, N.Y.

Harmanus Schuyler letters to Philip Schuyler

Dartmouth College Library, Hanover, N.H.

Benedict Arnold correspondence with his first wife, Margaret Mansfield Arnold

Josiah Bartlett Papers

Kenneth Roberts Collection

Eleazer Wheelock Papers

David Library, Washington's Crossing, Pa. (Material on Micro-film and Micro-fiche)

Letters of Benedict to: Margaret Mansfield Arnold; Capt. John Denny; Dr. John Dickinson; John Graves Simcoe; Jacob Thompson

Benedict Arnold's "Table Expenses" for April 1779

Winthrop Atwill: "Arnold the American Traitor," 1881. (Lecture)

Benedict Arnold's Memorandum Book

Isaac N. Arnold: "Benedict Arnold at Saratoga, a reply to J. A. Stevens and new evidence of Bancroft's error"

Jonathan Rathbun: "Account of Groton Fort Attack," 1840

Fort Ticonderoga Library, Ticonderoga, N.Y.

Benedict Arnold's Regimental Memorandum Book, 1775

Benedict Arnold's Proclamation following the capture of Fort Ticonderoga, 1775

Simon Metcalf's Book

Godfrey Memorial Library, Middletown, Conn.

Genealogical Collections of local people includes family of Comfort Sage, Arnold's friend.

Greenwich Maritime Museum Library, Greenwich, England

Admiralty Records

Ship Logs: Charlestown; Prince Edward; Greyhound; Robust

Henry Huntington Library, San Marino, California

Philip Schuyler Orderbook

Philip Schuyler Papers

Herst, Herman, Jr., Boca Raton, Fla. (Private Collection)

Letter of William Paget, October 12, 1780

Historical Society of Pennsylvania, Philadelphia, Pa.

Henry Carey Baird Papers

Balch Papers

Biddle Collection

Cadwalader Collection

Ferdinand Dreer Collection: Generals of the Revolution

Edward Carey Gardiner Collection

Simon Gratz Collection

Charles Hildeburn Collection

Lossing Papers

Robert Morris Papers

Journal of Dr. Isaac Senter, Physician and Surgeon on the March to Quebec

Society Collection

Stauffer Collection

Anthony Wayne Papers

James Wilson Papers

Houghton Library, Harvard University, Cambridge, Mass.

Collected Manuscripts of Jared Sparks

Lawrence, Kenneth R., No. Miami, Fla. (Private Collection)

Benedict Arnold letter, September 4, 1780

Library of Congress, Manuscript Division, Washington D.C.

John Adams Papers

Samuel Adams Papers (Photostats)

Continental Congress, Papers of

Peter Force Papers (Transcripts) : Material dated between 1774–1776

Horatio Gates Papers (Transcripts)

Alexander Hamilton Papers

John Hancock Papers

Journals of Congress

Robert Morris Papers

George Washington Papers

Litchfield Historical Museum, Litchfield, Conn.

Benedict Arnold Letters, 1786

Benjamin Tallmadge Letter, October 20, 1780

Literary and Historical Society of Quebec, Quebec, Canada

Hugh Finlay's Journal of the Siege and Blockade of Quebec, by the American Rebels in Autumn 1775 and Winter 1776

Sir John Hamilton's Journal of the Principal Occurrences during the Siege of Quebec

Manuscripts Relating to the Early History of Canada

Maass, Richard, White Plains, N.Y. (Private Collection )

> Various Letters of Benedict Arnold, 1775, 1777, and 1780

Massachusetts Historical Society, Boston, Mass.

> Jeremy Belknap Papers
>
> Jacob Bigelow Papers
>
> Henry Knox Papers
>
> William Livingston Papers
>
> Robert Treat Paine Papers
>
> Timothy Pickering Papers
>
> John Sullivan Papers
>
> Artemas Ward Papers
>
> Warren-Adams Papers
>
> Journals of Capt. Henry Dearborn and Major Return Jonathan Meigs (concerning the expedition to Quebec)

Massachusetts State Archives, State House, Boston, Mass.

> Revolutionary War Papers

Morristown National Historical Park Museum, Morristown, N.J.

> Halstead, John (Commissary under Benedict Arnold at Quebec, 1776) Expense Book
>
> Journal of Major Matthias Ogden
>
> Lord Francis Napier "Journal of the Burgoyne Campaign"
>
> Lloyd Wadell Smith Collection
>
> Anthony Wayne Papers

National Archives, Washington, D.C.

> Papers of the Continental Congress

New Brunswick Museum, Saint John, N.B. Canada

> 36 Letters between Benedict Arnold and His Attorney Jonathan Bliss, 1791–1800
>
> Ward Chipman Papers
>
> Jonathan Odell Papers

Edward Winslow Papers

*Royal Gazette* on Micro-film

New Hampshire Historical Society, Concord, N.H.

Josiah Bartlett Papers

Timothy Bedel Papers

Jeremy Belknap Papers

Diary of Major Henry Blake

Narrative of Joseph Gray: A Revolutionary Soldier

John Langdon Papers

Samuel Livermore Papers

Morris-Stark Papers

John Sullivan Papers

Meschech Weare Papers

New Haven Colony Historical Society, New Haven, Conn.

Business papers of Benedict Arnold

His "Waste Book," April 26, 1773, to March 1, 1780

Manuscript Essay Portfolio of his house on Water Street, by Christina Baker

New London County Historical Society, New London, Conn.

Letters between Benedict Arnold and Nathaniel Shaw, Jr., 1777–1781

The New York Historical Society, New York City

William Alexander Papers

Benedict Arnold Papers (Memorandum Book)

John Gruger Papers

James Duane Papers

William Duer Papers

Horatio Gates Papers

Robert R. Livingston Papers

William Livingston Papers

Colonel John Lamb Papers

Alexander McDougall Papers

Miscellaneous Papers

Gouverneur Morris Papers

Joseph Reed Papers

Philip Schuyler Papers

George Smyth Papers

Ebenezer Stevens Papers

Walter Stewart Papers

Marinus Willett Papers

New York Public Library, New York City

Samuel Adams Papers

Benedict Arnold Personal Miscellaneous Papers

George Bancroft Collection

Samuel Chase Papers

George Clinton Papers

Thomas A. Emmet Collection

Horatio Gates Papers (Transcripts)

Benjamin Lincoln Papers

Robert R. Livingston Papers (Transcripts)

Theodorous B. Myers Collection (contains papers of Daniel Morgan)

Philip Schuyler Papers (approximately 10,000 documents; letter-books of correspondence until July 1777; troop returns, journals, and diaries)

The Log of H.M.S. *Vulture*

New York State Library, Albany, N.Y.

John Burgoyne Orderly Book, 1777

Morgan Lewis Papers

Philip Schuyler Papers

John Williams Papers

Pennsylvania Historical and Museum Commission, Harrisburg, Pa.

> Division of Archives
>
> Benedict Arnold's Day Book 1777–1779

Public Archives of Canada, Ottawa, Ont., Canada

> Haldimand Papers
>
> Grants
>
> Ainslie Correspondence for 1781

Public Records Office, Kew, London, England

> American Loyalists Claims (60v. MS Books and papers of the Commission of Enquiry into the losses and services of the American Loyalists)
>
> Admiralty Records
>
> Audit Records
>
> Carleton Papers
>
> Colonial Office Papers
>
> Cornwallis Papers
>
> Grants of Land in America

Public Records Office, Chancery Lane, London, England

> Admiralty High Court Records
>
> State Papers

Rhode Island Historical Society, Providence, R.I.

> Collections, VI (1867), 1–104
>
> Simeon Thayer's Journal

Saratoga National Park, Stillwater, N.Y.

> Preliminary Documentary Report on Benedict Arnold at Saratoga, by John F. Luzader, Park Historian, October 27, 1958

The Spruance Library of the Bucks County Historial Society at the Mercer Museum, Doylestown, Pa.

> *The Pennsylvania Magazine of History and Biography*, 1877–1951. Publication of manuscripts and letters concerning Benedict Arnold, Peggy Shippen, and their families.

United States Army Military History Institute, Upton Hall, Carlisle Barracks, Pa.

> Benedict Arnold letters, also "Table Expenses," 1 April 1779

United States Military Academy Library, West Point, N.Y.

> Lecture on Arnold and André by Professor Ellsworth, illustrated by glass slides, 1899
>
> Anonymous Journal of the Burgoyne Campaign

University of NewBrunswick, Harriet Irving Library, Fredericton, New Brunswick, Canada

> The Archives and Special Collections

Virginia Historical Society, Richmond, Va.

> Letters concerning Benedict Arnold's sojourn in Virginia with the British army, following his defection.

Washington's Headquarters Museum, Newburgh, N.Y.

> John Burgoyne Order Book, 1777
>
> Miscellaneous Papers

Yale University, New Haven, Conn.

> Beinecke Library: Letters of Hannah Arnold (sister of Benedict Arnold)
>
> Sterling Memorial Library: Chauncey Family Papers; also, *The Connecticut Journal*, 6 May 1778 account of Benedict Arnold's return to New Haven.

## *Periodical Sources*

*Adirondack Bits'n Pieces*, Vol. 1, Number 1, Summer, 1983, pp. 6–9. "Benedict Arnold," by Hilda V. Finkbeiner.

*American Heritage Magazine*, October 1966, pp. 8–11; 87–91, "Battle at Valcour Island: Benedict Arnold As Hero" by Timothy William Hubbard.

*Army Magazine*, January 1983, pp. 46–52, "Benedict Arnold: An Epilogue," by Brenda Ralph Lewis.

———, July 1984, pp. 58–65, "Showdown at Newburgh," by B. Bruce-Briggs.

*Atlantic Advocate, The*, March 1963, pp. 33–43, "Benedict Arnold In New Brunswick," by Jean E. Sereisky.

*Atlantic Monthly*, March 1889, Vol. 63, pp. 398–418, "Ticonderoga, Bennington and Oriskany," by John Fiske.

Bicentennial Radio Series, New Haven, "The Era of the Revolution," by Thomas J. Farnham.

*Bulletin of the Fort Ticonderoga Museum*, Vol. 14, #3, Summer 1982, pp. 131–57, "The Fall of Ticonderoga In 1777: Who Was Responsible?" by Don R. Gerlach.

————, Vol. 14, #3, Summer 1982, pp. 158–83, "Troop Life at the Champlain Valley Forts during the American Revolution," by John W. Krueger. (This article is continued in Vol. 14, #4, Fall 1983, pp. 220–49, and in Vol. 14, #5, Summer 1984, pp. 277–310).

————, Vol. 14, #4, Fall 1983, pp. 250–59, "Trial at Quaker-Hill: Justice to an Injured Country or Justice to... Injured Gentlemen?" by Don R. Gerlach.

————, Vol. 14, #5, Summer 1984, pp. 311–21, "The British Invasion of 1780 and a Character...Debased beyond Description," by Don R. Gerlach.

————, Vol. 14, #2, Winter 1982, pp. 71–80, "Benedict Arnold's Regimental Memorandum Book."

————, Vol. 14, #2, Winter 1982, pp. 81–110, "The Northern Medical Department, 1776–1777," by Morris H. Saffron.

————, January 1, 1927, pp. 11–18; July 1927, pp. 26–33; January 1928, pp. 14–30; July 1928, pp. 21–55, "The Montgomery Expedition, 1775"; From a Manuscript Diary, Kept by the Reverend Benjamin Trumbull, in the Museum Library; Minutes or a Concise Journal of the Continental Army towards, and in the Country of Canada: of the Siege and Surrender of Chambly and the Forts at St. John's, etc., 1775.

*Connecticut Magazine*, October 1972, pp. 28–55, "The Battle of Ridgefield," by Sandra Foster.

*Connecticut Historical Society Collections*, Vol. 1, 1860, pp. 163–88, "Papers Relating to the Expedition to Ticonderoga," April and May, 1775 (includes Journal of Capt. Edward Mott).

*Coronet* Magazine, June 1950, "Girl behind Benedict Arnold," by E. I. Haines.

*Daily Kennebec Journal*, October 21, 1978, "Editorial Regarding a Pardon for Benedict Arnold."

*The Day,* New London Newspaper, September 8, 1981, "The Burning of New London and the Battle of Groton Heights." A special commemorative section featuring the recreation of these events.

————, October–November 1984 "Coverage of the Mock Trial of Benedict Arnold."

*The Galaxy*, December 1868, pp. 831–35, "The Galaxy Miscellany: Who Took Ticonderoga?" by B. F. DaCosta.

*Harper's Monthly* Magazine: January 1903, pp. 227–81, "Benedict Arnold — Naval Patriot," by John R. Spears.

*Hartford Daily Courant*, January 9, 1869, pp. 3–15, "The Origin of the Expedition against Ticonderoga in 1750," a paper read before the Connecticut Historical Society, January 5, 1869, by J. H. Trumbull.

*Harvard Magazine*, September 1975, pp. 38–46, "Who Is This Benedict Arnold and Why is He Storming Quebec?," by Christopher S. Johnson.

*History Today* (GB) December 1959, pp. 791–99, "The Battle of Valcour Island," by John A. Barton.

Lecture, on micro-fiche at the David Library, "Who Took Ticonderoga?" by George Sheldon.

Lecture, on micro-fiche at the David Library, "Treason of Benedict Arnold," by Winthrop Atwil.

*Magazine of American History*, Vol. 4, pp. 181–91 (1880), "Benedict Arnold and his Apologist," by James Austin Stevens.

————., Vol. 3 part 2 (1879) "Correspondence Between Jared Sparks and Benjamin Tallmadge" (concerning Arnold and André).

*Military Affairs:* 1973 37 (2) , pp. 41–47, "Legacy of Controversy: Gates, Schuyler and Arnold at Saratoga," 1777, by Paul David Nelson.

*New Brunswick Historical Society Collections*, 1971, #20, pp. 57–97, "Footprints of Benedict Arnold, Late Major Brigadier General, British Army," by Eric L. Teed, Q.C., M.L.A.

*Newsday*, April 25, 1982, p. 13, "Rallying 'Round the Powder-house," by Phil Mintz, Travel Section.

————, September 23, 1980, p. 21, "Who Foiled Benedict Arnold...and Took Off the Boots?" by Aileen Jacobson.

*New York History* Magazine, July 1976, pp. 339–66, "Guy Carleton versus Benedict Arnold: The Campaign of 1776 in Canada & On Lake Champlain," by Paul David Nelson.

*New York Historical Society Quarterly*, 55, 1971, pp. 235–52, "The Gates-Arnold Quarrel, September 1777," by Paul D. Nelson.

*New York State Historical Association Proceedings of XII (1913)*, pp. 139–57, "Benedict Arnold — Patriot," by Edgar W. Ames.

*New York Times, The,* April 25, 1976, "In the Footsteps of the Rebels Who Dared to Invade Canada," by Sol Stember (Sunday Travel Section).

————, September 21, 1975, "Invading Canada Again: A Motorized March and a Mock Battle," by Sol Stember (Sunday Travel Section).

————, September 15, 1968, "Seeking Benedict Arnold's 'Gold' In Canada," by Jacque Coulon (Sunday Travel Section).

————, July 20, 1975, "Spy Story along the Hudson," by Sol Stember.

————, July 1, 1977, "Ridgefield, Conn., Group Issues Medal Hailing Benedict Arnold," by Robert E. Tomasson.

————, October 8, 1977, "October 7, 1777; The Beginning of the End at Saratoga," by Drew Middleton, pp. 25–26.

————, October 5, 1952, "Thoughts on Visiting Saratoga Battlefield," by Frank Sullivan, pp. 22–24 (Sunday Magazine Supplement).

*Norwich Bulletin,* October–November 1984. "Data Coverage Of the Benedict Arnold Mock Trial."

*Pennsylvania Magazine of History and Biography, The Index (1877–1951),* edited by Eugene E. Doll, Philadelphia, Pa., The Historical Society of Pennsylvania, 1954. Tremendous listing of material on Benedict Arnold and members of his family.

*Pennsylvania State University, 1975,* 218 pp. "Benedict Arnold: The Traitor as Hero in American Literature," by David R. Johnson.

*The Portfolio ,* 4th Series, Vol. 21, Hall's 2nd Series, Vol. 1, July 1826, pp. 25–72, "Conspiracy of Arnold."

*Quebec Literary and Historical Society Canadian History: The Siege and Blockade of Quebec,* by Generals Montgomery and Arnold in 1775. "A paper read before.... Society," March 6, 1872, by William James Anderson.

Quebec: *Middleton and Dawson,* 1872. Paper 3, pp. 49–71 (Bound Separate).

*The Ridgefield Press,* April–May 1977 "Coverage of Recreation of the Battle of Ridgefield, 1777, with Notes on Research Concerning the Event and the Area. Interesting letters received in Editor's Columns concerning the affair and the issuance of the medallion are both pro and con.

*Saratoga County Bicentennial Times,* October 7, 1977, pp. 1–6, "Burgoyne Surrenders!"

*Saratogian, The Special Issue,* Friday, October 7, 1977, "Battle of Saratoga."

*Saturday Evening Post,* March 20, 1954, "So We Commemorate The Hero Who Got the Boot," by I. MacIvor.

*Scribner's Magazine,* February 1898, pp. 147–60, "The Naval Campaign of 1776 on Lake Champlain," by Capt. A. T. Mahan, USN.

*"Sleepy Hollow Restorations* — Hours with the Living Men and Women of the Revolution: A Pilgrimage," by Benson J. Lossing, Microfilm copy of interview with Mrs. Cornelia Beekman.

*Smithsonian Magazine,* December 1987, Vol. 18, #9, pp. 40–49, "Could Canada Have Ever Been Our Fourteenth Colony?" by Edwards Park.

*Southern Studies,* 1978, 17 (3), pp. 273–89, "Benedict Arnold: The Hero as Traitor," by Miriam J. Shillingsburg.

*Sunday News (New York),* January 12, 1958, "America's Greatest Traitor," by Dick Owen, p. 18.

*Times Union,* Sunday, April 7, 1968, and Sunday, April 14, 1968, "Benedict Arnold, Hero, or Traitor?," by V. R. Rolando and J. L. Trowill.

U.S. Naval Institute Proceedings: December 1929, pp. 10601–62 "Arnold's Retreat From Valcour Island," by L. H. Bolander.

———. January–April 1935, Vol. 61, pp. 337–44, "Paul Jones and Arnold," by Commander W. C. I. Stiles, U.S. Navy (Ret.).

———. October 1967, pp. 157–60, "The Battle of Valcour Island," by Arthur E. Gilligan.

———. October 1968, pp. 80–88, "Last in the Hearts of His Countrymen," by Philip B. Yeager.

*United Service Magazine,* September 1880, pp. 1–16, "Benedict Arnold at Saratoga," by I. N. Arnold.

*University of New Brunswick (Library Archives),* Fredericton, N.B., Canada — Arnold–Hayt Papers.

*University of Vermont, Bailey/Howe Library* (In Wilbur Collection, 5082), pamphlet, pp. 1–7, "General Arnold and the Congress Galley," by the late P. C. Tucker, Esq.

*Vermont Historical Society,* 1974, 42, #3, pp. 195–200, "With Benedict Arnold at Valcour Island: The Diary of De Angelis," by Charles M. Snyer.

———, Spring 1978, Vol. 55, #2, pp. 97–112, "An Incident Not Known to History: Squire Ferris and Benedict Arnold at Ferris Bay," by Art Cohn.

———, Summer 1978, Vol. 46, #3, pp. 141–50, "Dr. Robert Knox's Account of the Battle of Valcour, October 11–13, 1776."

*Virginia Magazine,* Col. 60, 1952, pp. 591–99, "Benedict Arnold in Richmond, January, 1781," by George Green Shackelford.

*Western Reserve Mason, The,* September, October and December, 1983, "Benedict Arnold: Patriot or Traitor," by Vincent Mahany, Past Master.

*Yankee Magazine,* November 1969, pp. 46–63, "By Way of the Kennebec," by Elmore B. Lyford.

———, January 1975, "Benedict Arnold Loves Peggy Shippen," by Dale M. Titler, pp. 40–138.

# Index

Illustrations are given in *italics*.
First names are listed when known.

**262**

Throughout history, man has done battle for many reasons including ideology, capture of land, and power. One of the greatest conflicts which affected not only the people who participated in it, but the entire world, was the American Revolution.

Designed as a quick reference for the researcher or the lover of history, this book is a chronological list of events relating to the American Revolution beginning with the accession of King George III, and ending with the death of George Washington.

**Harry J. Karapalides** received his B.A. in political science from Widener University in 1981 and his Juris Doctor from Delaware School of Widener in 1985. Since then, he has practiced law in Delaware County, Pennsylvania. He is a longtime enthusiast of the American Revolution.

**Little has been written on Henry Lee's exploits—but it can now be said that they have not been forgotten.**

➤ *The years 1776-1780 were the pivotal period during the Revolutionary War. At the center of practically every important military event during those four long years was a young cavalry officer, **Henry Lee, the father of Confederate General Robert E. Lee.***

➤ *Based extensively on **primary sources, many of them unpublished**, **The American Partisan** documents Henry Lee's remarkable military career—by 1780 Henry Lee had emerged a legend, a combat-hardened veteran of unparalleled daring and bravery.*

ISBN 1-57249-183-3    $24.95    HC
ISBN 1-57249-226-0    $17.95    PB
6" x 9", 246 pp., 13 phs., 3 maps, Bib, Index

The years 1776-1780 were the pivotal period during the Revolutionary War. It was during this time that the world's greatest experiment in democracy was saved and the groundwork laid for American independence.

At the center of practically every important military event during those four long years was a young cavalry officer, Henry Lee, the father of Confederate General Robert E. Lee. Henry Lee's exploits on and off the battlefield played a key role in not only contributing to American victories but also lifting the flagging spirits of his fellow countrymen, when it often appeared as though the war was almost lost. By 1780 Henry Lee had emerged a legend, a combat-hardened veteran of unparalleled daring and bravery.

Based extensively on primary sources, many of them unpublished, *The American Partisan* documents Henry Lee's remarkable military career. It details not only Lee's military exploits but examines the central role he played in both gathering intelligence and foraging for the Continental army. The book also delves into the unique personal relationship between Henry Lee and General George Washington, a relationship that was more akin to father and son than commander and soldier.

Little has been written on Henry Lee, and this is the first work that focuses on the years when Lee rose to become one of the true heroes of the American War for Independence. Henry Lee's exploits may have been largely ignored by historians, but it can now be said that they have not been forgotten.

**John W. Hartmann** received his B.A. from Georgetown University and his J.D. from Seton Hall University. In 1991 he was elected to the New Jersey State Assembly where he served for two years. He is a member of the New Jersey States Archives Commission, and manages his law practice in Princeton Junction, New Jersey.

**The mysterious discovery of an old, stained American flag reveals the courage & sacrifice of the small Connecticut town of Fairfield when their town becomes the target of a British shoreline raid.**

*The members of the Middleton family exhibit great determination and courage resisting the British raid on their town.*

➤ *THOMAS—member of the local militia*
  ➤ *BEN—tries to protect his mother*
    ➤ *SARAH—resolves to save her home & valuables*

The Forgotten Flag
REVOLUTIONARY STRUGGLE IN CONNECTICUT
FRANCES Y. EVAN

W\" ISBN 1-57249-338-0    $5.95
M 5-1/2" x 8-1/2" PB,
KIDS 92 pp., 3 phs., 1 map

In 1964 two young girls make a mysterious discovery. An old, stained American flag is found stuffed into the rafters of a historic farmhouse. The story of the flag is revealed as the events of July 1779 in the small town of Fairfield, Connecticut, unfold. The town becomes the target of a shoreline raid by British forces. The British intend to break the morale and spirit of the American patriots.

The members of the Middleton family exhibit great determination and courage resisting the British raid on their town. Thomas, a member of the local militia, carries with him a flag, the precious symbol of a proud new nation. Ben tries to protect his mother from approaching danger, as Sarah Middleton resolves to save her home and valuables from pillaging soldiers.

When Fairfield is pillaged and burned, Thomas must flee to safety, with help from his brother Ben. Pursued by the enemy, they struggle desperately through woods, across fields, into thickets and gullies. *The Forgotten Flag* is the story of the townsfolk of this small community as they stand against the British.

*"An interesting and lively account of the burning of Fairfield, Connecticut, by the British in 1779. It is good reading for middle school students and adults as well. The action is crisp and the characters sympathetic."*
    *—Lyn McNaught, Executive Dir., Horizons Student Enrichment Program*

*"Frances Evan's* The Forgotten Flag *brings the struggle to a small town and its families, homes, schools and churches. The assault of well-trained British and Hessian troops on the militia of Fairfield, a small Connecticut community, brings the battle to ordinary citizens. Conflicts between supporters of the Revolution and British loyalists divide the town and set the scene for betrayal and destruction. Mrs. Evan's characters are real and grow and develop as they respond to the threats of mercenary troops."*
    *—Barbara F. Kmetz, Ed.D., Dir. of Curriculum, Trumbull, Connecticut Public Schools*

**A professional storyteller, Frances Evan has been educating and entertaining children with original stories and activities about Connecticut for many years**. A native of Walthamstow, a suburb of London, England, Frances moved to a colonial farmhouse in Fairfield, Connecticut, and in 1964 her family actually found a stained American flag in the rafters of the attic. Currently a resident of Stratford **she visits classrooms and conducts programs about the history of Connecticut and the seashore.**